WORLD
INEQUALITY
REPORT
2022

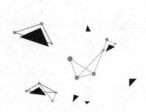

WORLD
INEQUALITY
REPORT
2022

Coordinated by

Lucas Chancel (Lead author)
Thomas Piketty
Emmanuel Saez
Gabriel Zucman

Foreword by
Esther Duflo and Abhijit Banerjee

The Belknap Press of Harvard University Press
Cambridge, Massachusetts, and London,
England
2022

WORLD
INEQUALITY LAB

Coordinated by:
Lucas Chancel
Thomas Piketty
Emmanuel Saez
Gabriel Zucman

Lead author:
Lucas Chancel

Research team:
Felix Bajard
François Burq
Rowaida Moshrif
Theresa Neef
Anne-Sophie Robilliard

Data coordinator:
Rowaida Moshrif

This report draws on recent research articles written by:

Facundo Alvaredo
Lydia Assouad
Luis Bauluz
Nitin Bharti
Thomas Blanchet
Lucas Chancel
Léo Czajka
Mauricio De Rosa
Carmen Durrer
Matthew Fisher-Post
Ignacio Flores
Bertrand Garbinti
Amory Gethin
Jonathan Goupille-Lebret

Thanasak Jenmana
Clara Martinez-Toledano
Marc Morgan
Rowaida Moshrif
Theresa Neef
Thomas Piketty
Anne-Sophie Robilliard
Emmanuel Saez
Alice Sodano
Li Yang
Tancrède Voituriez
Gabriel Zucman
Alvaro Zuniga-Cordero

The report also draws on the extensive work of researchers associated to the World Inequality Database available at www.wid.world/team

Communication manager:
Olivia Ronsain

Communication team:
Michael Luze
Top of mind

Design:
Latitude

Website:
La Quadrature du cercle

Editing:
Charlotte Graff
Kathleen Weekley

The authors thank the United Nations Development Programme for its role as a scientific partner in the production of this report. Special thanks to Achim Steiner, as well as to Pedro Conceição, Heriberto Tapia, Mansour Ndiaye and their teams.

CONTENTS

CONTENTS

FOREWORD

By Abhijit Banerjee and Esther Duflo

The job of holding up a mirror to the world can be a frustrating one. When the news is persistently bad, when the mirror highlights more wrinkles than we want to face up to, it is easy enough to find excuses—we are about to turn the corner, there is no other way to go, efficiency demands this, think of all the other good things that are happening, and the evergreen favorite, the data is wrong. Chasing down each of these narratives and slaying them takes stubborn-ness and hard work. Over the last twenty-five years, Thomas Piketty has been leading this fight, first by himself, then with Emmanuel Saez, Facundo Alvaredo, and the late Sir Tony Atkinson and, increasingly, with a growing team of collaborators, culminating in the World Inequality Lab.

This report is the current flagship product of the Lab, prepared under the leadership of Lucas Chancel and also coordinated by Thomas Piketty, Emmanuel Saez and Gabriel Zucman. It is the product of a relentless data amassment which makes it possible to provide better answers to almost every question we want to ask about what is happening to inequality world-wide. The answer is not pretty. In every large region of the world with the exception of Europe, the share of the bottom 50% in total earnings is less than 15% (less than ten in Latin America, Sub-Saharan Africa and MENA region) while the share of the richest 10% is over 40% and in many of the regions, closer to 60%. But what is perhaps even more striking is what is happening to wealth. The share of the bottom 50% of the world in total global wealth is 2% by their estimates, while the share of the top 10% is 76%. Since wealth is a major source of future economic gains, and increasingly, of power and influence, this presages further increases in inequality. Indeed, at the heart of this explosion is the extreme concentration of the economic power in the hands of a very small minority of the super-rich. The wealth of the top 10% globally, which constitutes the middle class in rich countries and the merely rich in poor countries is actually growing slower than the world average, but the top 1% is growing much faster: between 1995 and 2021, the top 1% captured 38% of the global increment in wealth, while the bottom 50% captured a frightening 2%. The share of wealth owned by the global top 0.1% rose from 7% to 11% over that period and global billionaire wealth soared. With the boom in the stock market, the picture does not seem to be getting better.

And yet, as the report makes clear, there is no case for giving up or opting to sit it out till the revolution. The period from 1945 or 1950 till 1980, was a period of shrinking inequality in many parts of the world (US, UK, France, but also India and China). For the countries of the West these were also covered the thirty odd years of fast productivity growth and increasing prosperity, never matched since—in other words there is no prima facie evidence for the idea that fast growth demands or necessarily goes hand in hand with growing inequality. The reason why that was possible had a lot to do with policy—tax rates were high, and there was an ideology that inequality needed to kept in check, that was shared between the corporate sector, civil society and the government. The same experience was repeated, if briefly, in the first years of this millennium in Latin America, when growth accelerated, poverty and wage inequality went down, thanks to a strong commitment to redistributive policies.

However, for most of the world, the defining experience turned out to be the panicked reaction to the slowdown of growth in US and UK in the 1970s, that led to the conviction that a big part of the problem was that the institutions that kept inequality low (minimum wage, union, taxes, regulation, etc.) were to blame, and that what we needed was to unleash an entrepreneurial culture that celebrates the unabashed accumulation of private wealth. We now know that as the Reagan-Thatcher revolution and it was the starting point of a dizzying rise in inequality within countries that continues to this day. When state control was (successfully) loosened in countries like China and India to allow private sector-led growth, the same ideology got trotted out to justify not worrying about inequality, with the consequence that India is now among the most unequal countries in the

world (based on this report) and China risks getting there soon.

Policy kept inequality in check, and policy changes let it run amok. This report once again makes it clear that profound policy changes are needed for things to fall back in place. The policy solutions often exist, and when they don't, we often know how to find them. Our own research, and that of the researchers in the network we helped create, has focused on how to get the plumbing right, so that policy can do its job. The World Inequality Lab and all those involved in this report are doing the same for how to collect taxes and redistribute better.

As the world comes out of the pandemic and there is renewed attention to economic policy, a report like this is extraordinarily timely. It has the potential to light a fire under us to do something now, before the cumulative concentration of economic (and other) power in the hands of a smaller and smaller minority makes it impossible to fight back. Read it, shout out its messages, find ways to act upon it.

WORLD
INEQUALITY
REPORT
2022

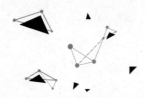

EXECUTIVE SUMMARY

Reliable inequality data as a global public good

We live in a data-abundant world and yet we lack basic information about inequality. Economic growth numbers are published every year by governments across the globe, but they do not tell us about how growth is distributed across the population – about who gains and who loses from economic policies. Accessing such data is critical for democracy. Beyond income and wealth, it is also critical to improve our collective capability to measure and monitor other dimensions of socio-economic disparities, including gender and environmental inequalities. Open-access, transparent, reliable inequality information is a global public good.

This report presents the most up-to-date synthesis of international research efforts to track global inequalities. The data and analysis presented here are based on the work of more than 100 researchers over four years, located on all continents, contributing to the World Inequality Database (WID.world), maintained by the World Inequality Lab. This vast network collaborates with statistical institutions, tax authorities, universities and international organizations, to harmonize, analyze and disseminate comparable international inequality data.

Contemporary income and wealth inequalities are very large

An average adult individual earns PPP €16,700 (PPP USD23,380) per year in 2021, and the average adult owns €72,900 (USD102,600).[1] These averages mask wide disparities both between and within countries. The richest 10% of the global population currently takes 52% of global income, whereas the poorest half of the population earns 8.5% of it. On average, an individual from the top 10% of the global income distribution

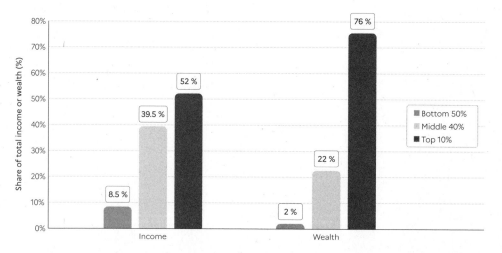

Figure 1 *Global income and wealth inequality, 2021*

Interpretation: *The global bottom 50% captures 8.5% of total income measured at Purchasing Power Parity (PPP). The global bottom 50% owns 2% of wealth (at Purchasing Power Parity). The global top 10% owns 76% of total Household wealth and captures 52% of total income in 2021. Note that top wealth holders are not necessarily top income holders. Incomes are measured after the operation of pension and unemployment systems and before taxes and transfers.* **Sources and series:** *wir2022.wid.world/methodology.*

earns €87,200 (USD122,100) per year, whereas an individual from the poorest half of the global income distribution makes €2,800 (USD3,920) per year (Figure 1).

Global wealth inequalities are even more pronounced than income inequalities. The poorest half of the global population barely owns any wealth at all, possessing just 2% of the total. In contrast, the richest 10% of the global population own 76% of all wealth. On average, the poorest half of the population owns PPP €2,900 per adult, i.e. USD4,100 and the top 10% own €550,900 (or USD771,300) on average.

MENA is the most unequal region in the world, Europe has the lowest inequality levels

Figure 2 shows income inequality levels across the regions. Inequality varies significantly between the most equal region (Europe) and the most unequal (Middle East and North Africa i.e. MENA). In Europe, the top 10% income share is around 36%, whereas in MENA it reaches 58%. In between these two levels, we see a diversity of patterns. In East Asia, the top 10% makes 43% of total income and in Latin America, 55%.

Average national incomes tell us little about inequality

The world map of inequalities (Figure 3) reveals that national average income levels are poor predictors of inequality: among high-income countries, some are very unequal (such as the US), while other are relatively equal (e.g. Sweden). The same is true among low- and middle-income countries, with some exhibiting extreme inequality (e.g. Brazil and India), somewhat high levels (e.g. China) and moderate to relatively low levels (e.g. Malaysia, Uruguay).

Inequality is a political choice, not an inevitability

Income and wealth inequalities have been on the rise nearly everywhere since the 1980s, following a series

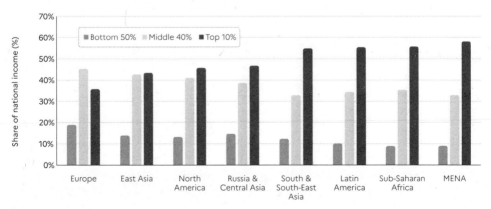

Figure 2 *The poorest half lags behind: Bottom 50%, middle 40% and top 10% income shares across the world in 2021*

Interpretation: In Latin America, the top 10% captures 55% of national income, compared to 36% in Europe. Income is measured after pension and unemployment contributions and benefits paid and received by individuals but before income taxes and other transfers. **Sources and series:** www.wir2022.wid.world/methodology.

of deregulation and liberalization programs which took different forms in different countries. The rise has not been uniform: certain countries have experienced spectacular increases in inequality (including the US, Russia and India) while others (European countries and China) have experienced relatively smaller rises. These differences, which we discussed at length in the previous edition of the World Inequality Report, confirm that inequality is not inevitable, it is a political choice.[2]

Figure 3   *Top 10/Bottom 50 income gaps across the world, 2021*

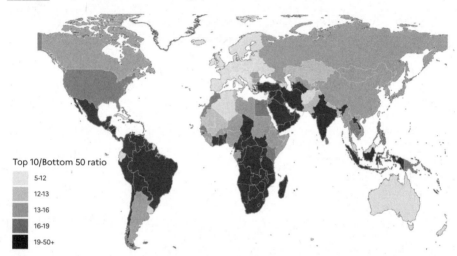

Top 10/Bottom 50 ratio

- 5-12
- 12-13
- 13-16
- 16-19
- 19-50+

*Interpretation: In Brazil, the bottom 50% earns 29 times less than the top 10%. The value is 7 in France. Income is measured after pension and unemployment payments and benefits received by individuals but before other taxes they pay and transfers they receive. **Source and series:** wir2022.wid.world/methodology.*

Figure 4   *The extreme concentration of capital: wealth inequality across the world, 2021*

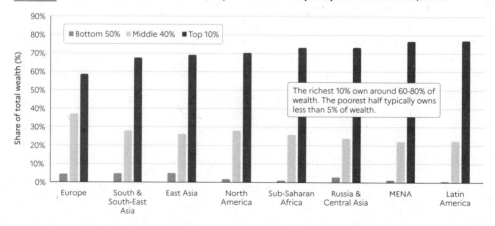

The richest 10% own around 60-80% of wealth. The poorest half typically owns less than 5% of wealth.

*Interpretation: The top 10% in Latin America captures 77% of total household wealth, compared with 1% captured by the bottom 50%. Net household wealth is equal to the sum of financial assets (e.g. equity or bonds) and non-financial assets (e.g. housing or land) owned by individuals, net of their debts. **Sources and series:** wir2022.wid.world/methodology.*

Contemporary global inequalities are close to early 20th century levels, at the peak of Western imperialism

While inequality has increased within most countries, over the past two decades, global inequalities between countries have declined. The gap between the average incomes of the richest 10% of countries and the average incomes of the poorest 50% of countries dropped from around 50x to a little less than 40x (Figure 5). At the same time, inequalities increased significantly within countries. The gap between the average incomes of the top 10% and the bottom 50% of individuals within countries has almost doubled, from 8.5x to 15x (see Chapter 2).This sharp rise in within country inequalities has meant that despite economic

catch-up and strong growth in the emerging countries, the world remains particularly unequal today. It also means that inequalities within countries are now even greater than the significant inequalities observed between countries (Figure 6).

Global inequalities seem to be about as great today as they were at the peak of Western imperialism in the early 20th century. Indeed, the share of income presently captured by the poorest half of the world's people is about half what it was in 1820, before the great divergence between Western countries and their colonies (Figure 7). In other words, there is still a long way to go to undo the global economic inequalities inherited from the very unequal organization of world production between the mid-19th and mid-20th centuries.

Figure 5   *Global income inequality: T10/B50 ratio, 1820-2020*

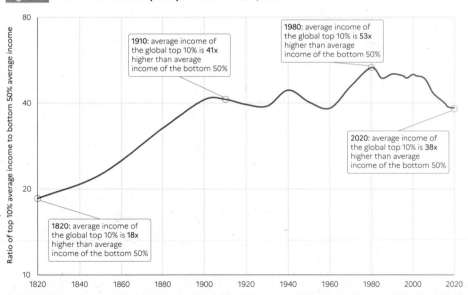

Interpretation: *Global inequality, as measured by the ratio T10/B50 between the average income of the top 10% and the average income of the bottom 50%, more than doubled between 1820 and 1910, from less than 20 to about 40, and stabilized around 40 between 1910 and 2020. It is too early to say whether the decline in global inequality observed since 2008 will continue. Income is measured per capita after pension and unemployement insurance transfers and before income and wealth taxes.* **Sources and series:** *wir2022. wid.world/methodology and Chancel and Piketty (2021).*

Figure 6   *Global income inequality: Between vs. within country inequality (Theil index), 1820-2020*

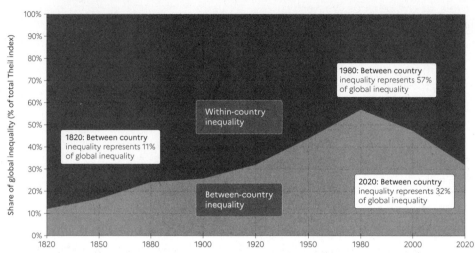

Interpretation: *The importance of between-country inequality in overall global inequality, as measured by the Theil index, rose between 1820 and 1980 and strongly declined since then. In 2020, between-country inequality makes-up about a third of global inequality between countries. The rest is due to inequality within countries. Income is measured per capita after pension and unemployement insurance transfers and before income and wealth taxes.* **Sources and series:** *wir2022.wid.world/methodology and Chancel and Piketty (2021).*

Figure 7   *Global income inequality, 1820-2020*

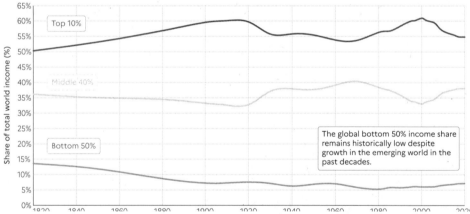

Interpretation: *The share of global income going to top 10% highest incomes at the world level has fluctuated around 50-60% between 1820 and 2020 (50% in 1820, 60% in 1910, 56% in 1980, 61% in 2000, 55% in 2020), while the share going to the bottom 50% lowest incomes has generally been around or below 10% (14% in 1820, 7% in 1910, 5% in 1980, 6% in 2000, 7% in 2020). Global inequality has always been very large. It rose between 1820 and 1910 and shows little long-run trend between 1910 and 2020.* **Sources and series:** *see wir2022.wid.world/methodology and Chancel and Piketty (2021).*

Nations have become richer, but governments have become poor

One way to understand these inequalities is to focus on the gap between the net wealth of governments and net wealth of the private sector. Over the past 40 years, countries have become significantly richer, but their governments have become significantly poorer. The share of wealth held by public actors is close to zero or negative in rich countries, meaning that the totality of wealth is in private hands (Figure 8). This trend has been magnified by the Covid crisis, during which governments borrowed the equivalent of 10-20% of GDP, essentially from the private sector. The currently low wealth of governments has important implications for state capacities to tackle inequality in the future, as well as the key challenges of the 21st century such as climate change.

Wealth inequalities have increased at the very top of the distribution

The rise in private wealth has also been unequal within countries and at the world level. Global multimillionaires have captured a disproportionate share of global wealth growth over the past several decades: the top 1% took 38% of all additional wealth accumulated since the mid-1990s, whereas the bottom 50% captured just 2% of it. This inequality stems from serious inequality in growth rates between the top and the bottom segments of the wealth distribution. The wealth of richest individuals on earth has grown at 6 to 9% per year since

Figure 8 *The rise of private wealth and the decline of public wealth in rich countries, 1970-2020*

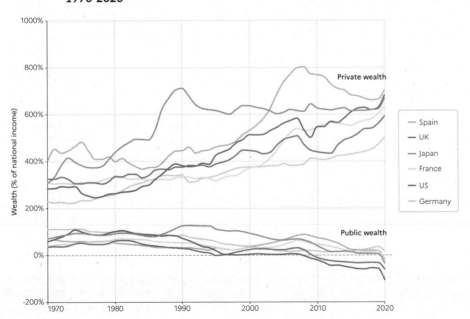

Interpretation: *In the UK, public wealth dropped from 60% of national income to -106% between 1970 and 2020. Public wealth is the sum of all financial and non-financial assets, net of debts, held by governments.*
Sources and series: *wir2022.wid.world/methodology, Bauluz et al. (2021) and updates.*

Figure 9   *Average annual wealth growth rate, 1995-2021*

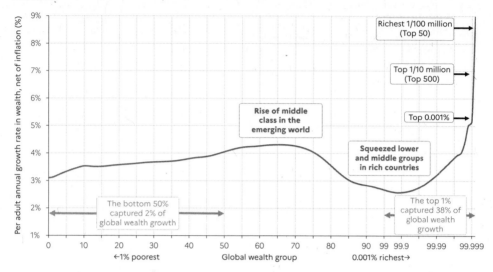

Interpretation: *Growth rates among the poorest half of the population were between 3% and 4% per year, between 1995 and 2021. Since this group started from very low wealth levels, its absolute levels of growth remained very low. The poorest half of the world population only captured 2.3% of overall wealth growth since 1995. The top 1% benefited from high growth rates (3% to 9% per year). This group captured 38% of total wealth growth between 1995 and 2021. Net household wealth is equal to the sum of financial assets (e.g. equity or bonds) and non-financial assets (e.g. housing or land) owned by individuals, net of their debts.* **Sources and series:** *wir2022.wid.world/methodology, Bauluz et al. (2021) and updates*

1995, whereas average wealth has grown at 3.2% per year (Figure 9). Since 1995, the share of global wealth possessed by billionaires has risen from 1% to over 3%. This increase was exacerbated during the COVID pandemic. In fact, 2020 marked the steepest increase in global billionaires' share of wealth on record (Figure 10).

Wealth inequalities within countries shrank for most of the 20th century, but the bottom 50% share has always been very low

Wealth inequality was significantly reduced in Western countries between the early 20th century and the 1980s, but the poorest half of the population in these countries has always owned very little, i.e. between 2% and 7% of the total

(Figure 11). In other regions, the share of the bottom 50% is even lower. These results show that much remains to be done, in every region of the world, if we are to reduce extreme wealth inequalities.

Gender inequalities remain considerable at the global level, and progress within countries is too slow

The World Inequality Report 2022 provides the first estimates of the gender inequality in global earnings. Overall, women's share of total incomes from work (labor income) neared 30% in 1990 and stands at less than 35% today (Figure 12). Current gender earnings inequality remains very high: in a gender equal world, women would earn 50% of all labor income. In 30 years, progress

Figure 10   **Extreme wealth inequality: the rise of global billionaires, 1995-2021**

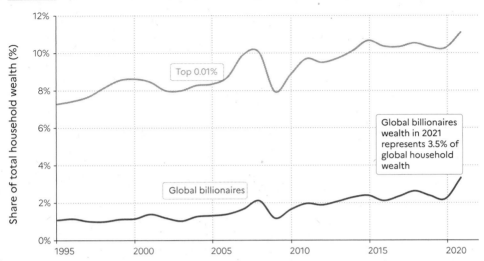

Interpretation: *The share of wealth detained by the global top 0.01% rose from 7% in 1995 to 11% in 2021. The top 0.01% is composed of 520 000 adults in 2021. The entry threshold of this group rose from €693,000 (PPP) in 1995 to €16,666,000 today. Billionaires correspond to individuals owning at least $1b in nominal terms. The net household wealth is equal to the sum of financial assets (e.g. equity or bonds) and non-financial assets (e.g. housing or land) owned by individuals, net of their debts.* **Sources and series:** *wir2022.wid.world/methodology, Bauluz et al. (2021) and updates.*

Figure 11   **Top 1% vs bottom 50% wealth shares in Western Europe and the US, 1910-2020**

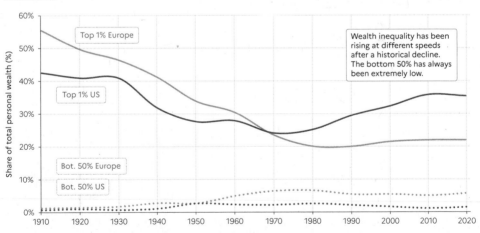

Interpretation: *The graph presents decennial averages of top 1% personal wealth shares in Western Europe and the US. In 1910, the top 1% in Europe owned 55% of wealth, vs. 43% in the U.S. A century later, the US is almost back to its early 20th century level. Net household wealth is equal to the sum of financial assets (e.g. equity or bonds) and non-financial assets (e.g. housing or land) owned by individuals, net of their debts.* **Sources and series:** *wir2022.wid.world/methodology, Bauluz et al. (2021) and updates.*

has been very slow at the global level, and dynamics have been different across countries, with some recording progress but others seeing reductions in women's share of earnings (Figure 13).

Addressing large inequalities in carbon emissions is essential for tackling climate change

Global income and wealth inequalities are tightly connected to ecological inequalities and to inequalities in

Figure 12   *Female share in global labor incomes, 1990-2020*

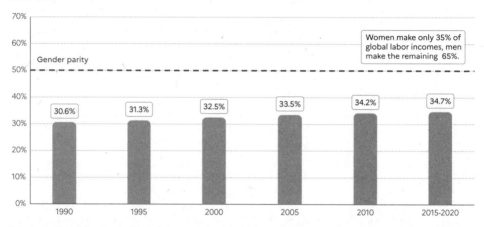

Women make only 35% of global labor incomes, men make the remaining 65%.

Gender parity

30.6% | 31.3% | 32.5% | 33.5% | 34.2% | 34.7%
1990 | 1995 | 2000 | 2005 | 2010 | 2015-2020

*Interpretation: The share of female incomes in global labour incomes was 31% in 1990 and nears 35% in 2015-2020. Today, males make up 65% of total labor incomes. **Sources and series:** wir2022.wid.world/ methodology and Neef and Robilliard (2021).*

Figure 13   *Female labor income share across the world, 1990-2020*

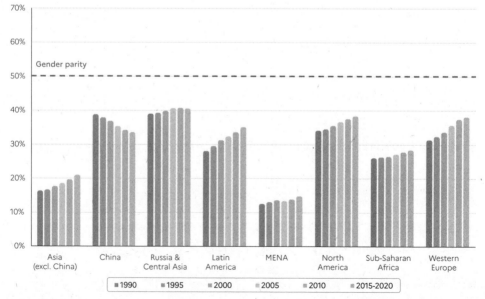

Gender parity

Asia (excl. China) | China | Russia & Central Asia | Latin America | MENA | North America | Sub-Saharan Africa | Western Europe

■1990   ■1995   ■2000   ■2005   ■2010   ■2015-2020

*Interpretation: The female labour income share rose from 34% to 38% in North America between 1990 and 2020. **Sources and series:** wir2022.wid.world/methodology and Neef and Robilliard (2021).*

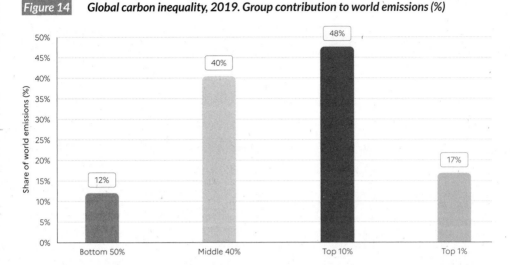

Figure 14 | *Global carbon inequality, 2019. Group contribution to world emissions (%)*

Interpretation: *Personal carbon footprints include emissions from domestic consumption, public and private investments as well as imports and exports of carbon embedded in goods and services traded with the rest of the world. Modeled estimates based on the systematic combination of tax data, household surveys and input-output tables. Emissions split equally within households.* **Sources and series:** *wir2022.wid.world/ methodology and Chancel (2021).*

contributions to climate change. On average, humans emit 6.6 tonnes of carbon dioxide equivalent (CO2) per capita, per year. Our novel data set on carbon emissions inequalities reveals important inequalities in CO2 emissions at the world level: the top 10% of emitters are responsible for close to 50% of all emissions, while the bottom 50% produce 12% of the total (Figure 14).

Figure 15 shows that these inequalities are not just a rich vs. poor country issue. There are high emitters in low- and middle-income countries and low emitters in rich countries. In Europe, the bottom 50% of the population emits around five tonnes per year per person; the bottom 50% in East Asia emits around three tonnes and the bottom 50% in North America around 10 tonnes. This contrasts sharply with the emissions of the top 10% in these regions (29 tonnes in Europe, 39 in East Asia, and 73 in North America).

This report also reveals that the poorest half of the population in rich countries is already at (or near) the 2030 climate targets set by rich countries, when these targets are expressed on a per capita basis. This is not the case for the top half of the population. Large inequalities in emissions suggest that climate policies should target wealthy polluters more. So far, climate policies such as carbon taxes have often disproportionately impacted low- and middle-income groups, while leaving the consumption habits of wealthiest groups unchanged.

Redistributing wealth to invest in the future

The World Inequality Report 2022 reviews several policy options for redistributing wealth and investing in the future in order to meet the challenges of the 21st century.

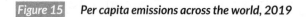

Figure 15   *Per capita emissions across the world, 2019*

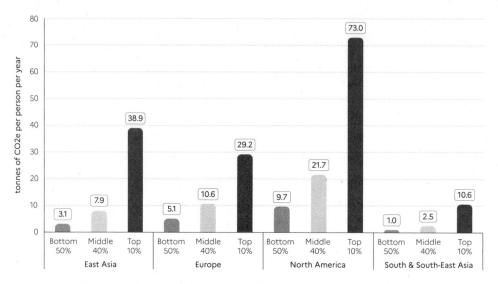

Interpretation: *Personal carbon footprints include emissions from domestic consumption, public and private investments as well as imports and exports of carbon embedded in goods and services traded with the rest of the world. Modeled estimates based on the systematic combination of tax data, household surveys and input-output tables. Emissions split equally within households.* **Sources and series:** *wir2022.wid.world/ methodology and Chancel (2021).*

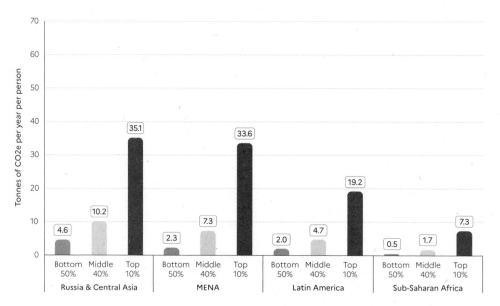

Interpretation: *Personal carbon footprints include emissions from domestic consumption, public and private investments as well as imports and exports of carbon embedded in goods and services traded with the rest of the world. Modeled estimates based on the systematic combination of tax data, household surveys and input-output tables. Emissions split equally within households.* **Sources and series:** *wir2022.wid.world/ methodology and Chancel (2021).*

Table 1 *Global millionaires and billionaires, 2021*

Wealth group ($)	Number of adults	Total wealth ($ bn)	Average wealth ($ m)	Global wealth tax	
				Effective wealth tax rate (%)	Total revenues (% global income)
All above 1m	62,165,160	174,200	2.8	1.0	1.6
1m - 10m	60,319,510	111,100	1.8	0.6	0.6
10m - 100m	1,769,200	33,600	19	1.3	0.4
100m - 1b	73,710	16,500	220	1.5	0.2
1b - 10b	2,582	7,580	2,940	2.3	0.2
10b - 100b	159	4,170	26,210	2.8	0.1
Over 100b	9	1,320	146,780	3.2	0.04

Interpretation: *In 2021, 62.2 million people in the world owned more than $1 million (at MER). Their average wealth was $ 2.8 million, representing a total of $174 trillion.* **Note:** *Numbers of millionaires are rounded to the nearest ten.* **Sources and series:** *wir2022.wid.world/methodology.*

Table 1 presents revenue gains that would come from a modest progressive wealth tax on global multimillionaires. Given the large volume of wealth concentration, modest progressive taxes can generate significant revenues for governments. In our scenario, we find that 1.6% of global incomes could be generated and reinvested in education, health and the ecological transition. The report comes with an online simulator so that everybody can design their preferred wealth tax at the global level, or in their region.

We stress at the outset that addressing the challenges of the 21st century is not feasible without significant redistribution of income and wealth inequalities. The rise of modern welfare states in the 20th century, which was associated with tremendous progress in health,

education, and opportunities for all (see Chapter 10), was linked to the rise of steep progressive taxation rates. This played a critical role in order to ensure the social and political acceptability of increased taxation and socialization of wealth. A similar evolution will be necessary in order to address the challenges of the 21st century. Recent developments in international taxation show that progress towards fairer economic policies is indeed possible at the global level as well as within countries. Chapters 8, 9 and 10 of the report discuss various options to tackle inequality, learning from examples all over the world and throughout modern history. Inequality is always political choice and learning from policies implemented in other countries or at other points of time is critical to design fairer development pathways.

NOTES

[1] Values expressed at Purchasing Power Parity (PPP). The Concept of income used is national income (i.e. the total income in the world) and the concept of wealth used is that of of household wealth. In this report, we will also use another concept of wealth: net national wealth (this is household wealth to which we add public wealth and wealth from non-profit sector). The average national wealth is €98,600 (USD139,000).

[2] World Inequality Report 2018, Harvard University Press, and online at wir2018.wid.world

INTRODUCTION

The aim of the World Inequality Report 2022 is to present the latest and most complete data available on inequality to inform democratic debate worldwide. It updates our 2018 World Inequality Report, adding new data with gender, environment, and tax justice dimensions.

Economic inequality is widespread, to some extent inevitable, and always at the center of debates about how societies should be organized. The unexpected COVID crisis illustrates this clearly. It has shut down large sectors of the economy, depriving many of their livelihood. Yet in many countries, compensatory income support systems were set in place very quickly, demonstrating the great power of societies, through their governments, to alleviate inequality and to avoid social and political catastrophes.

Generally speaking, how economies should distribute the incomes they generate, across national populations and across the world is the source of heated debate. Is economic growth distributed fairly? Is the social safety net wide and deep enough? Are low-income countries catching up with richer ones? Are racial and gender inequalities falling? Around the world, people hold strong and often contradictory views on what constitutes acceptable and unacceptable inequality, and what should be done about it.

Our objective is not to get everyone to agree about inequality: this will never happen, for the simple reason that no single, scientific truth exists regarding the ideal level of inequality, let alone the ideal social policies and institutions that would be required to achieve and maintain it. Ultimately, we can only make these difficult decisions through public deliberation, and via our political institutions. Our goal here then is more modest: we hope and believe that it is possible to agree about certain facts about inequality. The immediate goal of this report is to bring together new data series from the World Wealth and Income Database (WID.world) in order to document several new findings about global inequality and its evolution.

WID.world is a cumulative and collaborative research process that began in the early 2000s and now includes over one hundred researchers aiming to cover all countries in the world. WID.world provides open access to the most extensive available database on the historical evolution of the distribution of income and wealth, both within and between countries.

The 2022 report present novel findings in four main areas.

First, we provide truly comprehensive income inequality data for almost all countries in the world over long time periods. This allows us to present systematic data on inequality at the global level and to analyze how it has evolved over time. Global income inequality has always been very great, reflecting the persistence of a world economic system that is extremely hierarchical both between countries and within them. Global inequality increased between 1820 and 1910, in the context of the rise of Western dominance and colonial empires, and then stabilized at a very high level between 1910 and 2020. Since 1980, domestic inequality has grown, but inter-national inequality started to decline thanks to fast growth in the large so-called emerging economies. These two effects balance each other out so that in past few decades, global inequality has been basically stable, albeit at a very high level.

Second, our 2022 report provides much more in-depth evidence on wealth and its distribution worldwide than has been available until now. In recent decades, the weight of private wealth has increased at the expense of public wealth, due to deregulation, privatization, and increasing government debt. Furthermore, the concentration of private wealth has also increased, with the largest wealth increases occurring among the billionaire class.

Third, we analyze gender inequality by creating systematic data on the share of world labor income earned by women and how well represented women are at the top of the labor income distribution. Globally, the share of labor income paid to women stands at slightly under 35% and shows a positive trend over the past 30 years, up from around 31% in 1990. Men earn approximately twice as much as women across the world, on average. Further, the data reveal that women are significantly underrepresented at the top of the distribution, even though the fraction of women at the top has been increasing since the 1990s in many countries. Strikingly, women are now better represented at the top in some emerging economies such as Brazil than in advanced economies such as the United States.

Fourth, we present new evidence of inequality in carbon emissions across the world. Using a newly assembled set of carbon and energy accounts based on historical records, input–output tables and distributional statistics, we show how total carbon emissions are distributed not only between countries but also within them. Worldwide, carbon emissions are about as unequally distributed as income. The top 1% of carbon emitters contributed significantly more to global emissions growth than the entire bottom half of the global population. Policies aiming at reducing global emissions should, then, primarily target the very high emitters.

Finally, we discuss other policies that could reduce inequality. Progressive wealth taxes have (re)emerged in the debate as a promising tool for curbing extreme wealth concentration and generating much needed government revenue. Using our data, we analyze the revenue potential of wealth taxes and discuss how they could be successfully enforced based on lessons learned from existing and past progressive wealth taxes. Currently, multinational companies can easily escape paying corporate taxes by shifting their profits to tax havens, but there is an on-going international effort to set up a minimum tax agreement. We discuss the role of corporate taxation in fighting inequality, and global vs. unilateral approaches to

tax justice. We also offer broader perspectives on how to reinvent the social state in the 21st century.

As this report shows, WID.world has produced valuable inequality data in many dimensions, yet we are acutely aware that we still face important limitations in our ability to measure the evolution of income and wealth inequality. Our objective in WID.world and in the World Inequality Report is not to claim that we have perfect data series, but rather to make explicit what we know and what we do not know, and to flag clearly which countries are doing better in terms of data production and publication in their efforts to establish inequality statistics.

Part of our aim is to put pressure on governments and international organizations to release more raw data on income and wealth. In our view, the lack of transparency about income and wealth inequalities seriously undermines the possibilities for peaceful democratic discussion in today's globalized economy. In particular, it is crucial that governments provide public access to reliable and detailed tax statistics, which in turn requires that they operate properly functioning reporting systems for income, inheritance, and wealth. Without this, it is very difficult to have an informed debate about the evolution of inequality and what should be done about it.

Our most important reason for providing all the necessary details about data sources and concepts that underlie all our inequality estimates is to enable interested citizens to make up their own minds about these important and difficult issues. Economic issues do not belong to economists, statisticians, government officials, and business leaders. They belong to everyone, and it is our chief objective to contribute to the power of the many.

CHAPTER 1

Global economic inequality: insights

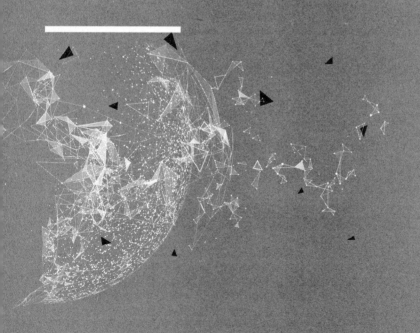

WORLD
INEQUALITY
REPORT
2022

What is the level of global economic inequality today?

Let us first define two key concepts for measuring economic inequality that we use in this report: national income and national wealth. National income is the sum of all incomes received by individuals residents in a given country over a year. Incomes takes various forms and we typically distinguish two broad sources: incomes stemming from individuals' labor (e.g. wages or salaries) and incomes stemming from individuals' wealth (e.g. interest and dividends). National wealth is the sum of the value of all assets owned by individuals in a given country. It is stock resulting from capital accumulation (from savings, i.e. income that has not been consumed) and price effects (see Box 1.3 on Economic concepts, and Chapter 3).[1] In 2021, global income amounts to €86 trillion ($122 trillion), while global net wealth amounts to six times this value, €510 trillion.[2] Global average income per adult in 2021 is €16,700 or PPP €1,390 per month (respectively $23,380 and $1,950), while the average adult individual owns €72,900 ($102,600) in wealth (or €98,600, i.e. $139,000, when all public assets and private non-profit assets are included).[3] These average values mask significant inequalities between countries and between citizens.

Global income and wealth inequality between individuals: initial insights

A straightforward way to describe the extent of global inequality is to focus on the shares of income captured by different groups of individuals in the distribution of income across the world. All the statistics presented in this report focus on the distribution of income or wealth across the global adult population of 5.1 billion individuals as of 2021, out of a world population of 7.8 billion when we include children.[4] In most statistics presented here, we split income and wealth equally across married couples.[5] The bottom 50% of the adult population, or the poorest half of the world population, today consists of 2.5 billion individual adults. The middle 40% represents the population earning more than the bottom 50% but less than the top 10%; it is made up of two billion individual adults. The global top 10% represents one tenth of the world population, i.e. 517 million individual adults. The global top 1% comprises the richest 51 million individual adults (Figure 1.0).

If all incomes were split perfectly equally across the world, i.e. if everybody earned €16,700 per year, then the global bottom 50% would capture 50% of global income and the global top 10% would capture exactly 10% of the total. Conversely, at maximum inequality, the global bottom 50% would capture 0% of the total and the global top 10% would capture 100% of it. These two situations are the extreme boundaries of global inequality. These levels of inequality have never been reported anywhere in the world and arguably never will be, but they provide a useful benchmark to help us to understand past and present levels of inequality observed within countries, and at the level of the world as a whole.

In practice, the global bottom 50% captures a very small share of global income, just 8.5%. This means that, on average, the bottom 50% earns slightly less than one fifth of the global average, i.e. just €2,800 per year or €230 per month. The global middle 40% earns 39.5% of the total: its income is very close to the global average, at €16,500 per year

Figure 1.0   *Adult population by group in 2021: Bottom 50%, middle 40%, top 10%, top 1%*

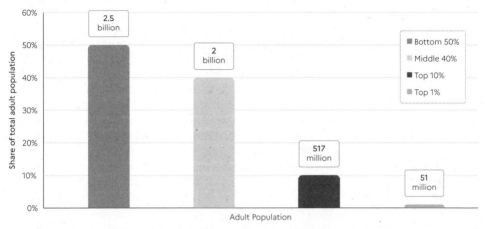

Interpretation: *The global bottom 50% among the adult population is composed of 2.5 billion individuals in 2021 and the global top 10% among the adult population is composed of 517 million individuals.* **Sources and series:** *wir2022.wid.world/methodology*

Figure 1.1   *Global income and wealth inequality, 2021*

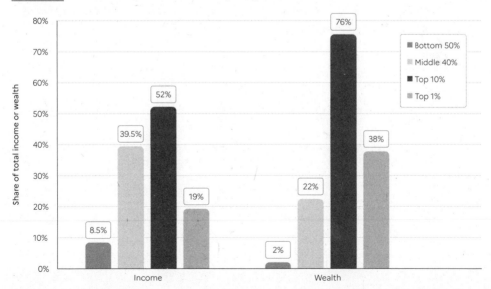

Interpretation: *The global 50% captures 8.5% of total income measured at Purchasing Power Parity (PPP). The global bottom 50% owns 2% of wealth (at Purchasing Power Parity). The global top 10% owns 76% of total Household wealth and captures 52% of total income in 2021. Note that top wealth holders are not necessarily top income holders. Income is measured after the operation of pension and unemployment systems and before taxes and transfers.* **Sources and series:** *wir2022.wid.world/methodology*

(€1,375 per month).[6] The global top 10% earns 52% of the total, which is slightly over five times the global average. Its average income per adult amounts to €87,200 per year or €7,300 per month. As we can see already, the world seems closer in 2020-2021 to the absolute inequality benchmark described above than to the absolute equality benchmark (see Table 1.1).

Global wealth appears to be even more unequally distributed than global income. The poorest half of the world population owns just 2% of total net wealth, whereas the richest half owns 98% of all the wealth on earth. The bottom 50% owns, on average, €2,900 of assets (typically in the form of land, housing, deposits or cash). Between the richest half of the global population, the middle 40% owns just 22% of total wealth (on average €40,900 per adult) and the top 10% owns 76% (i.e. €550,900 per adult, on average, including a large share of financial wealth such as stocks and bonds) (see Table 1.1). We should note that when we measure global wealth inequality using market exchange rates, rather

than purchasing power parities (see Box 1.3), then there is even more inequality: the global bottom 50% owns less than 1% of total wealth and the global top 10% nearly 82% of it. To summarize: as we write, the world is marked by a very high level of income inequality and an extreme level of wealth inequality. In Chapter 2, we show that beyond relatively small variations over the recent period, these extreme inequality levels persisted over the entire 1910-2020 period, despite profound transformations of the world economy over the past 100 years.

Global income and wealth inequality between countries

Global income and wealth inequality between individuals have two components: inequality *between* countries and regions (i.e. average income differences between, say, Indians and Germans) and inequality *within* countries (i.e. income differences between, say, rich and poor Indians). Let us be clear: in the contemporary global economy, these two components

Table 1.1   *The distribution of the world national income and wealth, 2021: Purchasing Power Parity*

	Avg. annual income per adult (PPP €)	Income threshold (PPP €)	Avg. wealth per adult (PPP €)	Wealth threshold (PPP €)
Full population	16,700		72,900	
Bottom 50%	2,800		2,900	
Middle 40%	16,500	6,700	40,900	12,000
Top 10%	87,200	37,200	550,900	125,500
Top 1%	321,600	123,900	2,755,200	807,300
Top 0.1%	1,300,800	446,000	14,133,400	3,333,700

Interpretation: *The global bottom 50% earns on average PPP€ 2,800 of income per adult and per year. Income is measured after pension and unemployment benefits are received by individuals, but before other taxes they pay and transfers they receive.* **Sources and series:** *wir2022.wid.world/methodology.*

of inequality are very substantial. Inequality within countries is at a historic high today (see Chapter 2), and inequality between countries remain particularly high despite the emerging world catching up somewhat over the past four decades.

What is the degree of inequality between world regions? We present key insights below. Figure 1.2a presents average incomes across world regions, expressed as a percentage of the global average income of €16,700 per year. Average income in Sub-Saharan Africa is 0.3, i.e. 31% of the global average, and in South and Southeast Asia it is 0.5, i.e. 50% of the global average. Latin America, East Asia, and Russia and Central Asia have average incomes at or near the global average. In Europe, the ratio is more than twice the global average (215%), and in North America it is three times the global average. This means that North Americans earn 6 to 10 times more, on average, than Sub-Saharan Africans, South and Southeast Asians, while East Asians earn half of what Europeans earn. Again, recall that these incomes are all expressed in purchasing power parity and not market exchange rates.

If we were to look at income earned per hour worked, the gap observed between rich and poor countries would be even wider (because Sub-Saharan Africans and Southeast Asians spend around 30% more time at work per year than Europeans and North Americans), and the difference in hourly income between Europeans and North Americans would be 30% lower because North Americans work longer hours.[7] This is the first note of caution: incomes are a powerful economic indicator of living standards, but must be complemented by other indicators (time spent at work, quality of public services and infrastructure, quality of civic and human rights,

Figure 1.2a   *Average income across world regions, 2021*

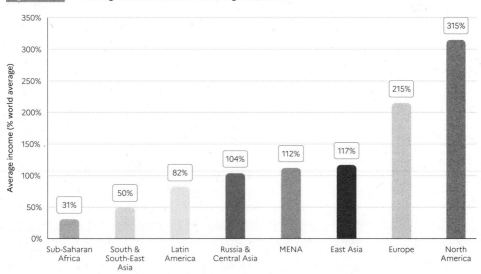

Interpretation: *In 2021, the average income of North America is 315% of world average wealth (at Purchasing Power Parity).* **Sources and series**: *wir2022.wid.world/methodology*

environmental quality, etc.) if they are to be a good representation of inequalities in living standards between countries. There is no silver bullet indicator for measuring inequality across nations and individuals across the world. We will come back to several of these complementary dimensions of inequality in the following chapters of this report.

Turning to wealth inequalities between world regions: it appears that wealth disparities between rich and poor regions are greater than income disparities. Poor regions are relatively poorer in terms of wealth: Sub-Saharan Africans, South and Southeast Asians and Latin Americans own just 20-50% of the global average (compared with 50%-100% for income) as shown in Figure 1.2b. It should be noted that for a given amount of capital, poor regions generate relatively more income than richer ones. It is sometimes argued that poor

countries are poor because they use their capital resources inefficiently. This is incorrect: poor countries are relatively efficient in their use of capital but have very little capital to start with. We discuss the various causes of global inequality between countries in Chapter 2.

Income inequality varies significantly across regions

Let us now turn to economic inequality within countries and regions. Figure 1.3 presents the top 10%, middle 40% and bottom 50% national income shares for various regions of the world. Nowhere in any of these regions does the bottom 50% gain above 20% or under 9-10%, meaning that it systematically earns between 40% and around 20% of the average. Regions with the smallest bottom 50% shares are Latin America, MENA, Sub-Saharan Africa and South and Southeast Asia, where the bottom 50% captures 9-12% of

Figure 1.2b   *Average wealth across world regions, 2021*

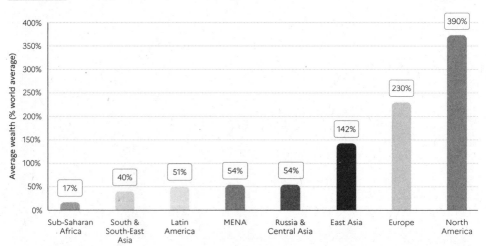

Interpretation: *In 2021, the average wealth of North America is 390% of world average wealth (at Purchasing Power Parity). Net household wealth is equal to the sum of financial assets (e.g. equity or bonds) and non-financial assets (e.g. housing or land) owned by individuals, net of their debts.* **Sources and series:** *wir2022. wid.world/methodology.*

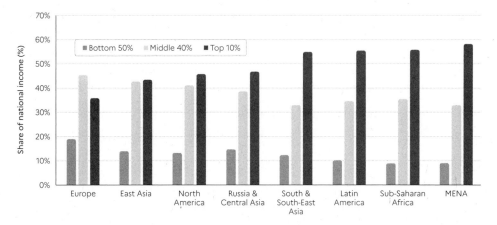

Figure 1.3   *The poorest half lags behind: Bottom 50%, middle 40% and top 10% income shares across the world in 2021*

Interpretation: In Latin America, the top 10% captures 55% of national income, compared with 36% in Europe. Income is measured after pension and unemployment benefits are received by individuals, but before income taxes and other transfers. *Sources and series:* wir2022.wid.world/methodology

national income. In these regions, inequality levels are on par with inequality levels recorded at the global level. Put differently, there is as much income inequality between world citizens as there is inequality between individuals living within Latin America or within Sub-Saharan Africa. This can be explained by the presence of dual societies within these regions – these are societies with a very affluent economic and political elite that enjoys high-income countries' levels of prosperity, living next to individuals in extreme poverty. In other world regions, the bottom 50% is not as poor, either relatively absolutely: in North America, East Asia, and Russia and Central Asia, the bottom 50% share is close to 13% and the European bottom 50% captures 19% of national income.

Turning to the other end of the distribution, the top 10% captures 36% of income in Europe while this is 55-58% in the world's most unequal regions. The ranking of top 10% income shares mirrors the ranking of regions on the relative position of the bottom 50%: regions with very low bottom 50% shares have very high top 10% shares. Europe stands out as a relatively equal region – the only one with a middle 40% (to simplify, a "middle class") that as a whole earns significantly more than the top 10%.

It is strikingly clear that average standards of living are a particularly unreliable determinant of inequality levels across the world. Europe and North America have broadly similar average incomes, but their inequality levels are markedly different.[8] MENA and East Asia also have similar per capita incomes, but very different income distributions. This is a key insight of this Chapter: there is a variety of possible inequality outcomes for any given average standard of living. Put differently, there is no trade-off between higher income levels and higher inequality levels. At the same time, higher average income levels by no means imply less inequality. The degree of inequality within a society is fundamentally a result of political choices: it is determined by how a society decides to organize its economy (i.e. the sets of rights given to and constraints imposed on firms, governments, individuals, and other economic actors).

Moving beyond the study of income shares, a simple way to compare overall inequality across countries is to focus on the gap between the top 10% average incomes and the bottom 50% average incomes. This indicator, which we call the **Top 10/ Bottom 50 (T10/B50) income gap** summarizes in a single metric how societies distribute incomes at both ends of the social ladder. Its interpretation is straightforward as it answers a relatively basic question: *"How many times more do the rich earn than the poorest half?"*

Note that if the top 10% income share were equal to 50% and the bottom 50% income share to 10%, then, as the bottom 50% is five times greater in number than the top 10%, the T10/B50 income gap would be exactly equal to 25, i.e. the rich would earn 25 times as much as the poorest half of the population. In other words, the T10/B50 gap is higher than 25 when the share that the top 10% earn is more than 50% of the total and the share of the bottom 50% is less than 10%, and lower than 25 when the opposite happens.

In practice, extremely unequal regions exhibit T10/B50 income gaps higher than 20. In East Asia, Russia and Central Asia, and North America, the top 10% earn 16 times more than the poorest half of the population. In Europe, the income gap is 10 in 2020-2021 (Figure 1.4). As we can see, inequality levels in Europe are nearly half those of in East Asia, Russia and Central Asia, and North America. Inequality levels are also nearly double between these latter regions and those marked by more extreme inequality levels.

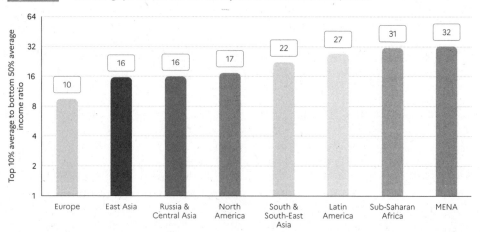

Figure 1.4   *Income gaps across the world: Top 10 % vs. Bottom 50%, 2021*

Interpretation: In Latin America, the bottom 50% earns 27 times less than the top 10%. The value is 10 in Europe. Income is measured after pension and unemployment benefits are received by individuals, but before other taxes they pay and transfers they receive. Numbers may not add up due to rounding.
Sources and series: *wir2022.wid.world/methodology*

Differences in inequality are not well explained by geographic or average income differences

Regional inequality levels mask significant variations in inequality between countries within regions, further demonstrating that inequality levels are not determined by geography or development levels. Figure 1.5 (see also online tables) presents T10/B50 income gaps for all countries across the world. In Africa, income gaps vary from 13 to 15 in Nigeria, Ethiopia, Guinea and Mali, for instance, to between 40 and 63 in the Central African Republic, Namibia, Zambia and South Africa. In South and Southeast Asia, India's T10/B50 income gap is 22, significantly above Thailand's value of 17. In Latin America, Argentina's income gap is 13 while it is 29 in neighboring Brazil and Chile. Between high-income countries, significant variations are also seen: in Germany, France, Denmark and the UK, the T10/B50 income gap is between seven and 10 while the

US income gap is over 17. For any given level of development, there is indeed a large variety of possible inequality levels.

The geographical repartition of global incomes

Figure 1.7 presents the relative size of the population of each region at different levels of the global income distribution in 2021. Each colored wedge is proportional to the total adult population of a region. Sub-Saharan Africa and South-South East Asia occupy the bottom of the distribution, with the bulk of their population between €1,000 and €7,000 per year. The bulk of East Asians, including Chinese, stands between €5,000 and €40,000. North Americans and Europeans are mainly represented between €20,000 and €70,000.

Figure 1.8 provides another type of geographical decomposition of global incomes. The graph presents, for each percentile of the global income distribution, the

---

Figure 1.5   *Top 10/Bottom 50 income gaps across the world, 2021*

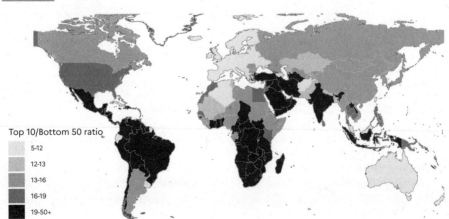

Top 10/Bottom 50 ratio

- 5-12
- 12-13
- 13-16
- 16-19
- 19-50+

Interpretation: *In Brazil, the bottom 50% earns 29 times less than the top 10%. The value is 7 in France. Income is measured after pension and unemployment benefits are received by individuals, but before other taxes they pay and transfers they receive.* **Sources and series:** *wir2022.wid.world/methodology.*

Figure 1.6a   *Top 10% income shares across the world, 2021*

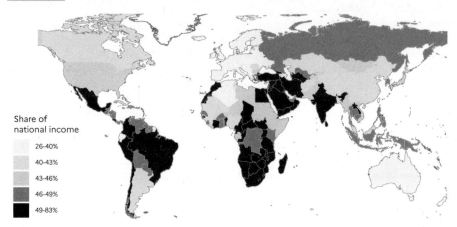

Share of
national income

- 26-40%
- 40-43%
- 43-46%
- 46-49%
- 49-83%

Interpretation: *In South Africa, the top 10% captures 67% of total national income, whereas the value is 32% in France. Income is measured after pension and unemployment benefits are received by individuals, but before other taxes they pay and transfers they receive.* **Sources and series:** *wir2022.wid.world/methodology.*

Figure 1.6b   *Bottom 50% income shares across the world, 2021*

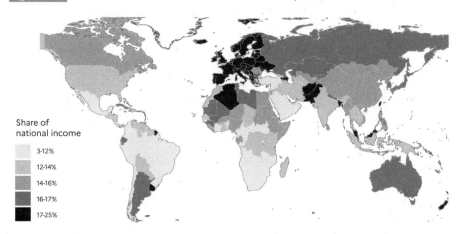

Share of
national income

- 3-12%
- 12-14%
- 14-16%
- 16-17%
- 17-25%

Interpretation: *In South Africa, the bottom 50% captures 5% of total national income, whereas the value is 23% in France. Income is measured after pension and unemployment are benefits received by individuals, but before other taxes they pay and transfers they receive.* **Sources and series:** *wir2022.wid.world/methodology.*

share of each region. Europe and North America are almost only present between the top 50% of the distribution and more so in the top 30%. The graph also shows that emerging and developing countries can combine both a very large share of extremely poor individuals and a relatively good representation among the world's top income groups.

The limited impact of redistribution on global inequality

It should be noted that the income figures reported above are measured after operations related to pension

Figure 1.7   *Global income distribution in 2021*

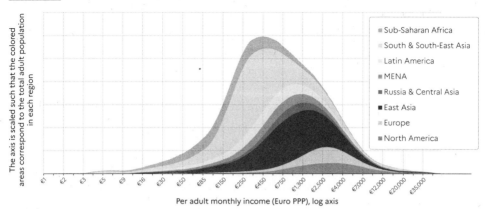

The axis is scaled such that the colored areas correspond to the total adult population in each region

Legend:
- Sub-Saharan Africa
- South & South-East Asia
- Latin America
- MENA
- Russia & Central Asia
- East Asia
- Europe
- North America

Per adult monthly income (Euro PPP), log axis

Interpretation: *The graph shows the size and geographical repartition of the global population at different levels of the income distribution. The relative size of each color wedge is proportional to the population in a region. Incomes are measured after pension and unemployment benefits are received by individuals, and before income and wealth taxes.* **Sources and series:** *wir2022.wid.world/methodology.*

Figure 1.8   *Geographic Breakdown of global income groups in 2021*

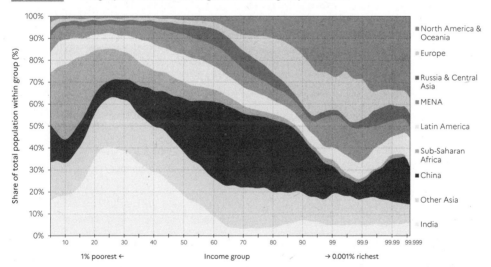

Share of total population within group (%)

Legend:
- North America & Oceania
- Europe
- Russia & Central Asia
- MENA
- Latin America
- Sub-Saharan Africa
- China
- Other Asia
- India

1% poorest ←   Income group   → 0.001% richest

Interpretation: *The graph shows the geographical breakdown of global income groups. In 2021, 18% of the population of the world's top 0.001% income group were residents of China. Income measured after pension and unemployment benefits are received by individuals, and before income and wealth taxes.* **Sources and series:** *wir2022.wid.world/methodology.*

and unemployment benefit systems (i.e. after contributions made and transfers received by individuals for their pensions and public unemployment insurance schemes, but before other taxes and transfers that they pay and receive). Taking pensions into account is necessary in order to reduce the influence of aging on inequality (as retirees earn little income through work but receive deferred earnings through pension schemes).

For reasons explained below, it is essential to measure inequality both before and after the operation of taxes and transfers if we are to arrive at a good understanding of how redistribution (through taxes and transfers) affects inequality.

Taxes, and the transfers that they finance, generally reduce inequality because they redistribute income (or wealth). We call such inequality reduction through taxes and transfers *redistribution*. Taxes include taxes on income (e.g., individual income taxes, and social contributions taken from labor earnings for health insurance), taxes on consumption (such as Value Added or Goods and Service Taxes) and taxes on wealth (e.g., property taxes).[9] Transfers include all social transfers received by individuals (except pensions and unemployment insurance, which are included in our definition of income before taxes, in order to make international comparisons more meaningful).[10]

Pre-distribution can be defined as the set of policies and institutions that reduce pre-tax income inequality. Pre-distribution policies include minimum wages rules (applied in some countries to prevent earnings from being too low), free/accessible education (which make it possible for children from low-income backgrounds to receive high quality education and have good earnings as adults), rent controls (which regulate the rents that landlords can charge), antitrust laws (which limit the power and profits of monopolies), and the like.[11] Significantly, the impact of pre-distribution policies on inequality is less directly visible than the impact of redistribution through taxes and transfers, but the very large variation in pre-tax income inequality across countries at similar stages of economic development shows that pre-distribution is critically important in controlling inequality.

Figure 1.9a shows T10/B50 income gaps across world regions before and after the operation of tax

Figure 1.9a   *Inequality across the world, 2018-2021: the uneven impact of redistribution on inequality*

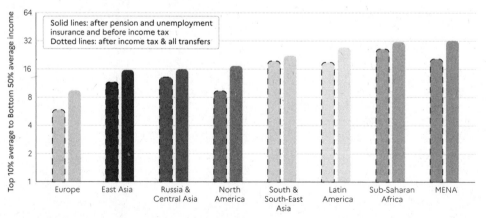

Interpretation: *In North America, the bottom 50% earns 17 times less than the top 10% before income tax, whereas after income tax and all transfers, the bottom 50% earns 10 times less than the top 10%.* **Sources and series:** *wir2022.wid.world/methodology*

and transfer systems. Solid lines show the level of inequality before redistribution but after the operation of pre-distribution mechanisms, whereas broken lines show the level of inequality after redistribution. Three results stand out. First, inequality after redistribution is lower than inequality before taxes in all regions of the world: taxes and transfers reduce inequality everywhere. While this may seem self-evident to readers today, historically this was not always so. In pre-modern or ternary societies, taxes were paid by the working classes to finance the standards of living of the political and religious elite as well as expensive wars.[12] In the 19th and early 20th century, progressive tax systems started to appear in European countries but, at the same time, European colonial powers implemented regressive tax and transfer systems in colonial societies.[13] The development of a progressive tax system was one of the clear social improvements of the 20th century but this system is by no means irreversible. In several countries, tax systems have become regressive over the past four decades, meaning that the rich pay less tax, as a share of their income, than the middle or working classes (more on this in Chapters 7, 8 and 9).

Second, even if taxes and transfers reduce inequality across the world, their impact seems relatively modest. In regions that are extremely unequal before taxes and transfers, inequality remains extremely high after taxes and transfers. Latin America and Sub-Saharan Africa for instance, with T10/B50 income gaps, move from 25-32 before to 18-26 after the operation of the redistribution system. In East Asia, North America

and Central Asia, T10/B50 income gaps reduce from 15-17 before taxes to 9-11 after taxes. Redistribution in these regions does not lower their inequality levels to close to the values observed in Europe (where the T10/B50 income gap decrease from around nine to six). We can therefore conclude that the biggest share of the inequality gap that exists between relatively equal regions (such as Europe) and relatively unequal regions is explained by pre-distribution, rather than by redistribution per se. In other words, inequality before taxes is a relatively good determinant of inequality after taxes and transfers. Redistribution is important in explaining inequality levels across regions, but pre-distribution matters even more. Third, redistribution is quite high in high-income regions (Europe, North America) and almost non-existent in low-income regions (South and Southeast Asia and Sub-Saharan Africa). Poor countries lack the fiscal capacity to reduce inequality. This has implications for current debates about state building and trade liberalization, as well as for the discussion about North–South revenue sharing in relation to the taxing of profits of multinational companies, which we discuss in the final chapter of this report.

The complementarity between predistribution and redistribution

Another way to look at redistribution across the world's regions is to plot the degree of inequality before taxes on the horizontal axis, and the degree of inequality reduction on the vertical axis. We do this in Figure 1.9b. The lower the inequality before taxes, the higher the level of redistribution.

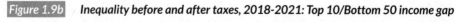

Figure 1.9b *Inequality before and after taxes, 2018-2021: Top 10/Bottom 50 income gap*

*Interpretation: In 2018-2021, the bottom 50% in Europe earns 10 times less than the top 10%, and Inequality decreases by 38% after taxes. **Sources and series:** wir2022.wid.world/methodology*

In regions where market inequality levels are relatively low (i.e. where pre-distribution is relatively high), there tend to be more social forces pushing for higher redistribution as well. Conversely, when the institutional and policy set-up does little to reduce inequality in the first place, there are fewer mechanisms to reduce inequality after taxes as well. An important conclusion from this global observation is that high levels of redistribution are difficult to attain with low levels of pre-distribution. These two forms of inequality reduction go hand in hand. In economics speak, they are complements rather than substitutes.

Figure 1.10 shows the relationship between inequality before taxes and transfers (as measured by our T10/B50 income gap, on the horizontal axis) and inequality after taxes transfers (on the vertical axis) across countries. The main observations made at the regional level are confirmed by this more detailed country level representation. Inequality differences after taxes and transfers are mainly driven by inequality differences before taxes and transfers. Pretax inequality explains most of the variations in post-tax inequality levels observed across countries. In other words, redistribution matters to reduce inequality but does not significantly change country rankings. This has important implications for contemporary debates about taxation and social policies, which we return to later in this report.

The extreme concentration of capital

We now turn to regional and national level wealth inequality. Figure 1.11 presents the top 10%, middle 40%

Figure 1.10   *Inequality before and after taxes 2018-2021: Top 10/Bottom 50 income gap*

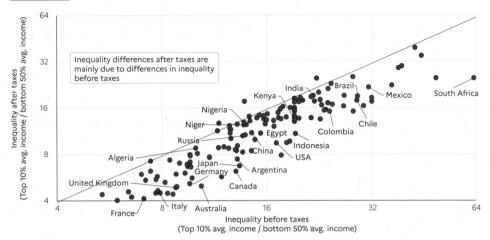

Interpretation: *Before taxes, the bottom 50% in South Africa earns 63 times less than the top 10%, whereas after taxes, the bottom 50% earns 24 times less than the top 10%. Income is measured after pension and unemployment payments and benefits received by individuals but before other taxes they pay and transfers they receive. Data for 2018-2021.* **Sources and series:** *wir2022.wid.world/methodology*

Figure 1.11   *The extreme concentration of capital: wealth inequality across the world, 2021*

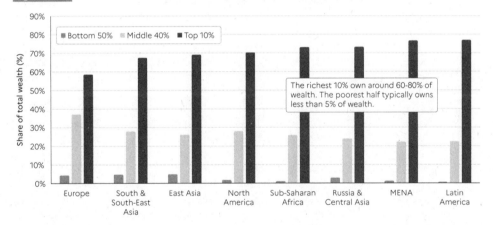

Interpretation: *The top 10% in Latin America captures 77% of total household wealth, compared with 1% captured by the bottom 50%. Net household wealth is equal to the sum of financial assets (e.g. equity or bonds) and non-financial assets (e.g. housing or land) owned by individuals, net of their debts.* **Sources and series:** *wir2022.wid.world/methodology*

and bottom 50% wealth shares for the major regions. It is striking that top 10% wealth shares fall broadly in the 60-80% range in all regions. This reveals the persistence of extremely hierarchical private property systems on all continents, irrespective of the political institutions the societies have opted for and irrespective of their level of economic development. North America, the world's richest region, is also one of the most unequal when it comes to wealth ownership.

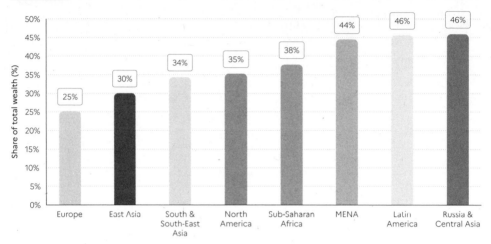

Figure 1.12 *The extreme concentration of capital. Top 1% wealth share across the world, 2021*

Interpretation: *The Top 1% in Russia and Central Asia captures 46% of total household wealth. Net household wealth is equal to the sum of financial assets (e.g. equity or bonds) and non-financial assets (e.g. housing or land) owned by individuals, net of their debts.* **Sources and series:** *wir2022.wid.world/ methodology*

Yet, there are notable differences between the regions. In particular, the middle 40% wealth group owns 20-30% in all regions except in Europe, where its share is close to 40%. This means that, in Europe, the patrimonial middle class owns close to the average wealth of this region. This European middle class emerged in the 20th century and has persisted since. In Chapter 3, we show that the wealth of the middle class in the US has considerably eroded since the 1980s with the rise of the top 1% wealth holders that has captured a disproportionate share of capital accumulated since then.Looking at the bottom 50% of wealth holders, it is striking that this group holds close to no wealth at all in all regions. Its share in total wealth varies from 1% in Latin America to 4-5% in Europe, East and Central Asia. The bottom half of the population, in all societies of the world, is almost entirely deprived of capital. Even in advanced economies, whatever modest wealth they own (such as housing or retirement funds) is almost entirely offset by debt. Moreover, this situation is particularly worrying for future income inequality levels because inequality in asset ownership has direct consequences on income inequality through capital income, and indirect consequences through unequal inheritances.

To get a better sense of the extreme wealth inequalities observed across the world, it is also useful to zoom in on the top 10% of wealth holders. Figure 1.12 presents the top 1% wealth shares across world regions. The richest 1% own between one quarter in Europe and 35-46% in North and Latin America of total wealth.

In order to compare the magnitude of wealth inequality with that of income inequality, Figure 1.13 presents T10/B50 wealth gaps, i.e. the average wealth of the top 10% divided by the average wealth of the bottom 50% - similar to the indicator used for income. The wealth gaps thus obtained are particularly extreme, with the richest 10% owning around 65 times more wealth than the poorest

half of the population in the less unequal regions of the world, and over 100 times more in the most unequal regions of the world. Note that, by definition, such wealth gaps become very great as bottom

Figure 1.13   *The extreme concentration of capital: Top 10/Bottom 50 wealth gaps, 2021*

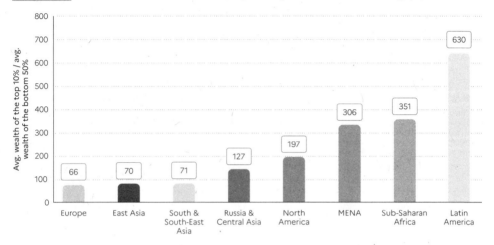

Interpretation: The Bottom 50% in Latin America holds 630 times less of household wealth than the Top 10%. Net household wealth is equal to the sum of financial assets (e.g. equity or bonds) and non-financial assets (e.g. housing or land) owned by individuals, net of their debts. **Sources and series:** wir2022.wid.world/methodology

Figure 1.14a   *Top 10% wealth shares across countries, 2021*

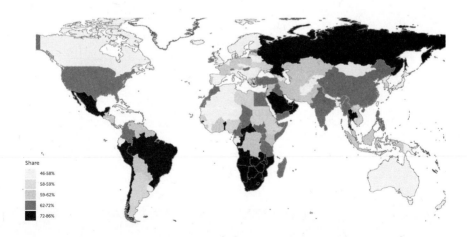

Interpretation: In Mexico, the Top 10% captures 79% of total household wealth, whereas the value is 52% in Norway. Net household wealth is equal to the sum of financial assets (e.g. equity or bonds) and non-financial assets (e.g. housing or land) owned by individuals, net of their debts. **Sources and series:** wir2022.wid.world/methodology

50% income shares approach zero, which, unfortunately, is the state of wealth inequality almost everywhere.

Figures 1.14abc present the top 10%, middle 40% and bottom 50% wealth shares across countries. As for income inequality, there are significant variations in wealth inequality within regions and between groups of countries with similar average wealth levels. The wealth share of the top 10% in the US is higher than 70%, a level closer

Figure 1.14b   *Bottom 50% wealth shares across countries, 2021*

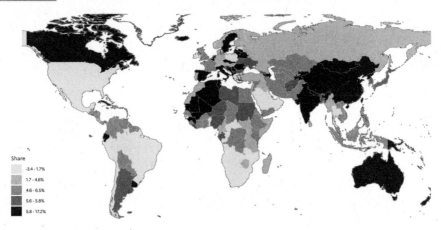

Share
- -3.4 - 1.7%
- 1.7 - 4.6%
- 4.6 - 6.5%
- 5.6 - 5.8%
- 5.8 - 17.2%

Interpretation: *In Spain, the Bottom 50% captures 17% of total household wealth, whereas the value is -2% in Greece: individuals from the bottom 50% have more debt than wealth on average. Net household wealth is equal to the sum of financial assets (e.g. equity or bonds) and non-financial assets (e.g. housing or land) owned by individuals, net of their debts.* **Sources and series:** *wir2022.wid.world/methodology*

Figure 1.14c   *Middle 40% wealth shares across countries, 2021*

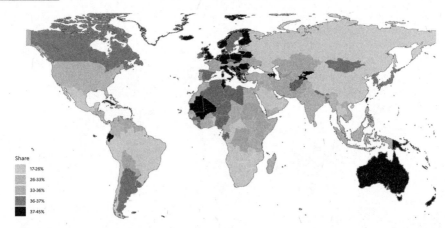

Share
- 17-26%
- 26-33%
- 33-36%
- 36-37%
- 37-45%

Interpretation: *In Australia, the Middle 40% captures 38% of total household wealth, whereas the value is 23% in Russia. Net household wealth is equal to the sum of financial assets (e.g. equity or bonds) and non-financial assets (e.g. housing or land) owned by individuals, net of their debts.* **Sources and series:** *wir2022. wid.world/methodology* to that of many extremely unequal Latin American or Sub-Saharan African countries than to European countries.

Figure 1.15 presents the global distribution of wealth and the size of the population of each world region at different levels of the wealth distribution.

Figure 1.16 provides a geographical breakdown of the global wealth distribution.

Figure 1.15   *Global wealth distribution in 2021*

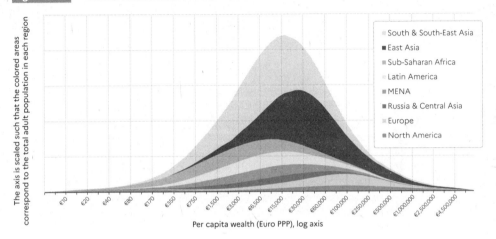

Interpretation: *The graph shows the size and geographical repartition of the global population at different levels of the wealth distribution. The relative size of each color wedge is proportional to the population in a region. Distribution of household wealth, net of debts.* **Sources and series:** *wir2022.wid.world/methodology*

Figure 1.16   *Geographic Decomposition of global wealth groups in 2021*

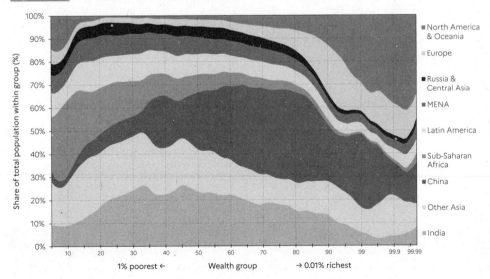

Interpretation: *The graph shows the geographical repartition of the global population at different levels of the wealth distribution. In 2021, 34% of the top 0.01% wealth group were residents of North America and Oceania. Distribution of household wealth, net of debts.* **Sources and series:** *wir2022.wid.world/methodology*

| Box 1.1 | Income and wealth inequality concepts used in this report |

There are different ways to define the income of individuals and therefore multiple ways to measure inequality, depending on the concepts of income used. To some extent, the same is true for wealth. When making international comparisons of income or wealth inequality levels, it is essential to measure the same concepts across countries to avoid any misleading conclusions.

The international network of researchers associated with the World Inequality Database (see Box 1.2) works hard to ensure that the income concepts presented in this report can be compared from one country to another and that they correspond to internationally recognized standards. Our benchmark income concept corresponds to the value that individuals read on their pay checks in many countries across the world, i.e. it is income measured before income and wealth taxes and after the operation of pension and retirement systems. We call this "**post-replacement, pre-income tax**" income. Another important income type corresponds to income measured after all income, wealth and consumption

taxes are deducted, and after all non-replacement transfers (e.g. healthcare, disability and housing benefits) are added. We call this "**post-tax income**". In this report, we alternate between the two concepts, using "post-replacement, pre-income tax" as the benchmark. As a general rule, we report incomes of adult individuals only and we split incomes equally between married couples.

Household wealth is defined as the sum of financial assets (e.g. deposits, stocks, bonds, equity) and non-financial assets (e.g. housing, business), net of debts, possessed by individuals. Interested readers should refer to the World Inequality Database and the Distributional National Accounts Guidelines for a discussion of the methods and other concepts associated with the data presented in this report.

The report contains several QR codes, which direct readers to relevant sections of the World Inequality Database. By clicking on the codes, readers will access additional methodological information, as well as the latest updates of the data presented in the report.

| Box 1.2 | The WID.world and Distributional National Accounts Project |

The World Inequality Database and the Distributional National Accounts Project

Producing inequality data in a context of extreme data opacity is difficult and so results are necessarily

imperfect and preliminary. And yet, income and wealth dynamics must be tracked as systematically as possible. The World Inequality Lab seeks to combine different data sources in a fully transparent and consistent way in order to map the distributions of national income and national wealth. We also work hard to publish all this information online, and in open-access form on the World Inequality Database (WID. world).

The Distributional National Accounts project originates from renewed interest in the use of tax data to study the long-run dynamics of inequality, following the pioneering work on income and wealth inequality series developed by economists Simon Kuznets, Anthony Atkinson and Alan Harrison.[14] Top income shares, based on fiscal data, were initially produced for France and the US by Thomas Piketty and Emmanuel Saez, and rapidly expanded to dozens of countries, thanks to the contribution of over 100 researchers involved in the World Inequality Database and its earlier version, the World Top Income Database.[15] These series had a very great impact on the global inequality debate because they made it possible to compare the income shares of top groups (for example, the top 1%) over long periods of time, revealing new facts and refocusing the discussion on the rise in inequality seen in recent decades.[16]

More recently, the Distributional National Accounts project, led by the World Inequality Lab, in partnership with a number of national statistical offices and international organizations, has sought to go beyond the study of top income shares to produce estimates consistent with macroeconomic growth rates. The objective is to be able to produce annual income and wealth growth rates of different groups of the population alongside the publication of growth statistics

by governments every year. Without such data, it is impossible really to know which social groups are losing and which are winning from economic policies.

The complete DINA methodological guidelines, as well as all computer codes and detailed data series and research papers, are available online on WID.world.[17] We summarize some of the methods below. The basic principle of the DINA project is that properly tracking income and wealth dynamics requires a systematic and transparent combination of different data sources, including fiscal, survey, wealth and national accounts data.

Household surveys have been used as the standard source to track income and wealth inequality over the past decades. While they provide a rich set of socio-demographic information about respondents, these sources tend to misrepresent top income and wealth levels in a population (due to misreporting and statistical biases). Because of this, inequality estimates in certain countries are at odds with the actual dynamics of income and wealth.

To track the evolution of top incomes and wealth, administrative data on income and wealth (e.g. data from tax authorities) tend to be more reliable sources of information than surveys. Unfortunately, in many countries these sources provide information on only a subset of the population—namely, those who file tax returns. Another limitation of tax data is that they are subject to changes in fiscal concepts over time and across countries. Typically, depending on whether income components (such as labor income, dividends, and capital income) are subject to tax, they may or may not appear in the tax data from which distributional statistics can be computed. These differences can make international and historical comparisons difficult.

The DINA project provides a series of systematic rules and methods to reconstruct comparable estimates. To some extent, the harmonization problems can be resolved by using national account data—and in particular, the concepts of national income and national wealth—as a benchmark. Our choice of these concepts for the analysis of inequality does not mean that we consider them perfectly satisfactory. On the contrary, our believe that national accounts statistics are insufficient and need to be greatly improved.In our view, however, the best way to improve on the national accounts is to confront them with other sources and to attempt to distribute national income and wealth across income and wealth groups. The key advantage of national accounts is that they follow internationally standardized definitions for measuring national economic activity. As such, they allow for a more consistent comparison over time and across countries than do fiscal data. National accounts definitions, in particular, do not depend on local variations in tax legislation or other parts of the legal system. They are the most widely used concepts for comparing economic prosperity across nations.

Today, the World Inequality Database brings together over 100 inequality scholars located on all continents. We work hand in hand with partner research groups (see Box 1.3), statistical institutions and international organizations to define internationally agreed standards, and to improve statistical capacities all over the world.

Box 1.3   The rich ecosystem of global inequality data sets

There are many different inequality databases across the world and even more research groups working on inequality. These inequality databases include, for instance, the World Bank's PovcalNet, which provides consumption inequality data from household surveys; the Luxembourg Income Study (LIS), which harmonizes a great deal of detail, income and wealth concepts using household surveys; the OECD Income Distribution Database (IDD) with distributional survey data for advanced economies; the University of Texas Income Project Database using industrial and sectoral data to measure inequality; and the Commitment to Equity Database (CEQ), which provides information on tax incidence, i.e., the impact of taxes and transfers on different income groups. The UNU-WIDER's World Income Inequality Database provides income inequality data sets for a vast number of countries. There are also relatively detailed regional databases such as the Socio-Economic Database for Latin America and the Caribbean (SEDLAC), and the European Survey of Income and Living Conditions database.

These databases have proven extremely useful to researchers, policymakers, journalists, and the general public interested in the evolution of inequality over past decades. There does not exist and there will never exist one perfect database on inequality: the different data sets bring complementary insights into inequality, and whether one should use one or another largely depends on the specific issues one wants to study. Some, like PovCalNet are relied upon to compute global poverty measures. Others, like the LIS database, have been used by generations of researchers to study economic inequality and its interactions with other dimensions of welfare, from an international perspective. Regional databases like SEDLAC and EU-SILC enable detailed regional analyses of inequality, while the CEQ database can be used to analyze the impact of tax and transfer policies.

A central issue for most of these sources is that they essentially rely on a specific information source—namely, household surveys—which are critical for measuring income and wealth inequality, but which also have important limitations. Household surveys consist mostly of face-to-face or virtual interviews with individuals who are asked questions about their incomes, wealth, and other socio-economic aspects of their lives. Surveys are particularly valuable because they gather information about not only income or assets, but also about social and demographic dimensions. They thus allow for a better understanding of the determinants of income and wealth inequality, and help to place income and wealth inequality in broader contexts—including racial, spatial, educational, and gender inequality.

The main problem with household surveys, however, is that they usually rely entirely on self-reported information about income and wealth. As a consequence, they tend to misrepresent top income and wealth levels, and therefore overall inequality. This can also contribute to inconsistencies between macroeconomic growth (as recorded by GDP statistics) and household income growth (as recorded by surveys for the bottom and middle parts of the distribution). The World Inequality Database seeks to address this issue by combining, in a systematic manner, household surveys, administrative data, rich lists, and national accounts – to bridge the gap between micro-economic statistics and the study of income and wealth economic growth.Over the years, researchers associated with the WIL have developed many partnerships and projects with other inequality data providers (e.g. LIS, CEQ, PovCal) in order to develop synergies and to improve global public statistics. The WIL has also developed partnerships with national and international statistical organizations (e.g. the United Nations and several national statistical offices and tax authorities) to develop new international inequality measurement standards, in the context of revisions of the national accounts system.[18]

Box 1.4   Impact of the Covid crisis on inequality between countries

The global Coivd-19 pandemic and the economic crisis that followed hit all world regions, but it hit them with varying intensity. Europe, Latin America, and South and Southeast Asia recorded the largest drops in national income in 2020 (between -6% and -7.6%) while East Asia (where the pandemic began) succeeded in stabilizing its 2020 income at the level of 2019. What has happened in the year 2021? Growth estimates are largely projections (based on April 2021 IMF forecasts, published before the rapid development of the Delta variant in the summer of 2021). It is quite clear, though, that the effects of the economic crisis continue to be unequally distributed across the world in 2021. In East Asia, projected growth for 2021 is 8% higher than in 2019, whereas Latin America will continue to suffer severely from the economic crisis (-6% growth). Europe is also projected to have lower incomes in 2021 than in 2019, but this region nevertheless shows a significant improvement over the 2020-2019 situation (-2% in 2021-2019). Other regions are expecting positive 2021-2019 growth, in contrast to with their negative values over 2020-2019 (see Figure B1.1).

Figure B1.2 shows how much of the drop in global income in 2020 occurred in each region. Europe and North America both experienced a little less than half of the average drop in global income (with 30% and 17% of the total recession, respectively), while South and Southeast Asia, Latin America, MENA and Central Asia all took a similar share of the global recession. So, what was the impact of the recession on global inequality between countries? To the extent that about half of the drop accrued in rich countries and the other half in low-income and emerging regions, no clear pattern emerges in the global top 10% income share. If anything, the share of the global bottom 50% halted its progression. We observe that this drop is entirely due to the impact on South and Southeast Asia, and more precisely on India. When India is removed from the analysis, it appears that the global bottom 50% income share actually slightly increased in 2020. These estimates assume that inequality within countries in 2020 has not been affected by the Covid crisis (see Box 1.5 for a discussion of known impacts within countries).

Box 1.5   Impact of the Covid shock on inequality within countries

The Covid-19 pandemic has exacerbated several forms of health, social, gender and racial inequality within countries. It is still too early for a systematic understanding of the intra-country impact of the crisis on income and wealth inequality due to the lack of real-time data on the distribution of growth across all countries.

However, some high-frequency data sources help us to understand the interplay between the Covid crisis and inequality within countries. From billionaire wealth records,

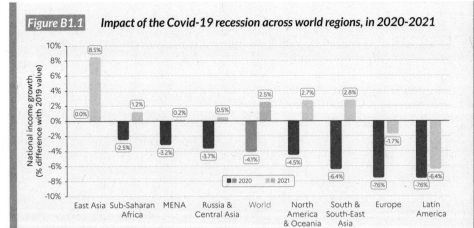

Figure B1.1 *Impact of the Covid-19 recession across world regions, in 2020-2021*

Interpretation: *In 2020, national income in Europe decreased by 7.6%, compared with 0% in East Asia. In 2021, national income in East Asia grew by 8.5% compared with 2019 values.* **Sources and series:** *wir2022.wid.world/methodology*

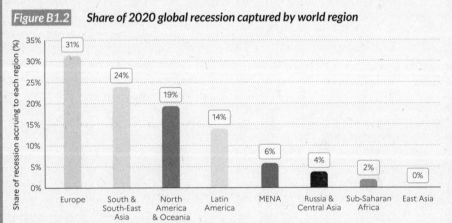

Figure B1.2 *Share of 2020 global recession captured by world region*

Interpretation: *In 2020, 31% of the total drop in global income was recorded in Europe.* **Sources and series:** *wir2022.wid.world/methodology*

we observe, for instance, that the gap between the very top of the wealth distribution and the rest of the population has widened dramatically during this pandemic. Between 2021 and 2019, the wealth of the top 0.001% grew by 14%, while average global wealth is estimated to have risen by just 1%. At the top of the top, global billionaire wealth increased by more than 50% between 2019 and 2021 (more on this in Chapter 4).

Income inequality data generally come less frequently than billionaire wealth data from rich lists. At this stage, it is therefore too early to produce global income inequality estimates that properly take into account the effect of Covid on income inequality within countries, but some country-level studies provide useful insights into these dynamics.

In certain high-income countries, real-time income and savings data are available and are already very informative. Studies reveal that the pandemic initially affected low-income and wealthy groups disproportionately but that government responses were able to counter this effect. In the US, for instance, Chetty et al. show that employment rates fell by 37% around the trough of the COVID recession (April 15, 2020) for workers paid wage rates in the bottom quartile of the pre-COVID wage distribution, while employment fell by 14% for those in the top wage quartile.[19] At the same time, the implementation of exceptional crisis responses in the US (including direct special. payments to households, unemployment benefits, and food stamps) is found to have had a substantial impact on poverty in the US. According to the Urban Institute, poverty dropped by 45% in 2020-2021 measured against 2018 levels (20 million people escaped absolute poverty in the US over the period).[20] This shows that Covid-related policies were critical to countering a rise in inequality and also that persistent poverty is not inevitable: it can indeed be countered with bold social policies.

In Europe, studies using micro-simulations and longitudinal surveys suggest similar results, i.e. without policy responses, a strong increase in income inequality would have occurred, but government support (partial unemployment guarantee, exceptional relief, etc.) tempered this impact and sometimes reduced income inequality.[21] Data on household savings show substantial inequality in the capacity to accumulate wealth during the pandemic, nevertheless. High income groups were able to save significantly more than other groups. In France, Bounie et al. , found that aggregate savings significantly increased in 2020 because of the lockdown.[22] Top wealth groups represent the bulk of this savings increase, and were able to reduce their debts over the course of 2020, while the bottom 10-20% of the distribution actually increased their level of indebtedness.

One important remark should be made at this stage. The large stimulus packages implemented by rich countries were both essential and successful in preventing a sharp rise in poverty and inequality at the bottom of the distribution. It should be noted, however, that these programs were costly and increased public debt by the order of 5-20% of national income (See Chapter 3). This public debt will have to be repaid by individuals in one way or another. At this stage, no one knows how this debt will be repaid. Different strategies can be pursued and each of them will have different consequences for the overall impact of the pandemic on inequality. The impact might be felt over several years or decades, as has been the case with major economic shocks in the past. Governments could, for instance, be tempted by a mix of austerity measures (such as were imposed in the aftermath of the 2008 financial crisis) and regressive taxes (such as increased value-added taxes), which would disproportionately hurt low-income groups. Conversely, should governments implement progressive taxes or pursue partial debt cancellations or restructuring, these measures would help to lower inequality. It is too early to say which of these paths will be followed.

In emerging countries, where social security systems are less developed, the effect of the pandemic on low-income groups has been more severe.[23] The World Bank estimates that the pandemic drove about 100 million people into extreme poverty, raising the global total to 711 million in 2021, up from 655 million in 2019. Without this crisis, the number of people in extreme poverty in 2021 would have been 613 million.[24]

Looking at inequality across the entire population, the International Monetary Fund has also estimated that, in 2020, income inequality grew in emerging markets and low-income countries as a consequence of the Covid crisis.[25] It could increase to a level comparable to that in 2008, reversing all gains made since then. In these countries, fiscal resources and borrowing capacities remain low, safety nets are patchy, and social protection programs sometimes almost non-existent.

Generally speaking, the weaker the social protection system, the more unequal the impacts of a crisis are likely to be, and households that have relatively limited access to markets, capital, and basic services will be most severely hit. Studies suggest that the early phases of the pandemic (the lockdowns) had a greater effect on vulnerable individuals, including those on lower incomes and with lower education levels, minorities, and women. In developing countries, informally employed workers tend to face a higher risk of losing their jobs than workers with formal contracts.[26] However, evidence in developing countries, and particularly low-income countries, remains incomplete due to the paucity of data on informal labor income, despite recent efforts to improve the measurement of distributional effects, such as the UN's Socio-Economic Impact Assessment conducted in several emerging countries during the crisis.[27] Such studies support the assumption that the pandemic has resulted in a loss of household labor income, both formal and informal, a decline in remittances, and price inflation triggered by food price hikes, with spillover effects through rising household debt levels, unaffordable out-of-pocket payments for healthcare services, and reduced access to public healthcare and education. In other words, the crisis hit low-income households disproportionately hard.

The World Bank has also set up a monitoring dashboard composed of harmonized indicators from high-frequency phone surveys conducted in over 45 countries in response to the Covid pandemic. These surveys show higher rates of income loss in low and middle-income countries than in high-income countries. These losses seem to be linked to the formality/informality of the labor market.[28] The farm vs. non-farm family business dichotomy might be another driver of increased inequality, pointing to the buffer role played by the agricultural sector.

At the other end of the distribution, it appears that emerging and low-income countries are no exception to the exceptional rise in top wealth inequalities observed over the period. While incomes dropped at the bottom of the distribution, capital rose steeply at the top.

Box 1.6	What is the relationship between Gross Domestic Product, National Income and National Wealth?

Economic growth is at the heart of contemporary economic policy debates. What does it mean exactly? "Growth" typically refers to the growth rate, or annual evolution, of Gross Domestic Product in a given country. Gross Domestic Product (GDP) is the value of all goods and services produced in an economy over a year, minus the value of goods and services needed to produce them, called intermediary production. Since its conceptual development in the 1940s, GDP has been criticized for its many limitations: it is blind to environmental degradation, it poorly captures variations in human well-being, and ignores inequality. Therefore, increases in GDP by no means indicate that the overall standards of living in a country are improving. This has led over the years to the creation of several alternative indicators, including the Human Development Index, which factors in education and healthcare, and GDP indicators that factor in environmental degradation.

In the aftermath of the 2008 financial crisis, a new wave of research and policy discourses, exemplified by the Stiglitz-Sen-Fitoussi Commission on measuring well-being, stressed the need to move beyond GDP.[29] Their report is fully in line with the work of the World Inequality Lab. We seek to improve measurement of inequalities in human well-being by looking at how economic production actually benefits different groups of individuals (rich and poor, men and women...), and also factoring in the environmental impacts of production.

We stress however that economic growth indicators remain essential to studying inequality worldwide, but to do that, we prefer to use national income rather than GDP. Here is why: GDP not only has key limitations to its measurement of well-being for the reasons indicated above, but also has several pitfalls from a purely economic point of view. In particular, the indicator filters out the depreciation of capital used in production processes (not only for roads and computers, but also, in principle, for forests and other natural resources to the extent that their value can be monetized). Put differently, if a country increases its production by depleting its capital stock (its forests, for instance), GDP will grow, even though the country is arguably getting poorer. In addition, GDP is blind to flows of income coming in to the country from abroad and being sent out to other countries. In certain countries, outward flows reduce actual incomes received by nationals by a large margin, while in others, they increase income significantly. Typically, capital income flows go from poor nations to rich countries, which own capital abroad. It is essential to have a proper sense of these dynamics when looking at global inequality. National income is a better concept than GDP for studying global economic inequality because it takes into account both the depreciation of capital stock and net income flows from abroad. Formally, national income is equal to GDP minus the depreciation of the capital stock used in production processes, plus net incomes received from (or paid to) the rest of the world.

In addition to national income, it is also crucial to focus on national wealth to fully understand the level and dynamics of global economic inequalities. Income is a flow, wealth is a stock. National wealth is equal to the stock of assets owned by nationals of the country (both in that country and abroad). This wealth can be privately owned (by individuals) or publicly owned (by the state). Studying the dynamics of wealth is necessary to understanding contemporary debates about debt, the relative sizes of the public and private sector in the economy, the amount and the quality of infrastructure (public schools, roads, hospitals), and the role of inheritance in the reproduction of inequality. Focusing on the dynamics of national wealth inequality is also necessary to complement our understanding of income inequality, in particular at the top of the distribution. Recent debates about taxation reveal that some billionaires appear to pay low or no individual income taxes because they can report modest incomes relative to the size of their wealth.[30] In fact, many of these individuals have actually become richer (i.e. their wealth increased) thanks to capital gains (i.e. the value of their stock increased). In many countries, capital gains are not treated as taxable income until they are cashed (e.g. until shares are sold). Capital gains are also excluded from the measurement of GDP and national income because they reflect changes in asset values rather than new production. At the same time, when they increase individual wealth, they are a form of income in the pure economic sense of the term. This is also why it is necessary to complement our understanding of aggregate and distributional income measures with aggregate and distributional wealth numbers, as we do in this report.

Box 1.7   Comparing incomes, assets and purchasing power across the globe

How to compare income levels and asset ownership across the world, knowing that the costs of living differ so much between (and within) nations? Market exchange rates do not take into account these differences and hence may not properly account for inequalities in living standards across the globe. A standard way to compare inequality in purchasing power across the globe is to deflate (or inflate) incomes earned in a given country by the cost of goods and services in that country relative to that of others: Purchasing Power Parity (PPP). For instance, housing is relatively cheap in India compared with France, but red wine is relatively less expensive in France than in India. In order properly to compare costs of living across the world, we need information about both the relative prices of goods and services (e.g. wine and housing), and the relative volume of each good and service in the consumption baskets of individuals. This has been the aim of the International Comparison Programme (ICP) since the 1970s. The ICP combines the major international statistical agencies and statistical administrations of more than 190 countries. The group conducts surveys to collect prices and expenditure levels for various goods and services purchased across the world. Its last round was published in May 2020 using data on 2017. Such an enterprise is not perfect (in particular, numbers are national averages, while there may be strong regional variations, as well as differences across income groups) but they provide a better view of inequality in purchasing power than does income at market exchange rates.

At the same time, Market Exchange Rates (MER) can be useful (and increasingly so) for tracking global inequality. While PPP numbers give a more accurate picture of global inequality from the point of view of individuals who spend their incomes in their own countries, MER are perhaps more informative about inequality in a world where individuals can easily spend their incomes wherever they want. This is particularly relevant when one looks at the wealth of global multimillionaires or billionaires, who can easily buy goods and services all over the world. When comparing their wealth levels, it can make a lot of sense to look at MER.

Focusing on MER rather than PPP can also be useful when focusing on how tourists spend their incomes and anyone making purchases in other countries via the internet. MER are also useful when focusing on the incomes of migrants and workers sending remittances back to their home countries.

To summarize, both purchasing power parity and market exchange rates can be valid measures for tracking global income and wealth inequalities, depending on the object of study, or on which countries are being compared. In this report, we generally use purchasing power parity for income comparisons, and a combination of MER and PPP for wealth in order to provide as complete a view of inequality as possible.

NOTES

[1] In this report, and unless stated otherwise, we express incomes in terms of Purchasing Power Parity (PPP), i.e. we take into account differences in the cost of living across countries when we compare incomes earned in different parts of the world. At PPP, EUR 1 = USD 1.4 = CNY 5.0. **See Box 1.7 on purchasing power parities.**

[2] This value is expressed at PPP. At Market Exchange Rates (MER), global wealth is equal to €392 trillion. At MER, EUR1= USD1.2 = CNY7.

[3] Global net wealth is the sum of global net private wealth and global net public wealth. Global net private wealth is equal to the sum of all financial and non-financial assets, net of debts, held by the private sector. See Chapter 3.

[4] Children generally generate very little or no income and have very little wealth. This is why we focus on the adult population. Of course, the welfare of children and whether they grow up in poor or affluent families is also very important as well but outside the scope of this report.

[5] Naturally, not all couples share economic resources equally but data on intra-family resource sharing is scarce. Some of our statistics, however, will focus specifically on the gender gap in labor income, where we attribute labor income to the person who earns it (without splitting it within couples).

[6] Unless stated otherwise, all values are expressed at Purchasing Power Parity.

[7] In Bangladesh, Myanmar, and South Africa, full-time employees work around 2,100 hours per year, compared with 1,600 in rich countries. In Europe, employees work around 1,550 hours per year compared with 1,750 hours in the US. See Feenstra, R. C., R. Inklaar and M. P. Timmer. 2015. «The Next Generation of the Penn World Table.» *American Economic Review*, 105(10), 3150-3182.

[8] Especially when controlling for time spent at work differences.

[9] Beyond healthcare contributions, all "non-contributory social contributions" are taken into account at this stage; these are all social

contributions, except those which contribute to the financing of delayed incomes (i.e. retirement income or unemployment insurance, which we do not count as redistribution strictly speaking).

[10] In order to compare inequality levels across the world, it is arguably better to focus on redistribution independent of the pension and unemployment insurance system. Indeed, before the operation of the pension schemes, retired individuals in countries with large public pension schemes have virtually no income and appear extremely poor in statistics. In these countries, prior to tax and pension transfers, inequality would seem to be extremely high (to a large extent for artificial reasons). After pension transfers, these individuals have an income and inequality levels drop. The drop in inequality is particularly large in countries with many elderly and hence is very sensitive to aging patterns. We choose to use pre-tax income after the operation of pensions systems precisely to control for such aging effects.

[11] For a discussion on redistribution and predistribution, see Blanchard, O., and D. Rodrik, (Eds.). 2021. *Combating Inequality: Rethinking Government's Role.* Cambridge: MIT press. See also Blanchet, T., Chancel, L. Gethin, A. « Why is Europe More Equal than the US?" *American Economic Journal: Applied Economics,* 2021 (forthcoming). See also Bozio, A. Garbinti, B., Goupille-Lebret, J., Guyot, M., and Piketty, T. "Predistribution vs. Redistribution: Evidence from France and the U.S", World Inequality Lab working paper 2020/22.

[12] That is, societies with a nobility, a clergy and a labor class. See Piketty, T. 2020. *Capital and ideology.* Cambridge: Harvard University Press.

[13] See also Piketty (2020).

[14] See Kuznets, S. 1953. "Shares of Upper Income Groups in Income and Savings." New York: National Bureau of Economic Research; Atkinson, A. B., and A. J. Harrison. 1978. *Distribution of Personal Wealth in Britain.* Cambridge: Cambridge University Press

[15] See Piketty, T. 2001. *Les hauts revenus en France au XXème siècle.* Paris: Grasset; Piketty, T. 2003. "Income inequality in France, 1901–1998." *Journal of political economy, 111*(5), 1004-1042; Piketty, T., and E. Saez. 2003. "Income inequality in the United States, 1913–1998." *The Quarterly Journal of Economics*, 118(1), 1-41.

[16] See e.g. Piketty, T. 2014. Capital in the Twenty-First Century. Cambridge: Harvard University Press; Alvaredo, F., L. Chancel, T. Piketty, E. Saez, and G. Zucman. 2018. *World Inequality Report 2018.* Cambridge: Harvard University Press.

[17] See Blanchet, T., L. Chancel, I. Flores, M. Morgan et al. 2021. "Distributional National Accounts Guidelines, Methods and Concepts Used in the World Inequality Database." World Inequality Lab.

[18] See United Nations Development Programme (UNDP). 2019. "Beyond Income, Beyond Averages, Beyond Today: Inequalities in Human Development in the 21st Century." New York: UNDP; see also Germain J.-M. et al. 2021. "Rapport du groupe d'experts sur la mesure des inégalités et de la redistribution." INSEE.

[19] Chetty, R., J. N. Friedman, N. Hendren, M. Stepner and The Opportunity Insights Team. (2020). "How did COVID-19 and stabilization policies affect spending and employment? A new real-time economic tracker based on private sector data." Cambridge: National Bureau of Economic Research.

[20] See Wheaton, L., S. Minton, L. Giannarelli and K. Dwyer. 2021. "2021 Poverty Projections: Assessing Four American Rescue Plan Policies". Washington, DC: Urban Institute, 500.

[21] See Clark, A., C. D'Ambrosio, and A. Lepinteur. 2020. "The Fall in Income Inequality during COVID-19 in five European Countries". Working Paper 565, ECINEQ Society for the Study of Economic Inequality; Palomino, J. C., J. G. Rodriguez, and R. Sebastian. 2020. "Wage inequality and poverty effects of lockdown and social distancing in Europe". *European Economic Review* 129, 103564. October; Almeida, V., S. Barrios, M. Christl, S. De Poli, A. Tumino, and W. van der Wielen. 2020. "Households' income and the cushioning effect of fiscal policy measures during the Great Lockdown". JRC Working Papers on Taxation & Structural Reforms 2020-06, Joint Research Centre; Brunori, P., M. L. Maitino, L. Ravagli, and N. Sciclone. 2020. "Distant and Unequal. Lockdown and Inequalities in Italy". Technical Report wp2020, Universita' degli Studi di Firenze, Dipartimento di Scienze per l'Economia e l'Impresa; O'Donoghue, C., D. M. Sologon, I. Kyzyma, and J. McHale. 2020. "Modelling the Distributional Impact of the COVID-19 Crisis*". *Fiscal Studies* 41 (2), 321–336. For a review of these studies, see Stantcheva, S. 2021. "Inequalities in the Times of a Pandemic", *Economic Policy*, 73rd Economic Policy Panel Meeting, April.

[22] Bounie, D., Y. Camara and J. W. Galbraith. 2020. "Consumers' Mobility, Expenditure and Online-Offline Substitution Response to COVID-19: Evidence from French Transaction Data". Available at SSRN 3588373.

[23] See Voituriez T, and L. Chancel. 2020. "Developing countries in times of COVID: Comparing inequality impacts and policy responses", World Inequality Lab. Issue Brief 2021/01.

[24] See Lakner, C. et al. 2021. "Updated estimates of the impact of COVID-19 on global poverty: Looking back at 2020 and the outlook for 2021", World Bank.

[25] See Voituriez and Chancel (2021) for a longer discussion.

[26] See also Voituriez and Chancel (2021).

[27] See United Nations Development Programme (UNDP). 2020. "COVID-19 and Central Asia: Socio-economic impacts and key policy considerations for recovery". New York: UNDP; United Nations Development Programme (UNDP). 2020. "COVID-19 and the countries of South Caucasus, Western CIS and Ukraine Implications for Business Support, Employment and Social Protection Policies and Programming for Sustainability." New York; United Nations Development Programme (UNDP). 2020. "Analysing long-term socio-economic impacts of COVID-19 across diverse African contexts." New York; United Nations Development Programme (UNDP). 2020. "The next frontier: Human development and the Anthropocene. Human Development Report 2020." New York.

[28] See Jain, R., J. Budlender, R. Zizzamia, I. Bassier. 2020. "The Labor Market and Poverty Impacts of COVID- 19 in South Africa". CSAE Working Paper WPS/202014, Center for the Study of African Economies, Cambridge: Harvard University Press.

[29] Stiglitz, J. E., A. K. Sen, and J.-P. Fitoussi. 2009. Rapport de la Commission sur la mesure des performances économiques et du progrès social.

[30] See the June 2021 leak of US billionaires' individual income and tax. Eisinger, J., J. Ernsthausen and P. Kiel. 2021. "The Secret IRS Files: Trove of Never-Before-Seen Records Reveal How the Wealthiest Avoid Income Tax." *ProPublica.* June 8.

CHAPTER 2
Global inequality from 1820 to now: the persistence and mutation of extreme inequality

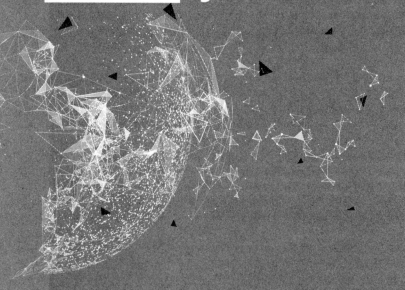

WORLD
INEQUALITY
REPORT
2022

This chapter is based on L. Chancel and T. Piketty. 2021. "Global inequality 1820-2020: The Persistence and Mutation of Extreme Inequality", Journal of the European Economic Association.

In Chapter 1 we provided a snapshot of current global inequality levels. In this chapter, we turn to global inequality trends. For this, we use a historical perspective to understand how current levels of inequality compare with those observed in earlier times. Looking at the past (whether a few decades back or a century ago), is critical to understanding the present. Historical perspectives on inequality make it possible to discuss questions such as: have there been lower inequality levels than now and how did societies deal with them? How extreme could inequalities be in the future?

Let us be clear: comparing inequality levels from one century to the next requires caution. A given level of global inequality can mask very different realities, between say, the European-dominated world economic order of 1910 and contemporary multi-polar capitalism (more on this below). It is not only the very notions of income and wealth that differ across times and cultures, but also forms of economic and political power. That said, some basic characteristics of human societies can be compared over time. Economic resources owned by individuals are not infinite and have to be shared, more or less equally. Constructing indicators to

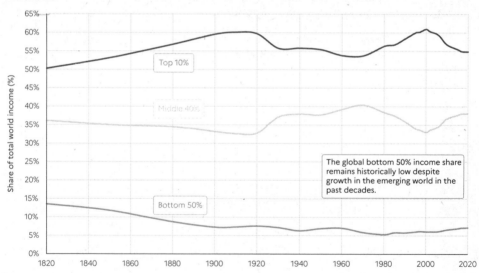

Figure 2.1   *Global income inequality: bottom 50%, middle 40% and top 10%, 1820-2020*

The global bottom 50% income share remains historically low despite growth in the emerging world in the past decades.

Interpretation: The share of global income going to top 10% highest incomes at the world level has fluctuated around 50-60% between 1820 and 2020 (50% in 1820, 60% in 1910, 56% in 1980, 61% in 2000, 55% in 2020), while the share going to the bottom 50% lowest incomes has generally been around or below 10% (14% in 1820, 7% in 1910, 5% in 1980, 6% in 2000, 7% in 2020). Global inequality has always been very large. It rose between 1820 and 1910 and shows little change over the long term between 1910 and 2020. Income is measured per capita after pension and unemployement insurance transfers and before income and wealth taxes. Sources and series: wir2022.wid.world/methodology and Chancel and Piketty (2021).

understand how this distribution of economic resources has evolved over time improves our collective understanding of the roots of justice and injustice across societies.

Global inequality rose between 1820 and 1910, and stabilized at a high level since then

Using similar inequality indicators as in Chapter 1, we start here with the basic breakdown of the shares of world income going to the global top 10%, middle 40% and bottom 50% groups between 1820 and 2020 (see Figure 2.1). The first striking finding is that the level of global income inequality has always been great. The global top 10% income share oscillated around 50-60% of total income between 1820 and 2020, while the bottom 50% share has generally

remained around 5-15%. This corresponds approximately to the level of inequality that we currently observe in the most unequal countries in the world, such as South Africa, Brazil, Mexico and the United Arab Emirates (see Chapter 1).

In brief: in terms of inequality and concentration of resources and economic power, the world today is and has long been like a giant South Africa.

We can also see in Figure 2.1 a clear rise in global inequality between 1820 and 1910. The top 10% share rose from 50% to 60%, while the bottom 50% share dropped from 14% to 7%. In contrast, the shift observed between 1910 and 2020 involves a number of contradictory changes and compensating trends. The bottom 50% share further

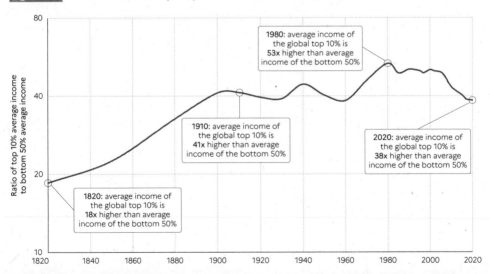

Figure 2.2   *Global income inequality: T10/B50 ratio, 1820-2020*

Interpretation: *Global inequality, as measured by the ratio T10/B50 between the average income of the top 10% and the average income of the bottom 50%, more than doubled between between 1820 and 1910, from less than 20 to about 40, and stabilized around 40 between 1910 and 2020. It is too early to say whether the decline in global inequality observed since 2008 will continue. Income is measured per capita after pension and unemployement insurance transfers and before income and wealth taxes.* **Sources and series:** *wir2022. wid.world/lmethodology and Chancel and Piketty (2021).*

dropped from 7% in 1910 to 5% in 1980, before rising to 7% in 2020, so that it is today very close to what it was in 1910.[1] The top 10% share dropped from 60% in 1910 to 54% in 1970, before rising back to 61% by 2000, and declining again to 55% in 2020. If we look at the overall change between 1910 and 2020, there is no clear long-run trend in inequality, either downward or upward, except maybe a small improvement in the share of the global middle 40%.

We reach the same conclusion if we look at global inequality indicators such as the top 10/bottom 50 (T10/B50) income gap between the average incomes of the top 10% and the bottom 50%. The global T10/B50 income gap more than doubled between 1820 and 1910, from 18 in 1820 to 41 in 1910 (see Figure 2.2).

It reached an all-time high of 53 in 1980 and 50 in 2000, before declining to 38 in 2020. It is striking that the decline in the global T10/B50 income gap occurred for the most part after the 2008 financial crisis. It is too early to say whether that decline will continue in the future.

We reach the same conclusion when we look at other indicators, such as the global Gini coefficient. In effect, the global Gini increased from 0.60 in 1820 to 0.72 in 1910, again 0.72 in 2000 and 0.67 in 2020 (see Figure 2.3). Note that the global inequality peak was reached in 2000 according to the Gini coefficient, while it was reached in 1980 (almost on par with 2000) according to the T10/B50 ratio. Whatever the indicator consulted, a global inequality peak was

Figure 2.3   *Global income inequality: Gini index, 1820-2020*

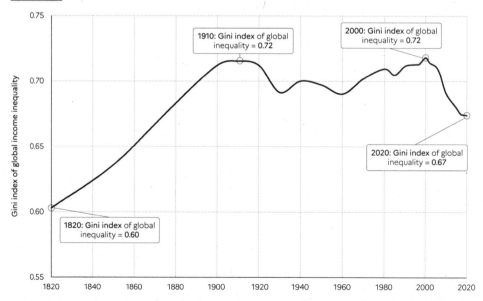

Interpretation: *Global inequality, as measured by the global Gini coefficient, rose from about 0.6 in 1820 to about 0.7 in 1910, and then stabilized around 0.7 between 1910 and 2020. It is too early to say whether the decline in the global Gini coefficient observed since 2000 will continue. Income is measured per capita after pension and unemployement insurance transfers and before income and wealth taxes.* **Sources and series:** *wir2022.wid.world/methodology and Chancel and Piketty (2021).*

reached twice, first around 1910 and then in 1980-2000, and most of the decline in global inequality took place after the 2008 financial crisis. In all cases, global indicators indicate very high inequality levels in 2020 (close to those observed around 1900-1910, and substantially larger than those observed in 1820).

Within-country and Between-country inequalities are as great in 2020 as in 1910

Figure 2.4 presents two versions of the T10/B50 inequality ratio: the "within-country" ratio and the "between-country" ratio. The T10/B50 inequality ratio within countries was computed by canceling the component of inequality between countries, i.e. by assuming that all countries have the same average income, and by aggregating the resulting country-level distributions. In effect, this is almost equivalent to computing a form of average of all country-level T10/B50 inequality ratios (weighted by national population size). We find that within inequality (as measured by this indicator) increased gradually between 1820 and 1910, then sharply declined between 1910 and 1980, and finally rose again between 1980 and 2020. This is the familiar pattern, found in the United States and Western Europe in the context of the new wave of historical research on inequality. A similar pattern has also been found in Japan, India, Russia, China, Latin America, South Africa, among other places, so it is not surprising that we find it here at the global level. Note that the rise of within-country inequality since 1980 apparently reached a sort of plateau between 2010 and 2020 (and has not turned back so far). This plateau appears to be comparable in magnitude (or slightly lower) to the plateau of 1910.

In contrast, the T10/B50 ratio of inequality between countries follows a very different pattern. It was calculated by canceling the within-country inequality component, i.e. by assuming that all inhabitants in any given country have the same income as their country average, and by aggregating the resulting country-level distributions. We find that between-country inequality (as measured by this indicator) increased continuously between 1820 and 1980. In particular, it increased enormously between 1820 and 1950, during the period of colonial empires. In effect, the between-country T10/B50 more than quadrupled, from less than four in 1820 to almost 16 in 1950. It continued to increase at a slower pace between 1950 and 1980. The between-country T10/B50 income gap was over 20 in 1980, after which it started to decline quickly, down to nine in 2020. It is worth noting that China ceased to be part of the bottom 50% of the world in 2010, so the continuation of the decline after 2010 is due to the high-growth performance of countries like India, Indonesia, Vietnam and some (but not all) Sub-Saharan African countries relative to growth rates in rich countries. We should also stress that despite this decline, Between-country inequality remains very high in absolute terms: in 2020, it is roughly at the same level as it was in 1900.

By comparing the evolution of the global T10/B50 income gap (Figure 2.2) with the evolution of the within-country and between-

Figure 2.4   *Global income inequality: Between-country vs Within-country inequality (ratio T10/B50), 1820-2020*

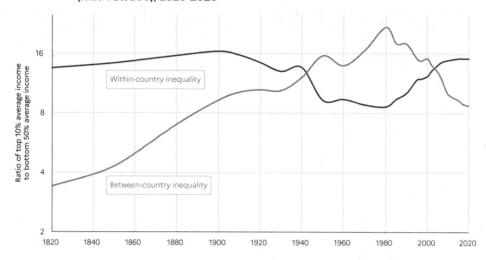

Interpretation: *Between-country inequality, as measured by the ratio T10/B50 between the average incomes of the top 10% and the bottom 50% (assuming everybody within a country has the same income), rose between 1820 and 1980 and has since strongly declined. Within-country inequality, as measured also by the ratio T10/B50 between the average incomes of the top 10% and the bottom 50% (assuming all countries have the same average income), rose slightly between 1820 and 1910, declined between 1910 and 1980, and rose since 1980. Income is measured per capita after pensions and unemployement insurance transfers and before income and wealth taxes.* **Sources and series:** *wir2022.wid.world/methodology and Chancel and Piketty (2021).*

country components (Figure 2.4), we now have a clear picture of the long-term transformation of the world income distribution over the past two centuries. Between 1820 and 1910, both components were rising: between-country inequality was rising, as Western countries were establishing their economic and political supremacy over the rest of world, and within-country inequality was also rising (or was quasi-stable at a very high level), reflecting very unequal and hierarchical domestic political and economic systems. Between 1910 and 1980, within-country inequality was greatly reduced, largely due to rising social spending and progressive taxation, but between-country inequality continued to increase, so that the impact on global inequality was ambiguous.

The opposite occurred between 1980 and 2020: within-country inequality started to rise again, while between-country inequality declined, so that the effect on synthetic inequality indicators like the global T10/B50 income gap was again ambiguous. In the most recent period, however, and especially since the 2008 financial crisis, the declining inequality effect clearly dominates. This is because the rise of within-country inequality seems to have reached a plateau between 2010 and 2020 (in both the North and the South), while simultaneously, the decline in between-country inequality accelerated (due in part to relatively poor growth performance in rich countries post-2008, especially in Europe, compared with growth rates in developing and emerging countries). At the same time, global inequality remains very high in absolute terms: in 2020 it is close to the level observed around 1900.

We reach the same conclusion regarding the breakdown of global inequality trends into within-country and between-country components if we use other indicators, such as the Theil index (which allows for additive decompositions, see Figure 2.5). Namely, the between-country component was relatively small in 1820 (around 10% of global inequality).

It rose substantially between 1820 and 1980 (when it was quantitatively larger than the within-country component, reaching more than 55% in 1980), before declining sharply since then (to arrive at around 30% in 2020).[2]

The global economic elite never fully recovered its *Belle Époque* opulence

Our global inequality series also allow us to study finer inequality indicators focusing on specific segments of the distribution, such as very top incomes. According to our estimates, the global top 1% share rose from 20% of total income in 1820 to 26% in 1910, before dropping to 16% in 1970 and rising again to 21% in 2020. Between 1880 and 2020, the global top 1% share was generally three to four times larger than the share of the bottom 50% (6%-9% of total income), which has typically been of the same order of magnitude as the top 0.1% share (see Figure 2.6). For instance, both the bottom 50% income share and the top 0.1% share are about 8% of total income in 2020. This illustrates the

Figure 2.5   *Global income inequality: Between-country vs Within-country inequality (Theil index), 1820-2020*

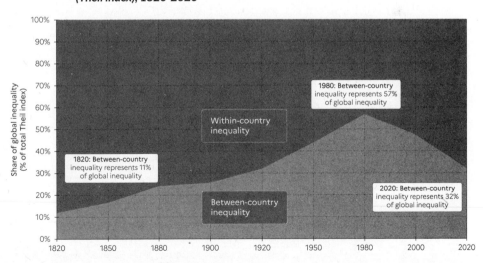

Interpretation: *The importance of between-country inequality in overall global inequality, as measured by the Theil index, rose between 1820 and 1980 and strongly declined since then. In 2020, between-country inequality makes-up about a third of global inequality between individuals. The rest is due to inequality within countries. Income is measured per capita after pension and unemployement insurance transfers and before income and wealth taxes.* **Sources and series:** *wir2022.wid.world/methodology and Chancel and Piketty (2021).*

| Figure 2.6 | **Global income inequality: top 1% and top 0.1% vs bottom 50% income shares, 1820-2020** |

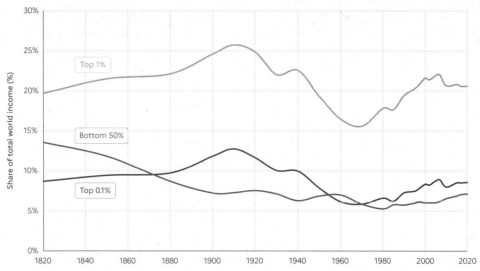

Interpretation: *The share of global income going to the top 1% highest incomes at the world level has hovered around 15-25% between 1820 and 2020 (20% in 1820, 26% in 1910, 16% in 1970, 21% in 2020) and has always been substantially greater than the share going to the bottom 50%, which has generally been of the same order of magnitude as the share going to the top 0.1%. Income is measured per capita after pension and unemployement insurance transfers and before income and wealth taxes.* **Sources and series:** *wir2022.wid. world/methodology and Chancel and Piketty (2021).*

| Figure 2.7 | **Global income inequality: T1/B50 ratio, 1820-2020** |

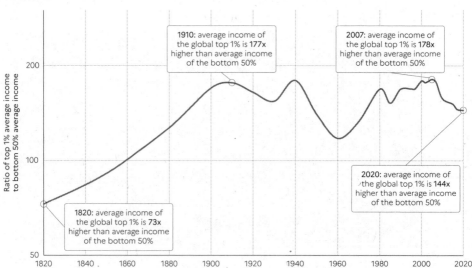

Interpretation: *Global inequality, as measured by the ratio T1/B50 between the average income of the top 1% and the average income of the bottom 50%, more than doubled between between 1820 and 1910, from about 70 to about 180, and stabilized around 150 between 1910 and 2020. It is too early to say whether the decline in global inequality observed since 2008 will continue. Income is measured per capita after pension and unemployement insurance transfers and beofre income and wealth taxes.* **Sources and series:** *wir2022. wid.world/methodology and Chancel and Piketty (2021).*

extreme degree of global income inequality. It implies, for example, that a redistributive policy based on a reduction of one quarter or one third of the incomes of the top 0.1% could have a very significant impact on the incomes of the bottom 50% and on global poverty rates.

Looking at the ratio between the average incomes of the global top 1% and the global bottom 50%, we see that this inequality indicator rose from about 70 in 1820 to 180 in 1910, and then stabilized around 150 between 1910 and 2020 (see Figure 2.7). Note that the T1/B50 ratio is always much larger than 50, which is simply another way to say that the top 1% share is much bigger than the bottom 50% share. If we look at the ratio between the

average incomes of the global top 0.1% and the global bottom 50%, we find that this indicator rose from about 300 in 1820 to 900 in 1910, before stabilizing around 500-700 between 1910 and 2020 (see Figure 2.8). A ratio T0.1/B50 equal to 500 would mean that each of social classes has the same income share. What is notable is that the T0.1/B50 ratio reached its historical peak in 1910, while other inequality indicators like the T10/B50 ratio, the Gini coefficient, and the T1/B50 ratio reached their historical peaks around 1980-2010. This illustrates the fact that top-end inequality never fully returned to its Belle Époque 1910 high point, especially in Europe, which dominated the world economy and the top of the distribution at the time.

Figure 2.8   *Global income inequality: T0.1/B50 ratio, 1820-2020*

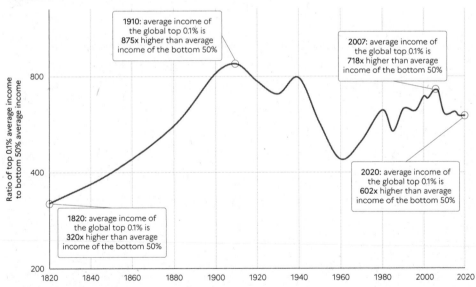

Interpretation: *Global inequality, as measured by the ratio T0.1/B50 between the average income of the top 0.1% and the average income of the bottom 50%, almost tripled between between 1820 and 1910, from about 300 to about 900, and stabilized around 500-700 between 1950 and 2020. It is too early to say whether the decline in global inequality observed since 2008 will continue. Income is measured per capita after pension and unemployement insurance transfers and before income and wealth taxes.* **Sources and series:** *wir2022.wid.world/methodology and Chancel and Piketty (2021).*

The evolution of the global T1/B50 ratio can also be broken down into two components: inequality between the top and the middle of the distribution, as measured by the ratio T1/M40, and inequality between the middle and the bottom of the distribution, as measured by the ratio M40/B50. If we do this, we see that the two components moved in opposite directions between 1980 and 2020: global inequality between the top and the middle of the distribution increased, but it declined between the middle and the bottom of the distribution (see Figure 2.9). Another way to visualize this is the well-known "elephant curve" of global inequality between 1980 and 2020.[3] That is, if we look at cumulative income growth over the 1980-2020 period, we find that the two groups that have benefited from the highest growth performance are the bottom 50%

and the top 1% (see Figure 2.10). In contrast, if we look at the growth incidence curve over the entire 1820-2020 period, we find that it is upward sloping: the global top 30% have benefited from an increase in their purchasing power over the past two centuries roughly twice as great as that for the global bottom 50% (see Figure 2.11). This reflects the fact that global inequality in 2020 is still substantially greater than in 1820.

The regional decomposition of global inequality: back to 1820?

If we look at the regional composition of the global top 10%, we find that the undisputed dominant position that Europe occupied between 1880 and 1910 has been shared with North America since the 1920s (see Figure 2.12). The share of top 10% income holders coming from

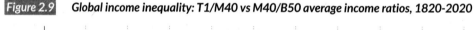

Figure 2.9   *Global income inequality: T1/M40 vs M40/B50 average income ratios, 1820-2020*

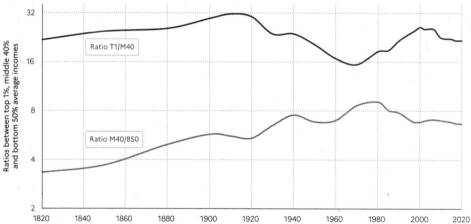

Interpretation: *Bottom-end global inequality, as measured by the ratio M40/B50 between the average incomes of the middle 40% and the bottom 50%, rose from 3.3 in 1820 to 9.1 in 1980, down to 6.7 in 2020. Top-end global inequality, as measured by the ratio T1/M40 between the average incomes of the top 1% and the middle 40%, rose from 22 in 1820 to 32 in 1910, went down to 15 in 1970, then up to 22 in 2020. Income is measured per capita after pension and unemployement insurance transfers and before income and wealth transfers.* **Sources and series:** *wir2022.wid.world/methodology and Chancel and Piketty (2021).*

Figure 2.10   **The elephant curve of global inequality, 1980-2020**

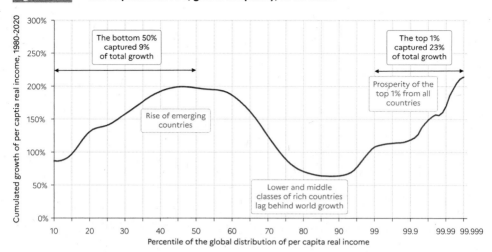

Interpretation: *The bottom 50% incomes of the world saw substantial growth between 1980 and 2020 (between +50% and +200%). The top 1% incomes also benefited from high growth (between +100% and +200%). Intermediate categories grew less. In sum, inequality decreased between the bottom and the middle of the global income distribution, and increased between the middle and the top. In effect, the top 1% captured 23% of total world growth between 1980 and 2020, vs. 9% for the bottom 50%. Income is measured per capita after pension and unemployement insurance transfers and before income and wealth taxes.* **Sources and series:** *wir2022.wid.world/methodology and Chancel and Piketty (2021).*

Figure 2.11   **The global growth incidence curve, 1820-2020**

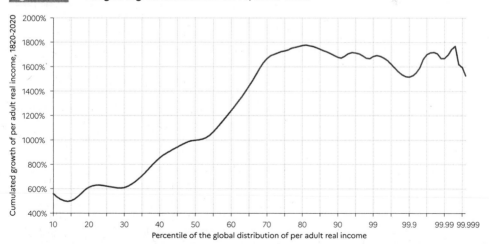

Interpretation: *The bottom 50% incomes of the world saw substantial growth between 1820 and 2020 (between +600% and +1000%). The top 30% incomes benefited from even higher growth (between +1600% and +1800%). Income is measured per capita after pension and unemployement insurance transfers and before income and wealth taxes.* **Sources and series:** *wir2022.wid.world/methodology and Chancel and Piketty (2021).*

Figure 2.12   *The regional composition of the global top 10%, 1820-2020*

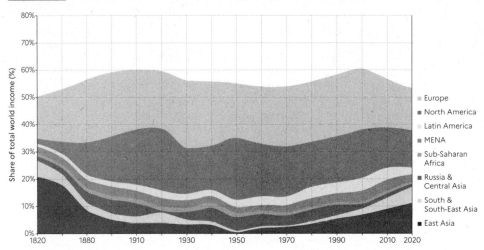

*Interpretation: The regional composition of the global top 10% has changed significantly between 1820 and 2020. In particular, the share of East Asia and South and South-East Asia within the global top 10% collapsed between 1820 and 1950, before gradually rising again between 1950 and 2020. Income is measured per capita after pension and unemployement insurance transfers and before income and wealth taxes. **Note:** Oceania is included in North America. **Sources and series:** wir2022.wid.world/methodology and Chancel and Piketty (2021).*

East Asia, and South and Southeast Asia has increased gradually since 1950, with an acceleration since 1980, but the Western dominance of the global top 10% remains striking.

We find the same general pattern for the regional composition of the global top 1%, with two interesting caveats.

First, the dominant position of Europe largely collapsed after World War I (and never fully recovered), so that North America has been the undisputed leader of the global top 1% since around 1930. Next, it is worth noting that the global top 1% includes, in recent decades, a relatively large fraction of people from the Middle East, Latin America and Russia. In effect, these regions play a substantially bigger role in the global top 1% than in the global top 10%, reflecting the fact that their

rates of within-country inequality are very high.

Looking at the regional composition of the global bottom 50%, we see the declining importance of East Asia, and the rising shares of South and Southeast Asia, and especially Sub-Saharan Africa in recent decades (see Figure 2.13). Note also that almost nobody from Europe or North America has set foot in the global bottom 50% since the mid-20th century. The European poor did, however, constitute a significant proportion of this group back in the 19th century. In contrast, the global middle 40% today is very diverse and draws significant populations from all regions: the regional shares are relatively close to the shares of the total population.

Figure 2.14 presents the relative size of the population across the global income distribution for the two centuries. Comparing the global

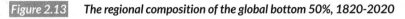

Figure 2.13   *The regional composition of the global bottom 50%, 1820-2020*

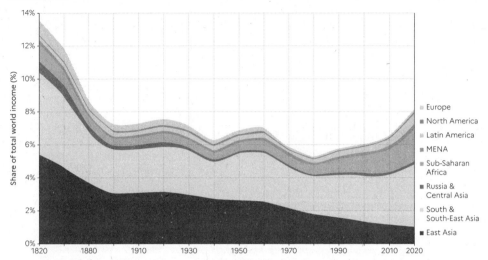

Interpretation: The regional composition of the global bottom 50% has changed significantly between 1820 and 2020. In particular, the share of South/South-East Asia and Sub-Saharan Africa within the global bottom 50% increased substantially between 1980 and 2020. Income is measured per capita after pension and unemployement insurance transfers and before income and wealth taxes. **Note:** *Oceania is included in North America.* **Sources and series:** *wir2022.wid.world/methodology and Chancel and Piketty (2021).*

income distribution between 1820 and 1910, we notice the rise of between-country inequality, where Sub-Saharan Africa, South and South-East Asia and East Asia occupy the bottom of the distribution and North Americans and Europeans occupy the top of the distribution.

Between-country inequality continued to rise until 1980 and started declining between 1980 and 2020. Over this period of time, we notice that the gap between regions narrows down as East Asia (mainly China) moves up along the global distribution and catches up with North America and Europe.

Figure 2.14   *Global income distribution, 1820-2020*

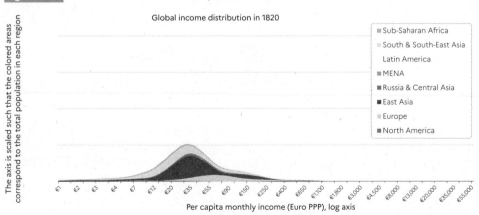

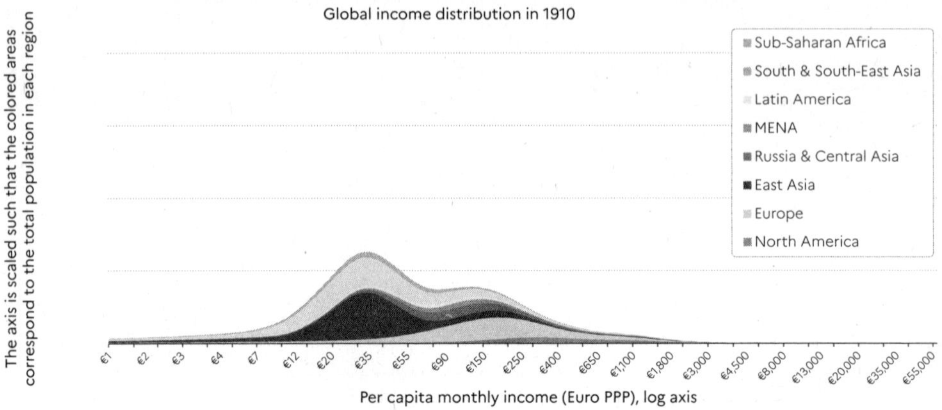

Global income distribution in 1910
The axis is scaled such that the colored areas correspond to the total population in each region
Sub-Saharan Africa
South & South-East Asia
Latin America
MENA
Russia & Central Asia
East Asia
Europe
North America
€1
€2
€3
€4
€7
€12
€20
€35
€55
€90
€150
€250
€400
€650
€1,100
€1,800
€3,000
€4,500
€8,000
€13,000
€20,000
€35,000
€55,000
Per capita monthly income (Euro PPP), log axis

Global income distribution in 1950
The axis is scaled such that the colored areas correspond to the total population in each region
Sub-Saharan Africa
South & South-East Asia
Latin America
MENA
Russia & Central Asia
East Asia
Europe
North America
€1
€2
€3
€4
€7
€12
€20
€35
€55
€90
€150
€250
€400
€650
€1,100
€1,800
€3,000
€4,500
€8,000
€13,000
€20,000
€35,000
€55,000
Per capita monthly income (Euro PPP), log axis

Global income distribution in 1980
The axis is scaled such that the colored areas correspond to the total population in each region
Sub-Saharan Africa
South & South-East Asia
Latin America
MENA
Russia & Central Asia
East Asia
Europe
North America
€1
€2
€3
€4
€7
€12
€20
€35
€55
€90
€150
€250
€400
€650
€1,100
€1,800
€3,000
€4,500
€8,000
€13,000
€20,000
€35,000
€55,000
Per capita monthly income (Euro PPP), log axis

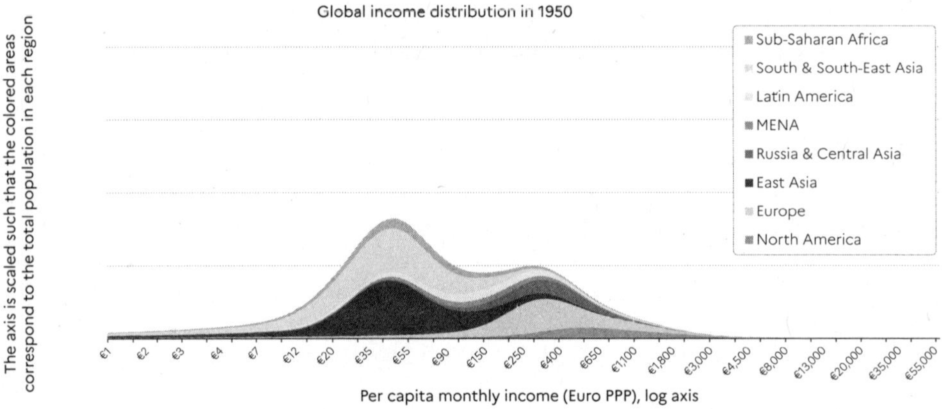

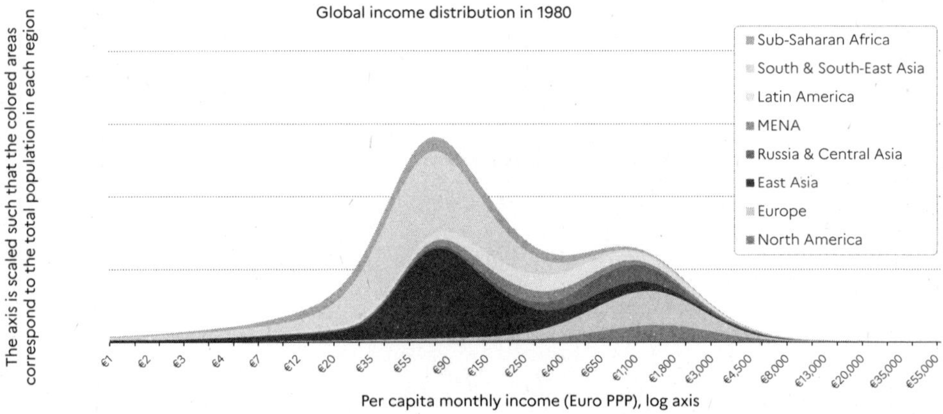

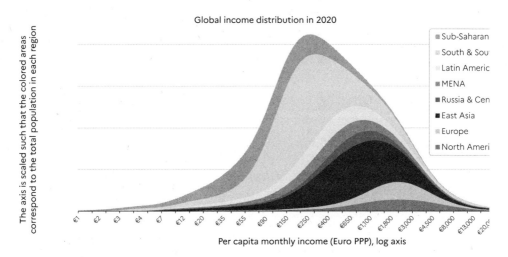

Global income distribution in 2020

The axis is scaled such that the colored areas correspond to the total population in each region

Per capita monthly income (Euro PPP), log axis

Legend:
- Sub-Saharan
- South & Sou
- Latin Americ
- MENA
- Russia & Cen
- East Asia
- Europe
- North Ameri

Interpretation: *The graph shows the size and geographical repartition of the global population at different levels of the income distribution. The relative size of each color wedge is proportional to the relative population in a region. Incomes are measured after pension and unemployment insurance transfers and before income and wealth taxes.* **Note:** *Distribution of per capita incomes (for the distribution of per-adult incomes, see Chapter 1).* **Sources and series:** *wir2022.wid.world/methodology.*

Taxes and transfers do not reduce global inequality that much

Our benchmark income concept is pre-tax, post-replacement national income, which in the framework of distributional national accounts refers to income before taxes and transfers, except for operations of the social insurance system (pensions and unemployment benefits), which in practice in most countries constitutes the largest component of redistribution. All series presented so far use this definition of income. We have also produced estimates using the concept of post-tax national income, wherein we deduct all taxes and add all transfers (including in-kind transfers and collective expenditures).[4] These calculations involve a number of assumptions and should be viewed as exploratory and incomplete. Our main finding is described in Figure 2.15. The bottom line is that taxes and transfers (other

than pensions and unemployment benefits) have little impact on 1820-1910 series and a limited impact on 1910-2020 series. In particular, whether we look at pre-tax, post-replacement national income or at post-tax national income, we find that the level of global inequality in 2020 is close to the level observed around 1880-1900. The results for within and between country inequality trends and regional decomposition are virtually unchanged.

Understanding the roots of global economic inequality: center and periphery imbalances

How do we account for the rise of global inequality between 1820 and 1910, and for the persistence of high levels of global inequality between 1910 and 2020, and what are the lessons for the future? Put briefly, our main conclusion is that political and institutional factors, and the ideological strife between

Figure 2.15 *Global income inequality: pre-tax vs post-tax T10/B50 income ratio, 1820-2020*

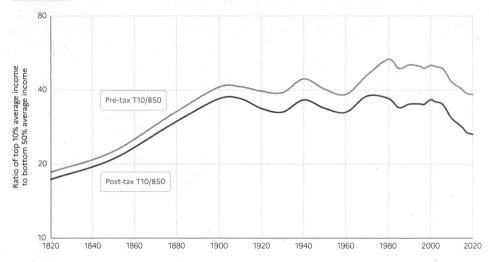

Interpretation: *Global inequality, as measured by the post-tax ratio T10/B50 between the average income of the top 10% and the average income of the bottom 50%, more than doubled between between 1820 and 1910, from less than 20 to about 40, and stabilized around 35 between 1910 and 2020. It is too early to say whether the decline in global inequality observed since 2008 will continue. Pre-tax Income is measured per capita after pension and unemployement insurance transfers and before income and wealth taxes. Post-tax income is income per capita after income tax and all transfers. **Sources and series:** wir2022.wid.world/methodology and Chancel and Piketty (2021).*

competing state powers and social classes have played major roles in past shifts and that this is also likely to be so in the future.

We should first stress that people in countries with relatively low average incomes also tend to work longer hours, both in the cross-section and over time, so that the global inequality of hourly income is even higher than the global inequality of income and has followed the same evolution over the long run (in an even more pronounced manner).[5] From the viewpoint of standard neoclassical economics, the most obvious explanation for the extreme and persistent inequality in hourly income (productivity) is the inequality in capital endowments. That is, if the poorest economic groups at the global level were to receive sufficient capital investment, both in terms

of physical capital (equipment, machinery, infrastructure, etc.) and human capital (education, skills, health, etc.), then global income inequality would shrink tremendously. At some level, this must be right. If there were sufficient redistribution of wealth from the richest global economic groups to the poorest, allowing for massive investment in physical and human capital benefiting the world's poorest groups, then global inequality would certainly shrink. However, there are obvious reasons of political economy why this is unlikely to take place in the form of a simple wealth transfer.

Unless they are forced to, through revolution, land reform or permanent systems of progressive taxation and redistribution of wealth, the richest economic groups are unlikely to give away their assets. They will, rather, attempt to lend resources and earn the highest possible returns out of their capital investment. This has several consequences. First, the fact that the poorest are borrowers who need to repay large sums, rather than asset owners, implies that they have less economic autonomy and fewer incentives to produce. Next, because lenders fear expropriation (and often rightly so), they will tend to regulate their relationships with the poorest groups through colonial and military domination, and to organize investment patterns so as to keep control of the most valuable production processes.

There is ample evidence that "center–periphery" relations developed between 1800 and 1950 with the establishment of Western dominance and colonial empires, and that this process largely explains the extraordinary rise of between-country inequalities in this period. In particular, Kenneth Pomeranz has shown the extent to which the Industrial Revolution of the late 18th and 19th century, first in Britain and then in the rest of Europe, depended on large-scale extraction of raw materials (especially cotton) and energy (especially in the form of wood) from the rest of the world – extraction that was achieved through coercive colonial occupation.[6] In Pomeranz's view, the more advanced parts of China and Japan had attained a level of development in the period 1750-1800 more or less comparable to certain regions of Western Europe. Specifically, we find similar forms of economic development, based in part on demographic growth and intensive agriculture (made possible by improved agricultural techniques and a considerable

increase in cultivated acres thanks to land clearing and deforestation); we also find comparable processes of proto-industrialization, particularly in the textile industry. Two key factors caused European and Asian trajectories to diverge. First, European deforestation, coupled with the presence of readily available coal deposits, especially in England, led Europe to switch quite rapidly to sources of energy other than wood, and to develop corresponding technologies. Furthermore, the fiscal and military capacity of European states, largely a product of their past rivalries, and reinforced by technological and financial innovations stemming from interstate competition, enabled them to organize the international division of labor and supply chains in particularly profitable ways. The exploitation of land in North America, the West Indies, and South America, using slave labor brought from Africa, produced the raw material that not only earned handsome profits for the colonizers but also fed the textile factories that developed rapidly in the period 1750-1800. Military control of long-distance shipping routes allowed the development of large-scale complementarities. By 1830, British imports of cotton, wood, and sugar required the exploitation of more than 10 million hectares of cultivable land, according to Pomeranz's calculation, or 1.5-2 times all the cultivable land available in the UK. If the colonies had not made it possible to circumvent the ecological constraint, Europe would have had to find other sources of supply. We are, of course, free to imagine scenarios of historical and technological development that would have enabled an autarkic

Europe to achieve a similar level of industrial prosperity, but it would take considerable imagination to envision fertile cotton plantations in Lancashire and soaring oaks springing from the soil outside Manchester. In any case, this would be the history of another world, having little to do with the one we live in.

Subsequent work has largely confirmed the central role of military and colonial domination in accounting for the rise of global inequality during the 19th century. Sven Beckert's work on the "empire of cotton" has shown the crucial importance of slave extraction and cotton production for the seizure of control of the global textile industry by the British and other Europeans. Half of the African slaves shipped across the Atlantic between 1492 and 1882 sailed in the period 1780-1860 (especially 1780-1820).[7] This late phase of accelerated growth in the slave trade and cotton plantations was key to the rise of the British textile industry. The natural reproduction of slaves also played a major role, particularly on US soil, where the number of slaves quadrupled between 1800 and 1860, and the production of cotton was multiplied by 10. On the eve of the American Civil War, 75 percent of the cotton imported by European textile factories came from the southern United States. . Prasannan Parthasarathi also emphasizes the role played by anti-India protectionist policies in the emergence of the British textile industry in the 18th and early 19th centuries.[8] It was only after acquiring a clear comparative advantage in textiles that the UK began in the mid-19th century to adopt a more full-throated free trade rhetoric (though not without ambiguities, as in the case of opium exports to China). The British also relied on protectionist measures in the shipbuilding industry, which was flourishing in India in the 17th and 18th centuries. According to available estimates, the Chinese and Indian share of global manufacturing output, which was still 53 percent in 1800, had fallen to five percent by 1900, largely as a consequence of military and colonial coercion.[9]

Between 1820 and 1910, at the same time as global between-country inequality was rising at an accelerated pace, within-countries inequality was also very high and rising slowly (see Figure 2.4). We have to wait until the World War I to see the beginning of a significant decline of income and wealth inequality within Western countries and in other parts of the world. That within-country inequalities remained so high until 1910-1920 can be accounted for by a mixture of ideological and institutional factors. In a country like Sweden, for instance, the electoral system that applied between 1865 and 1910 was the embodiment of proprietary ideology: only the top 20% (male) property owners had voting rights, and within this group, each person was granted between one and 100 votes, depending on the size of his fyrkar (a formula based upon asset ownership, income and tax payments). A few decades later, the entire system had been turned upside down: universal suffrage was introduced, the Social Democrats took power in 1932 and put the state's capacities at the service of a completely different political project, based on socioeconomic equality.[10] More generally, the large decline in within-countries inequalities that took place between 1910 and 1980 was the consequence of large-scale political mobilization and institutional change. In little more than 30 years (1914-1945), the balance of power between capital and labor was considerably transformed, thanks to worker mobilization as well to the combined impact of World Wars I and II, the Great Depression and a number of revolutionary events (including the Russian Revolution of October 1917). Various coalitions of social democrats, labor parties, democrats, socialists and communists took power in a great many countries, and implemented combinations of redistributive policies, manifest in the building of the welfare state and policies of progressive taxation on income and wealth. The expansive and inclusive investments in public infrastructure, education and health that followed contributed not only to a sharp reduction in inequalities but also to increased growth and prosperity in post-war Western countries.[11]

The political shocks that occurred between 1914 and 1945 also contributed to the end of colonial empires and to Western dominance, but with substantial delays. In a first step, Europe's colonial expansion reached its peak between 1910 and 1950, especially the British and French Empires, which inherited the remains of the Ottoman Empire and the German colonies in 1919-1920. In the longer run, World Wars I and II strongly contributed to the weakening of European state powers, the development of strong independence movements, and finally to the end of European colonialism in 1950s-1960s. Between 1950 and 1980, North–South inequality continued to rise, first because it was a period of exceptionally rapid growth in the North, and next because it took a few decades for the newly independent countries to emerge from independence wars and civil unrest, and to design suitable development strategies, which then led in some cases to the reduction of between-country inequalities between 1980 and 2020 (as illustrated for instance by the cases of China and Vietnam). within-country inequalities started to rise again globally around 1980-1990, following the demise of state-led socialism in China and Russia, and the conservative revolution in the West (leading to serious reductions in progressive taxation, union power, and minimum wages, and an historical interruption in the rise of the social state). After the 2008 financial crisis, neoliberal policies became less and less attractive, and between-country inequality seems to have reached a plateau. It is too early to tell whether the 2020 pandemic and the growing awareness of the environmental crisis will lead to a new wave of state interventions and inequality reduction in the future.

Global inequality within countries is higher than inequality between countries – which remains significant

On the matter of inequality among world citizens, our findings offer a novel perspective on the relative importance of within- and between-country inequalities. Francois Bourguignon and Christian Morrisson recently found that most global inequality was explained by between-country differentials over the 1950-1990 period.[12] This finding was also supported by Christoph

Lakner and Branko Milanovic, who extended Bourguignon and Morrisson's series up to the early 2010s.[13] Our new series reveal that, around the turn of the 21st century, the within-country component of global inequality has become greater than the between-country component.[14] In contemporary capitalism, an individual's income group (i.e. whether they belong to the bottom 50%, top 1%, etc. in their own country) now matters more than their nationality (where they live) in the determination of global inequality levels. The basic implication of this finding is that the pre-distribution and redistribution of incomes and capital within countries, both rich and emerging, is essential to reducing global inequality. We should stress, however, that inequality between countries is still very high in absolute terms in 2020 (roughly at the same level as in 1900), and that reducing average income (or capital endowment) differences between countries still matters significantly. Put differently, within-countries inequalities now dominate in relative terms, but disparities between countries are still very great, which explains why overall inequalities are so marked, in a way that is comparable to the situation in 1900-1910. In addition, while between-country inequality has been declining since 2008, there is no guarantee at all that it will keep declining in the future.

In the European colonial empire period, the world economic system was explicitly organized in a highly hierarchical manner, and the reproduction of inequality directly derived from there. For instance, in French Algeria, until 1962, expenditure on education for the children of Muslim Algerians was on average 40 times less than expenditure on the children of European settlers.[15] This specific type of political structure is now gone, but that does not mean that extreme inequalities in education expenditures and other capital investments have disappeared. In particular, center–periphery relations are still alive and well in the sense that dominant economic state powers, whether they are European, North American, Japanese or Chinese, tend to organize the international division of labor in a way that best suits their interests, and which often involves selective state protection and support for the production sectors that they view as crucial to their national interest and development strategy.[16] Periphery countries and weaker states, especially in Sub-Saharan Africa and South Asia, tend to be relegated to less productive activities, requiring less equipment and human capital, so, for example, they can obtain loans for certain types of capital investment but not others. Although this kind of neo-colonialism takes different institutional forms from those of classic colonialism, we can imagine circumstances in which this would lead to a stabilization of between-country inequality at a high level. Indeed, this will happen if it fits the interests and world views of the dominant states, and if periphery countries are not powerful enough to obtain the capital investments needed to improve their positions.

When he was writing in the 1980s, prominent historian and theorist of comparative development and core–periphery relations Immanuel Wallerstein famously hypothesized that the relative position of the world's bottom 50% individuals might have deteriorated continuously between 1500 and 1980, thereby demonstrating the validity of Marxist predictions about increasing polarization under capitalism at the global level.[17] Things look somewhat different from the viewpoint of 2020, but not completely different: between-country inequality declined sharply between 1980 and 2020, but it is still much greater in 2020 than it was in 1820. Whether the trend toward more global equality will continue depends on several political, social and economic factors. Between 1910 and 1980, the march toward more within-country equality was led by socialist political movements that were also pushing to some extent for more equality at the international level, at least through their support for independence and an end to colonialism. New forms of internationalist egalitarian political mobilization around alternative economic system, and grassroots movements like Black Lives Matter, Fridays for Future and MeToo might play a similar role in the future. Novel challenges like climatic disasters, migration pressures and competition among China, Europe and the US might also trigger major political, ideological and institutional change. What seems fairly clear, however, is that an accelerated compression of inequality among and within countries will require a massive redistribution of wealth. For instance, we could think of allocating a fraction of global tax revenues paid by multinationals and billionaires to countries on the basis of their population. In the Sub-Saharan African and South Asian regions, this would radically transform the capacity of national states to finance investment in human capital, equipment and infrastructure.[18] Short of that, historical evidence suggest that extreme levels of global inequality can be highly persistent.

Box 2.1   **Global inequality: beyond income measures**

The series presented in this chapter are exploratory in many ways. First, we need more refined country studies on income inequality trends, both from a long-term perspective and for recent changes. In particular, access to adequate tax data is very constricted in large parts of the world, so in a number of regions our corrections to raw survey data often rely on a limited set of countries in which we have access to more diverse data sources (household surveys, tax data, inheritance and wealth records, national accounts). As better country series become available, we will refine our estimates of global inequality dynamics. The many robustness checks that we have performed demonstrate that this will not affect our general conclusions regarding the long-term shifts in global inequality. But it certainly might effect some of the finer breakdowns for the more recent period, and allow us to understand better the mechanisms behind global inequality trends.

Second, a deeper understanding of the transformation of global inequalities will also require detailed breakdowns by production sector. For instance, we emphasize the key role of the power structure of the global textile sector (Beckert's empire of cotton) in order to understand changing power structures and core–periphery relations in the 19th century. It would be equally instructive to look more closely at the changing global dominance structure of the automobile sector in the 20th century, or the high-tech digital sector in the early 21st century. In relation to this perspective on global production systems, it is also crucial to analyze the evolution of the structures of energy extraction and consumption, carbon emissions and environmental damage.[19] This material perspective on global inequality is highly complementary to the income perspective adopted in this paper. Indeed, factoring in environmental pollution may reinforce the level of global inequality between countries in 2020 (as the effects of climate change are more pronounced in low-income countries) as well as within countries (as low-income groups also tend to be disproportionately impacted by environmental damages).[20]

Finally, the global income inequality perspective ought to be supplemented by a global wealth inequality perspective. We already know from previous research that private wealth-to-income ratios have increased enormously in recent decades and are now close to their early 20th century peak (around 500-600% of national income by 2020, compared with about 300% of national income in the 1970s, and about 600% of national income in 1910).[21] On the eve of World War I, net foreign wealth held by British property owners was as much as 200% of national income. It was over 100% of national income for their French counterparts. A very large share of top incomes around 1910 was made of capital income flows coming from colonial assets and other foreign investment. In other words, the between-country inequality structure and the within-country inequality structure were tightly intertwined at the time of colonial empires.[22] Net foreign assets held by China, Germany and Japan increased significantly over the 1990-2020 period, but they remain more modest than those held by Britain and France in 1910 relative to GDP.[23] One major difference, however, is that gross foreign positions have reached much higher levels in our era of financial globalization than in any previous era. We should look more closely at gross positions in different production sectors (and not only at aggregate net foreign wealth), e.g. Chinese or Western investment patterns in construction, transportation, and mining in various African and Asian countries, in order to analyze properly the dynamics of ownership and power structures in the recent period. More research is needed on global wealth dynamics if we are to reach a better understanding of global inequality trends.[24]

NOTES

[1] All our benchmark series are based on income per capita values. For additional series, see our online data sets. Focusing on income per adult, we find a global bottom 50% income share slightly above 8% today. The difference is due to the fact that low-income countries have relatively fewer adults than rich countries. This contributes to (a slight) increase in the global bottom 50% income per adult share compared with per capita values. We prefer per capita values as benchmark series to be consistent with Maddison's population data.

[2] Technically, one advantage of using the Theil index is that it allows for additive decompositions, i.e. the global Theil index is exactly equal to the sum of the within-country Theil index and the between-country Theil index (which is not the case with other inequality indexes such as the T10/B50 income gap or the Gini coefficient). However, we prefer to focus attention on inequality indicators based on income ratios because these are more intuitive and easier to grasp. All substantial conclusions that we present in this paper hold, independent of the specific inequality indicator.

[3] For a more detailed discussion, see Alvaredo, F., L. Chancel, T. Piketty, E. Saez, G. Zucman. 2018. World Inequality Report 2018, Cambridge: Harvard University Press.

[4] See Blanchet, T., L. Chancel et al. 2021. "Distributional National Accounts Guidelines. Methods and Concepts Used in the World Inequality Database". World Inequality Lab.

[5] See A. Ahmed 2021. "Global Inequality of Hourly Income", 1980-2020, Paris School of Economics, Master Thesis.

[6] Pomeranz, K. 2000. The Great Divergence: China, Europe and the Making of the Modern World Economy. Princeton: Princeton University Press, 2000.

[7] Beckert, S. 2015. Empire of Cotton: A Global History. New York: Vintage.

[8] Parthasarathi, P. 2011. Why Europe Grew Rich and Asia Did Not: Global Economic Divergence, 1600-1850. Cambridge: Cambridge University Press.

[9] Note that the role of slave and colonial extraction in the development of industrial capitalism had already been analyzed by numerous 19th century observers (beginning with Karl Marx), and by Eric Williams (prime minister of Trinidad from 1956 to 1981) in Capitalism and Slavery (1944). By contrast, Max Weber, in The Protestant Ethic and the Spirit of Capitalism (1905), stressed cultural and religious factors, whereas Fernand Braudel in Civilisation matérielle, économie et capitalisme (1979) focused on the role of high finance in both Catholic and Protestant Europe. The recent work of Pomeranz, Parthasarathi, and Beckert is much less Eurocentric; to some extent it represents a return to Marx and Williams, but with the richer tools and sources associated with global and connected history.

[10] See Bengtsson E., A. Missiaia, M. Olssson, and P. Svensson.2017. "Wealth Inequality in Sweden, 1750-1900", Economic History Review.

[11] See Piketty T. 2014. Capital in the 21st century, Cambridge: Harvard University Press; Piketty T. 2020. Capital and ideology, Cambridge: Harvard University Press; See also Lindert. P. 2004. Growing Public. Social Spending and Economic Growth since the 18th Century, Cambridge: Cambridge University Press.

[12] Bourguignon, F. and C. Morrisson. 2002. "Inequality among World Citizens: 1820-1992." The American Economic Review, vol. 92 (4): 727-744.

[13] Lakner, C., and B. Milanovic. 2016. Global Income Distribution: From the Fall of the Berlin Wall to the Great Recession. Published by Oxford University Press on behalf of the World Bank. https://openknowledge.worldbank.org/handle/10986/29118 License: CC BY-NC-ND 3.0 IGO.

[14] The main difference from earlier series is the use of historical tax data, more precise than household surveys used in earlier long-run studies of global inequality. For an overview of our methodology, see Section 2, the online appendix as well as Blanchet T., L. Chancel et al. "Distributional National Accounts Guidelines" that provides a detailed description of the various sources used.

[15] Cogneau, D., Y. Dupraz, S. Mesplé-Somps, « Fiscal Capacity and Dualism in Colonial States: The French Empire 1830-1962 », Journal of Economic History, 2021; See Piketty, T. 2019. Capital et idéologie. Paris: Seuil. Figure 7.8.

[16] See Chang H.J. 2002. Kicking Away the Ladder: Development Strategy in Historical Perspective, Anthems. See Mazzucatto M. 2013. Entrepreneurial State: Debunking Public vs Private Sector Myths, Anthems.

[17] See Wallerstein, I. 1974-1989. The Modern World-System, 3 volumes, Academic Press. See also Balibar, E. and I. Wallerstein. 1988. Race, nation, classe : les identités ambiguës. Paris: La Découverte, where Wallerstein hinted that the absolute position (and not only the relative position) of the world's bottom 50% might also have deteriorated since the beginning of capitalism, while at the same time mentioning that the existence of communist and socialist alternatives led to some limited absolute progress in some cases.

[18] See Piketty, T. Une brève histoire de l'égalité, Paris: Seuil, 2021 (A Brief history of equality, Cambridge: Harvard University Press, 2022)

[19] See e.g. Chancel, L. 2020. Unsustainable inequalities. Cambridge: Harvard University Press.

[20] See Diffenbaugh, N. S., and M. Burke. 2019. "Global Warming has Increased Global Economic Inequality." Proceedings of the National Academy of Sciences, 116 (20): 201816020. https://www.researchgate.net/publication/332581715_Global_warming_has_increased_global_economic_inequality. See also Burke, M., S. M. Hsiang, and E. Miguel. 2015. "Global non-linear effect of temperature on economic production", Nature, 527 (235–239); Hallegatte, S., and J. Rozenberg. 2017. "Climate change through a poverty lens." Nature Climate Change 7 (4): 250-256; Chancel, L. Unsustainable inequalities.

[21] See Piketty, T., and G. Zucman. 2014. "Capital is Back: Wealth-Income Ratios in Rich Countries 1700-2010", Quarterly Journal of Economics.

[22] See Piketty, T., G. Postel-Vinay, and J-L. Rosenthal. 2006. "Wealth Concentration in a Developing Economy, Paris and France, 1807-1994." American Economic Review, 236-256; and Piketty, T. 2019. Capital et idéologie. Paris: Seuil. Table 4.1.

[23] See Piketty, T. 2019. Capital et idéologie. Paris: Seuil. Figure 7.9.

[24] For a global perspective on wealth, see Chapter 4 of this report.

CHAPTER 3

Rich countries,
poor governments

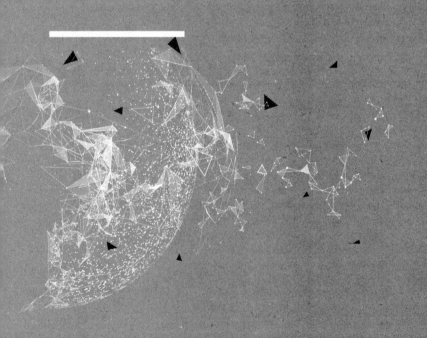

WORLD **INEQUALITY** REPORT **20**22

What is wealth and what does owning capital mean?

Contrary to national income, which is a flow, national wealth is a stock, an economic resource that has been accumulated over time. More precisely, wealth arises from both capital accumulation (made possible by savings that are invested) and price effects (reflecting changes in asset prices in the absence of any saving). Capital can be accumulated in many forms: residences and buildings, equipment and machinery, intangible capital such as software. Price effects reflect the dynamics of market perceptions of various types of assets. The value of a house might increase or decrease without any improvements being made by its owners, simply because there is a shortage of housing in the area.[1]

In national accounts, wealth can take either of two forms: financial or non-financial assets. Financial assets are contractual financial claims such as bank deposits, stocks, bonds and equities. Non-financial assets, by contrast, refer to assets such as land, housing, machinery and intangibles, which typically derive their value from their direct physical or immaterial properties. When studying wealth, it is always important also to think about financial liabilities, i.e. debts: the net wealth of a country or an individual is always the sum of their financial and non-financial assets, minus their debts (see Box 3.1).

Two types of actors can own wealth: private actors and public actors. By definition, the wealth of a country is equal to the sum of net private wealth and net public wealth. Private actors are individuals who own firms, bonds, housing, etc. in their own names, and private foundations and institutions such as religious organizations, which can also own assets and liabilities.[2] Public actors are local and central governments around the world. Their assets can take many forms: public hospitals and roads, as well as bonds and publicly owned firms, for instance. And what about the corporate sector, that is firms? Firms can indeed own capital, and other firms (and the assets of these firms) but ultimately, a private or a public actor has to own these firms.[3]

Given these definitions, it follows that behind every dollar, euro or yuan of asset owned in the world, there is an individual or a group of individuals controlling the asset and making decisions about how it should be used: wealth on earth is not kept by the planet Mars. Broadly speaking, being the proprietor of capital means two things: receiving the income generated by the capital, and choosing how and where this capital is to be invested. Ownership of capital can come with significant power over individuals who use that capital (workers using machines, tenants living in houses, drivers using roads, etc.). It is important to keep in mind that the very notions of private and public property, and the power relationships associated with them, can have very different meanings in different countries and at different times. For instance, private property in land or housing can take very different forms, depending on the extent of tenant rights, the length of the lease period, the capacity of landlords to change the rent or to expel the tenant unilaterally, etc. Similarly, corporate property may not have

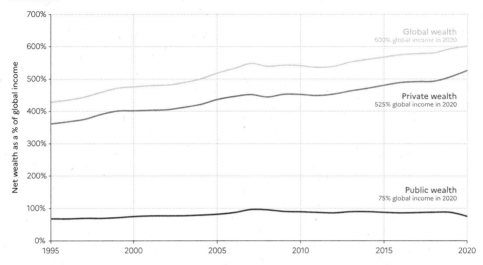

Figure 3.1   *Global, public and private wealth-income ratio, 1995-2020*

Interpretation: Global Public wealth dropped from above 87% of global national wealth in 2019 to 75% in 2020. Public wealth is the sum of all financial and non-financial assets, net of debts, held by governments. Private wealth is the sum of all financial and non-financial asset, net of debts, held by the private sector. National wealth is the sum of public wealth and private wealth. **Sources and series:** wir2022.wid.world/methodology, Bauluz et al. (2021) and updates.

the same meaning and implications for workers in countries where shareholders control all voting rights as in countries where workers' representatives have substantial voting rights on corporate boards (such as in the Nordic countries and Germany).

Public property can also have very different meanings depending on the country or period under consideration, and the prevailing political system: public property in Russia today, for example, is very different from public property there 40 years ago, or from Norway's public sovereign fund (see below). The details of the legal, political and governance systems are important in understanding the interplay between property structures and relationships of power among social groups. To understand these dynamics properly, sound data are necessary, but not sufficient. We also require a

good understanding of a country's institutions and how these affect political and social inequality.

Ultimately, decisions about what can be owned privately or publicly, and the various constraints placed on property, must be subject to democratic debate. Yet they are often neglected in public discussion, because of financial opacity and lack of data, because the discourse seems too technical, or because those who possess wealth see little interest in discussing such fundamental questions. This Report provides historical and international data and analysis in order to make such debates as informed as possible.[4]

Until recently, it was difficult to get a good grasp of the dynamics of wealth across countries and over time, because of a lack of data. In the previous Inequality Report, we presented harmonized annual series of wealth–income ratios for the largest industrialized economies in the World from 1700 onward, and for several emerging countries over the past four decades, including former communist countries, before and after their transition to capitalist regimes.[5] That work has been extended for this edition of the report, by researchers associated with the WID.world database. Thanks to the work of Luis Bauluz, Thomas Blanchet, Clara Martinez Toledano and Alice Sodano, in particular, the WID.world database now contains wealth information for nearly all countries in the world over the recent period.

We should stress, however, that this is an area where we still need to make a lot of progress. In particular, we know too little about the structures of public, private and foreign ownership in many areas of the developing and emerging world, especially in Africa, Latin America and Asia. This is why some of our data starts early in the 20th century (or before), while for other regions our estimates only begin in the 1990s.

Global private and public wealth: insights

The best way to study the volumes of and changes to wealth at the national and global levels is to focus on the ratio of national wealth to national income. The reason is simple: if the wealth of a country increases at the same speed as its national income, then the relative importance of wealth in the economy is unchanged, even though the level of wealth has increased. In this case, the growth in wealth simply reflects normal economic growth. Focusing on wealth–income ratios (the value of national wealth divided by national income) allows us to disentangle the growth of wealth from the growth rate of the economy. When wealth–income ratios increase, it means that the value of total assets is growing faster than incomes; societies are either accumulating more capital or the price of assets is increasing. We can also focus separately on the private wealth-to-income ratio (the value of private wealth divided by national income) and the public wealth-to-income ratio (the value of public wealth divided by national income). By definition, total wealth in a country is equal to the sum of private and public wealth. When private wealth-to-income ratios increase, it means that the relative weight of those who possess capital is overtaking the weight of those who only live off their incomes.

Global wealth is equal to around €510 trillion in 2020 or about 600% of national income. The ratio of total wealth to total income rose from around 450 % in the early 1990s to about 600% today (Figure 3.1). What do such values mean in practice? A wealth-to-income ratio of 450% (i.e. equivalent to 4.5 years of national income) implies that a country could decide to stop working for 4.5 years and still enjoy the same living standard as before, thanks to the sale of all its assets. After this period, the country would no longer have any assets and would have to start working again to meets its needs and to accumulate new capital. A rise from 4.5 years to six years at the global level is a very significant shift, indicating a return of the relative size of the stock of wealth vs. the flows of income in contemporary capitalism (more on historical trends below), after the drop of wealth-to-income ratios in the mid 20th century.

It is striking that this rise is almost entirely due to the increase in the global private wealth-to-income ratio. In 1995, this ratio was 360% and it rose to 510% before the Covid crisis. The trend seems to have been uninterrupted over the period. The change is notably different for the global public wealth-to-income ratio: it rose from 70% to 100% on the eve of the global financial crisis of 2008-9, before dropping back to 90%. The private sector has become significantly richer over the past decade while governments became poorer.

The return of private wealth in rich countries

A rise in private wealth income ratios is observed in most countries, both rich and emerging, but it occurred at different rates. In high income countries, we find that in 1970, private wealth–national income ratios ranged between 200% and 400%. By 2008, when the global financial crisis began, these ratios averaged 550% in the countries observed, peaking at 800% in the extreme case of Spain (Figure 3.2). Despite the fall in these ratios in some of the countries following the financial crisis and the decline in housing prices, the multi-decade trend seems to have been largely unaltered. By 2020, in the rich countries, market value aggregate private wealth was typically twice as large as in 1970. There have been cross-country variations in volume and level among rich countries, exemplified by the extreme cases of Japan and Spain, which experienced a dramatic rise in private wealth in the 1980s and

mid-2000s. These dynamics reflect asset booms (in particular in the real estate market), which burst after the peaks in 1990 in Japan and 2008 in Spain. Remarkably, despite the asset bubble bursts, the secular trend observed in these countries seems unaltered.

Putting this trend in historical perspective, it appears that rich countries are back to (or closely approaching) the wealth to income ratios reached in the late 19th and early 20th centuries, before the political, economic and war shocks of 1914-1945. National wealth then amounted to 700% of national income in France, Germany and the UK, before dropping to around 300% after the Second World War. A series of capital control policies (rent controls, financial market regulations) helped to keep national wealth at a much lower level between the 1950s and the 1970s.

The secular fall of public wealth was exacerbated by the Covid-19 crisis

The evolution of public wealth in rich countries since 1970 has been similarly dramatic (Figure 3.2). Public wealth has fallen in all countries over the past 50 years. Indeed, in the UK and the US, national wealth consists entirely of private wealth, as net public wealth has become negative (i.e. public assets now total less than public debt) (-30% of national income). France, Japan and Germany have also experienced significant declines in public wealth, which is now worth just about 10-25% of national income according to official estimates, a tiny fraction of total national wealth. The disappearance of

Figure 3.2   *The rise of private wealth and the decline of public wealth in rich countries, 1970-2020*

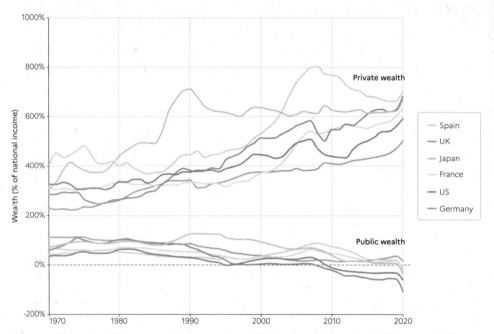

Interpretation: In the UK, public wealth dropped from 60% of national income to -106% between 1970 and 2020. Public wealth is the sum of all financial and non-financial assets, net of debts, held by governments.
Sources and series: *wir2022.wid.world/methodology, Bauluz et al. (2021) and updates.*

public wealth in national wealth represents a marked change from the situation that prevailed in the 1970s, when net public wealth was typically between 40% and 100% of national income in most developed countries (and over 100% in Germany). Today, with either small or negative net public wealth, rich countries' governments are constrained when they want to intervene in the economy, redistribute income and mitigate growing inequality.

The impact of the Covid crisis is clear in Figure 3.2. As economies shut down, national incomes dropped by 5-10% across rich nations. Governments responded by injecting large amounts of money into the economy, to counter the epidemics, and to

support workers and businesses affected by lockdowns, and running fiscal deficits close to 5-15% of national income in 2020. The value of net public wealth decreased by the same amount.

We should note that the decline in net public wealth in recent decades is mostly due to the rise of public debt (before Covid), while the ratios of public assets to national income have remained relatively stable in most countries. The relative stability of public assets – relative to national income – can be viewed as the consequence of two conflicting effects: on the one hand, a significant proportion of public assets were privatized (particularly shares in public or semi-public companies of the infrastructure, transport and telecommunication sectors, which were significant in a number of developed countries between the 1950s and the 1970s); and on the other hand, the market value of the remaining public assets – typically public buildings housing administrations, schools, universities, hospitals and other public services – increased in this period.

The rise of private wealth in emerging countries

In emerging countries, the rise in private wealth has been no less spectacular than in rich countries. In fact, large emerging economies such as China and India experienced faster increases than wealthy countries after they transitioned away from communism (in China and Russia) or from a highly regulated economic system (in India). While to some extent these increases are to be expected (as a large proportion of public wealth is transferred to the private sector), the scale of the change is striking (Figure 3.3).

China has had the largest increase in private wealth in recent decades. At the time of the "opening-up" reforms in 1978, private wealth in China amounted to just over 120% of national income; by 2020, it had reached 530%. Most of this increase was due to housing (which went from 50% private ownership to near 100% in that period), and corporate ownership (from 0% privately owned in 1978 to 30% today). These increases bring the overall level of private wealth in China, relative to national income, to levels similar to those found in the US and France.

The private wealth increase seen in India over this time is also remarkable (up from 290% in 1980 to 560% in 2020). While India's economy was highly regulated in the 1980s, and a very strong public sector controlled large segments of the economy, the private sector was significantly larger than in communist China (especially in the business sector). Today, both Asian giants have similar private wealth-to-income ratios. The speed and scale of the change in these

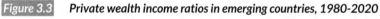

Figure 3.3 *Private wealth income ratios in emerging countries, 1980-2020*

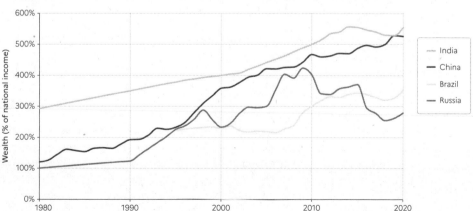

Interpretation: *Private wealth grew in India from 290% of national income in 1980 to 555% in 2020. Private wealth is the sum of all financial and non-financial assets, net of debts, held by the private sector.*
Sources and series: *wir2022.wid.world/methodology, Bauluz et al. (2021) and updates.*

economies surpasses that seen in industrialized countries: by way of comparison, we have to go back to the early 20th century to observe a similar magnitude of change in the wealth–income ratios in European countries (see above).

Private wealth also increased steeply in Russia following its transition to a market economy in 1990. Its private wealth-to-income ratio rose from 120% of national income to 280% today. Russia's private wealth-to-income ratio more than tripled, from around 120% to 390% between 1990 and 2008. The transition to a capitalist regime was accompanied by an asset price bubble, which burst in the aftermath of the financial crisis. Other factors, such as the impact of Western sanctions on Russia following the Crimean war explain why Russia's private wealth has not risen during the 2010s. All in all, private wealth in Russia today is at its level of 1998, about three times higher than its communist level. Other emerging countries, including Brazil, have experienced significant but smaller increases over these decades.

The decline of public wealth across the world

Let us focus on the secular decline in public wealth. As stated above, public wealth refers to the public ownership of infrastructure (such as school, hospitals, transport), firms and financial assets, minus public debt. Figure 3.4 expresses public wealth as a share of total wealth, meaning that if the public wealth share is equal to 30%, then the private wealth share must be equal to 70%.

In rich countries, public wealth typically amounted to 15-30% of total wealth in the early 1980s but these values have dropped to near 0% in most rich countries, and to around -10 to -20% in the US and the UK (Figure 3.4). In Western countries, zero or negative public wealth values effectively means that private actors control the whole of the economy through the assets they own. Put differently, if a Western country were to sell all its public assets to pay off its debt, then everything there is to own in that country (roads, schools, etc.) would end up in private hands. Citizens would then have to pay rents to the new private owners in order to use the privatized infrastructure (roads, schools, etc.). In the US, even this operation would not suffice to repay fully the public debt, since public wealth is currently negative. Let us also note that the higher the state debt, the greater the influence of debt holders on state budgets and tax policies. There is no clear limit to the decline of public wealth because the public sector can potentially incur an ever-increasing amount of debt.

The net public wealth position of emerging economies is markedly different. Former communist countries' public wealth positions are now similar to those observed in rich countries in 1980, at the end of the mixed economy period (1950-1980). China's and Russia's public wealth currently represent about 20%-30% of their total wealth, down from about 70% at the end of the communist period. Two remarks can be made at this stage: first, under communism in China and Russia, wealth was never totally publicly owned, as 20-30% of the economy belonged to private individuals then (largely in the form of housing wealth). Second, while public wealth has declined in most

Figure 3.4   *The decline in public wealth in rich and emerging countries, 1980-2020*

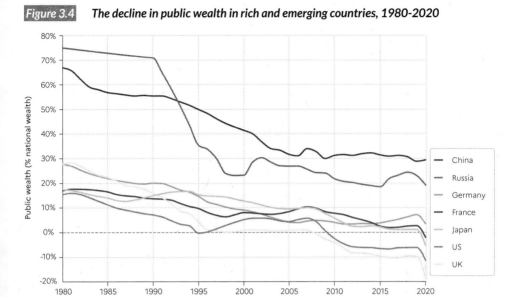

Interpretation: *Public wealth dropped in the UK from 28% of national wealth in 1980 to -18% in 2020. Public wealth is the sum of financial and non-financial assets, net of debts, held by the governments.* **Sources and series:** *wir2022.wid.world/methodology, Bauluz et al. (2021) and updates.*

countries, some have been able to maintain relatively high positions. In China, for instance, the relative persistence of public wealth is the result of strategic efforts to maintain control of economic assets, in particular in the business and infrastructure sectors. These have been coupled with a strict control of foreign private investments in the economy since 1978.

There are examples of high public wealth persisting in rich countries as well. In the Czech Republic for instance, the share of public wealth in national wealth has decreased from 70% to 30%, staying significantly above the levels observed in larger Western European countries. This case demonstrates that maintaining relatively high public wealth levels is not incompatible with Western political systems.

Another, extreme, counter-example to the decline of public wealth among Western countries is Norway. There, public wealth rose from around 100% of national income in the 1990s to nearly 500% of national income today. This growth followed the discovery of fossil fuel reserves, and the subsequent transformation of profits generated by oil and gas extraction into permanent public wealth, through investments made by the Norwegian sovereign wealth fund in financial markets all over the world. Obviously, this model of public wealth creation is singular, as most countries do not have large oil and gas resources. The Norwegian strategy also raises serious concerns from an environmental point of view, as most fossil fuel resources should be kept underground if we are to meet the objectives of the Paris Agreement on climate change.

That said, Norway's strategy should be considered from an international perspective. Russia has also been exporting fossil resources over the past decades but pursued a very different strategy than Norway, privatizing its resources at low cost to the private sector, with little gain for the public sector. The UK, which also discovered offshore gas in the 1970s, pursued a different strategy too. The UK did not reinvest the revenues in a large sovereign fund as Norway did. In sum, maintaining relatively high public wealth, whether in China, the Czech Republic or Norway, is always a matter of political choice.

Net foreign wealth has largely increased in East Asia and fallen in North America

Wealth held by private and public actors can be domestic or foreign.

The net foreign wealth positions of countries indicate whether the citizens and state of a country own more assets in foreign countries than foreign countries own assets in that country. In the US, net foreign wealth has been declining over the past decades, meaning that US assets possessed by foreigners now total more than all the US assets abroad. This gap has increased significantly since the 2010s. Today, net foreign wealth represents about -40 to -50% in the US, meaning that the overall value of US assets owned by the rest of the world is worth significantly more (i.e. the equivalent of 50% of national income) than the value of assets owned by Americans in other countries.

Conversely, net foreign assets significantly increased in China between the 1980s and 2000s, and have been maintained at a

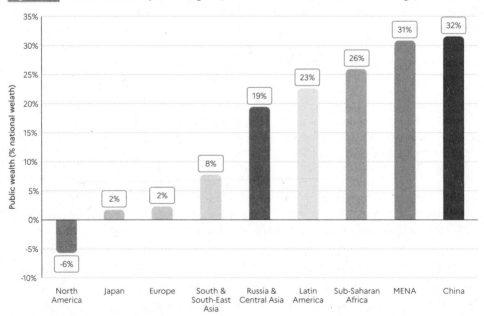

Figure 3.5   *Public wealth by world region (% national wealth, 2010-2020 average)*

Public wealth (% national welath)

North America	-6%
Japan	2%
Europe	2%
South & South-East Asia	8%
Russia & Central Asia	19%
Latin America	23%
Sub-Saharan Africa	26%
MENA	31%
China	32%

Interpretation: *Public wealth in China is 32% of national wealth for the 2010-2020 period. Public wealth is the sum of all financial and non-financial assets, net of debts, held by governments.* **Sources and series:** *wir2022.wid.world/methodology, Bauluz et al. (2021) and updates.*

high level since then (about 20%-25% of national income). What is striking though, is that net foreign income positions (i.e. the income generated by foreign assets) remain positive in the US and negative in China: assets owned by Americans in other countries are more profitable than assets owned by Chinese abroad – at least until now. This illustrates the power of the dollar in the international legal and monetary systems, which to some extent allows the US to accumulate large foreign deficits at limited cost. Interestingly, the net foreign wealth position of Europe deteriorated between the mid-1990s and 2010, before returning to equilibrium.

Financialization increased everywhere since 1980, but at different speeds

In principle, financial markets and intermediation are supposed to help to allocate capital where it is needed and therefore help to

boost national incomes across the world. Financialization has played a key role in the rise of private capital across the world over the past decades. How do we measure the weight of finance in contemporary capitalistic economies? One way is to look at the ratio between total financial liabilities – i.e., total debt and equity issued by households, the government, and the corporate sector combined – and national income. In China and in rich countries, this ratio has risen from 250%-500% in 1980, to 700-1800% in 2020 (Figure 3.7). In practice, the financialization of contemporary economies can have dire consequences because it makes them more vulnerable to financial crises, which in turn can become worldwide because of financial integration (e.g., the 2008-9 financial crisis started with subprime mortgages in the US and then spread). Financial intermediation also tends to disconnect investment decisions on the allocation and use of capital from where economic activity

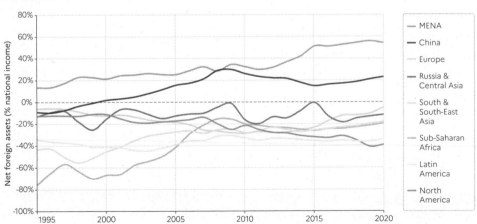

Figure 3.6   *Net foreign wealth positions across the world, 1995-2020*

Interpretation: *Net foreign assets have risen from -9% of national income to 23% of national income in China between 1995 and 2020. Net foreign wealth is equal to all foreign assets held by national citizens minus all national assets held by foreign citizens.* **Sources and series:** *wir2022.wid.world/methodology, Bauluz et al. (2021) and updates.*

actually takes place (more on this below). Investors in Singapore who decide to invest in the US inevitably pursue different motives than workers and capital owners living in the US. Financial intermediation thus raises important governance and regulation issues.

While financialization has greatly increased in countries like France and Japan over the past few decades, some countries have somewhat resisted the rising trend. In Germany, the ratio of financial liabilities to national income rose from 400% in 1980 to 800% in 2005 before dropping back to 700%, revealing that financialization has

little to do with overall economic performance.

Economies are increasingly owned by foreigners but some have resisted this trend more than others

With the rise of financialization, financial wealth is also increasingly owned by foreigners. One way to measure this phenomenon is to focus on the ratio of foreign financial liabilities to domestic financial liabilities. France and Germany (and European countries in general) have relatively large foreign ownership levels: foreign

Figure 3.7   *The rise of financial intermediation: in rich countries and China, 1980-2020*

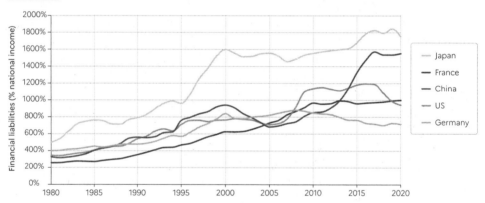

Interpretation: Financial liabilities in Japan rose from 500% of national income in 1980 to nearly 1800% in 2020. Sources and series: wir2022.wid.world/methodology and Bauluz et al. (2021).

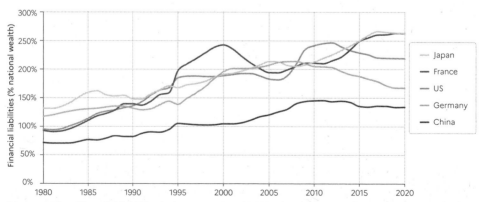

Interpretation: Financial liabilities in Japan rose from 130% of national wealth in 1980 to nearly 260% in 2020. Sources and series: wir2022.wid.world/methodology and Bauluz et al. (2021).

liabilities represent 25-30% of domestic financial liabilities in these countries, up from less than 10% in the early 1980s, and having increased especially in the 2000s.

Foreign financial liabilities have also increased in the US, but at 17% remain markedly lower than in Europe today. China and Japan show a different profile. Their foreign financial liabilities represent 5% (China) and 10% (Japan) of domestic financial liabilities. The East Asian economic giants are significantly less open to foreign financial ownership than the West (Figure 3.8). The dynamics observed in China are interesting. Between 1978 and the mid-1990s, foreign financial ownership increased rapidly in China, until it caught up with the US. After the mid-1990s, their trajectories diverged, as China strictly controlled foreign financial flows into the country.

The strong differences between European countries and others are partly the effects of size: European countries are smaller than the US, Japan and China, and if ownership were to be consolidated at the European level, then the rest of the world would own only about 15-20% of European wealth (so, like the levels in the United States). Even so, it appears to be true that some Asian countries – Japan, and particularly China – are less open to foreign ownership than European and North American countries. At this stage, it is too early to say whether the recent announcements made by US and European Union administrations aimed at curbing foreign ownership (in particular by China), will significantly alter foreign asset ownership positions in these countries.

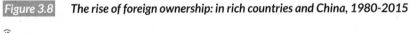

Figure 3.8   *The rise of foreign ownership: in rich countries and China, 1980-2015*

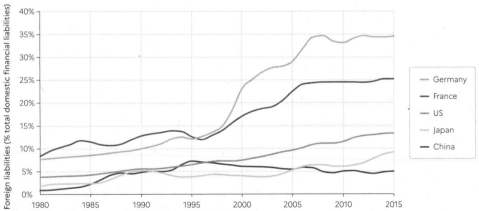

Interpretation: In 2015, 35% of total financial liabilities in Germany are owned by foreigners.
Sources and series: wir2022.wid.world/methodology and Bauluz et al. (2021).

Box 3.1   How do we measure wealth inequality within countries?

While the measurement of national wealth is a centuries' old tradition as monarchs were interested in evaluating wealth in their kingdoms for tax purposes, it is only recently that governments have started systematically to measure and publish aggregate wealth data called balance sheets. In many countries (in particular emerging and poor nations), such basic information is still missing today. Below, we briefly sketch the general method used to measure wealth across countries.

We begin with the set of concepts and guidelines of the System of National Accounts, which distinguishes between six institutional sectors that can own wealth, five resident sectors, and the foreign sector. The five resident sectors are households, non-profit institutions serving households, non-financial corporations, financial corporations, and the general government. We re-group these five sectors into three: (i) the private sector (the sum of households and non-profit institutions serving households), (ii) the corporate sector (financial plus non-financial corporations), and (iii) the general government.

Wealth can be broken down into four classes of assets and liabilities: housing assets, business and other non-financial assets, financial assets, and liabilities. Housing assets are defined as the sum of the market value of dwellings and land beneath dwellings: in practice, it is generally easier to measure the sum (as observed in real estate transactions) than the two components separately. Business assets (and other non-financial assets) are the difference between total non-financial assets and housing. Financial assets regroup for instance currency, deposits as well as bonds and loans, equity, life insurance or pensions funds. For all sectors, we report total liabilities, except for corporations, where we distinguish between equity and non-equity liabilities.

In order to measure total national wealth in each country of the world, we first collect and harmonize the available information on each of the classes of assets described above. In the past few years, there have been improvements in the publication of aggregate wealth data. Using empirical regularities observed in countries where all asset classes are available, we estimate asset class data in countries (typically, low-income ones) where some items are missing. The resulting database is the most extensive set of data on aggregate wealth across the world.[6]

NOTES

[1] The national accounts provide a measure of the capital stock reflecting only past savings poured into the capital stock, net of the depreciation of capital, and adjusted for general price inflation. This measure does not take into account changes in asset prices (such as increases in real estate prices or stock prices). In contrast, the measure of household wealth at market value published in the financial accounts captures such price effects.

[2] Whenever possible, it is preferable to study nonprofit institutions separately, and to distinguish between foundations serving private interests and those serving the general interest. Unfortunately, this line can sometimes be difficult to draw, and in practice the wealth of non-profit institutions is often mixed up with household wealth in existing national accounts. The share of nonprofit wealth in total private wealth is always less than 10% (and usually less than 5%). See Piketty T. and G. Zucman. 2014. "Capital is Back: Wealth-Income Ratios in Rich Countries 1700-2010", Quarterly Journal of Economics. 1255–1310. doi:10.1093/qje/qju018.

[3] In practice, national accounting distinguishes between two definitions of national wealth. Market value national wealth, and book value national wealth. Market value national wealth is the sum of the net wealth possessed by governments and the private sector in a given country. Book value national wealth is equal to national wealth plus the net wealth of the corporate sector when there is a difference between the market value of firms and the book value of these firms (i.e. a difference between the value of all the assets they possess and how markets evaluate this value). The standard concept used throughout this report to track wealth is "market value national wealth" (which we refer to as national wealth). At times, we explicitly refer to book value national wealth to make comparisons (see Box 4.1).

[4] Piketty, T.. 2020. Capital and ideology, Cambridge: Harvard University Press.

[5] See also Piketty and Zucman. "Capital is Back".

[6] For more information, see Blanchet T., L. Bauluz, A. Sodano and C. Martinez-Toledano. 2021. "Estimation of Global Wealth Aggregates in WID.world: Methodology". World Inequality Lab working paper.

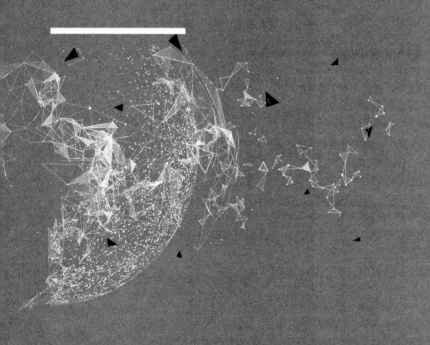

CHAPTER 4
Global wealth inequality: the rise of multimillionaires

Global wealth data remain opaque

The global financial system remains distinctly opaque in the 21ˢᵗ century, despite recent announcements about the end of tax evasion and financial secrecy. In practice, researchers, journalists, citizens, and public servants still encounter serious difficulties in tracking income and wealth flows across the world. Let us say at the onset that this situation is the consequence of policy choices and is not inevitable. In the digital age, inequality is omnipresent, but often missing from public statistics. It is paradoxical, for instance, that tax administrations and the general public across the world often learn about the extent of wealth inequality through fortune magazines. In principle, tax authorities should collect and publish information on how different wealth groups fare in the global and national economies, from the very poorest to the very richest.[1]

Without such information, it is impossible fully to understand the impacts of monetary, budget and tax policies on the economy, and impossible to make governments accountable for their choices. Certain magazines (Forbes, Bloomberg), and a handful of financial institutions (for instance, Credit Suisse) have been producing billionaire wealth estimates for several years. These studies find that the wealth of top wealth holders have been increasing at very high speed in recent decades—substantially faster than the size of the world economy— and we agree with this general conclusion. However, the methods used by these institutions often lack transparency; in particular,

they do not release their raw data sources or detailed methodologies, so it is impossible to reconstruct their statistical results. This is not merely a technical question; methodological choices can have a significant impact on the measured changes in wealth inequality, and transparency of methods and sources is crucial if we want to reach better agreement about the facts of inequality.

Moreover, while billionaire data is important, it is not sufficient for a full grasp of the dynamics of wealth inequality in a given country and around the world. It is equally important to understand the dynamics of wealth at the bottom of the distribution (say, the poorest half of the population), among the middle class, and among the very wealthy non-billionaires. In particular, we stress the importance of millionaires and multi-millionaires, i.e. individuals with a few million or sometime a few dozen or hundreds of millions—but not billions—of dollars in assets, and who collectively possess much more wealth than the billionaires, as we see below.

The WID.world project seeks to address these issues of scope and methodology by providing estimates on the entire distribution of wealth, from the poorest groups to the richest. We also make very clear what we know and do not know about wealth inequality, and we publish all our assumptions and methodology online so that anyone interested in contributing to this work can do so. In recent years, we have partnered with several statistical institutions, tax administrations, and international organizations to improve our common understanding of wealth inequality. A lot of work remains to be done before we fully understand the dynamics and drivers of wealth concentration worldwide, but we are starting to get a good picture of many important facts and trends about global wealth inequality, which we present below.

How large is global wealth and where is it held?

In Chapters 1 and 3, we presented some insights into global wealth inequality. In this chapter, we focus on the distribution of global household wealth, i.e. the inequality of private wealth among individuals. We also look

at how wealth inequality levels have changed in the past several decades, and more recently during the Covid-19 pandemic.

The total market value of household wealth possessed by individuals around the globe amounts to €377 trillion (or USD535 trillion), a value roughly equal to 4.4 times global income (factoring in the wealth of public actors and private foundations raises this value to €510 trillion, i.e. 5.9 times global income, see Chapter 1).[2] Figure 4.1 shows the amount of household wealth owned by the global top 10% of wealth owners, the middle 40% and the bottom 50%. The top 10% owns collectively €285 trillion (76% of the

Figure 4.1   *Regional composition for the top 10%, middle 40% and bottom 50% wealth groups, 2021*

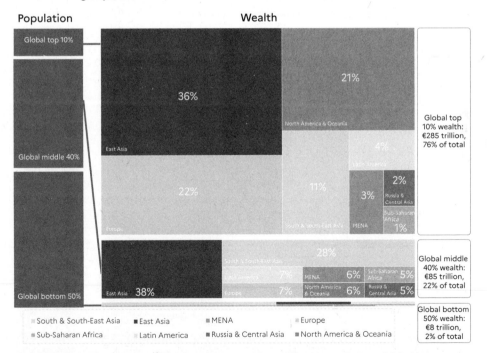

Interpretation: *The colored rectangles shows the wealth possessed by each group (global bottom 50%, middle 40% and top 10%). The size of colored rectangles is proportional to wealth owned by each group, and by each region within each group. In 2021, 22% of the wealth detained by the global top 10% was held in Europe. Net household wealth is equal to the sum of financial assets (e.g. equity or bonds) and non-financial assets (e.g. housing or land) owned by individuals, net of their debts.*
Sources and series: *wir2022.wid.world/methodology, Bauluz et al. (2021) and updates.*

world total), the middle 40% owns €85 trillion (22% of the total) and the bottom 50% owns €8 trillion (2% of the total).[3] As discussed in Chapter 1, wealth concentration levels are particularly extreme: half of the world's population is almost entirely deprived of wealth, while the top 10% owns nearly three quarters of it.

These statistics are based on wealth levels expressed at Purchasing Power Parity (PPP), in order to reflect differences in purchasing power across the world. Purchasing Power Parity definitely gives a more accurate picture of global inequality from the point of view of individuals who do not travel across the world and who essentially spend their incomes in their own countries. However, Market Exchange Rates (MER) are perhaps better to inform about inequality in a world where individuals can easily spend their incomes where they want. At Market Exchange Rates, the bottom 50% of the population owns just 1% of global wealth and the top 10% captures over three quarters of global wealth. While using PPP is standard practice when looking at global income inequality, it is less often used when discussing wealth inequality. But for talking about wealth, both PPP and MER can be relevant, depending on the question asked. When focusing on the bottom of the distribution of global wealth owners, using PPP values makes sense: €3,000 (at market exchange rates) in Ghana is a non-negligible amount of money, whereas €3,000 (at market exchange rates) in Germany is not very much. Using PPP helps us to grasp these differences: €3,000 in Ghana is worth the equivalent of a little more than €9,000 in Germany, given

differences in the costs of goods and services in the two countries.

For the cases of global multimillionaires and billionaires, PPP is less suited, and Market Exchange Rates are more informative. Individuals possessing one billion dollars, whether in Ghana or Germany, typically spend large portions of their incomes and wealth globally rather than only in their home country. It therefore makes more sense to use Market Exchange Rates to study the wealth of the very rich and its implications in terms of taxation and redistribution, for instance. In this chapter, numbers are expressed in PPP because we focus both on the bottom and top of the global wealth distribution. In Chapter 7, where we focus more specifically on global multimillionaires and billionaires, and taxation issues, we use Market Exchange Rates. The World Inequality Database allows anybody to check wealth inequality levels in all countries, both at PPP and at MER.

To return to Figure 4.1, the rectangles inform about the geographical composition of each global wealth group. Colored rectangles show the relative wealth share of each region within wealth groups. For instance, the East Asia rectangle tells us about the amount of wealth owned by East Asians relative to other regions. It appears that East Asians, North Americans and Europeans make up the bulk of the global top 10%. More precisely, East Asians own 36% of the wealth of the global top 10%, North Americans and those from Oceania own about 21% of it and Europeans 22%. If there were no wealth inequalities, then these shares would be equal to each region's share of the global population: about a third for East Asians, 15% for Europeans, and 21% for North Americans.

The uneven increase in wealth since the 1990s

At this stage, our data allows us to produce wealth estimates since 1995. As discussed above, wealth inequality data remain more opaque and scarcer than income inequality data. Therefore, we cannot produce global wealth inequality estimates starting in 1980 or earlier. We have series on the evolution of wealth starting in the early 20th century (and even late 18th century) in some countries, which we also discuss below to complement the analysis of global trends.

Since 1995, global wealth per adult has grown around 3.2% per year,

but global groups of wealth holders have not all grown at the same speed. Average wealth among the bottom 50% grew 3.7%, the middle 40% grew 3.8% and the top 10% 3.0%, while growth was much higher at the very top of the distribution (over 5% for the top 0.01%) (Table 4.1). The global bottom 50% (essentially composed of the lower and middle classes of emerging countries) recorded relatively high growth rates, but the levels are very low. This group started with just PPP €1,000 on average at the beginning of the period and ends with €2,908€. The wealth of the middle 40% grew at a relatively low rate, as did its income (see Chapter 2): this corresponds to squeezed lower and middle classes in industrialized nations, which have been largely cut off from economic growth in their own countries in the past few decades. In some countries,

Table 4.1   *Global distribution of wealth, 2021*

	Share in total wealth (%) (2021)	Avg. Per adult wealth (2021 €)	Threshold (2021)	Avg. annual growth rate (1995-2021)
Full population	100%	72,913		3.2%
Bottom 50%	2.0%	2,908		3.7%
Middle 40%	22.4%	40,919	11,954	3.8%
Top 10%	75.6%	550,920	124,876	3.0%
Top 1%	37.8%	2.8 million	893,338	3.2%
Top 0.1%	19.4%	14.1 million	3.6 million	4.0%
Top 0.01%	11.2%	81.7 million	18.0 million	5.0%
Top 0.001%	6.4%	469.0 million	119.4 million	5.9%
Top 1/1 million	3.5%	2.6 billion	674.7 million	6.9%
Top 1/10 million	1.9%	14.2 billion	3.7 billion	8.1%
Top 1/100 million	1.1%	77.4 billion	20.3 billion	9.3%

*Interpretation: The global top 1% own 38% of total household wealth, and have had an average annual growth rate of 3.2% since 1995. The global average wealth per adult was 72,910€ (at Purchasing Power Parity) in 2021. Net household wealth is equal to the sum of financial assets (e.g. equity or bonds) and non-financial assets (e.g. housing or land) owned by individuals, net of their debts. The top 1/100 million represents 52 persons. **Sources and series:** wir2022.wid.world/methodology, Bauluz et al. (2021) and updates.*

including the US, the poorest 50% (in terms of wealth) had barely recovered from the financial crisis of 2008-9 in 2020, when the Covid shock hit (more on this later). The wealth of the US bottom 50% has in fact recorded a very slow increase since the 1990s (see also below). Sluggish wealth growth rates at the bottom and at the middle of the distribution are also observed in most industrialized countries over the past two or three decades.

At the top of the global distribution, the global top 1% grew by 3.2%. Note that it takes PPP €893,000 today (USD1.3 million) to be part of the top 1%. What we see further up in the distribution confirms this general pattern: the wealthier the individuals, the higher the increase in their wealth. At the extreme end of the distribution, the wealth of the global top 0.01% grew 5% per year over 25 years,

the top 0.001% at 5.9%, and the top 0.00001% (one person in 10 million, 520 adults in 2021) saw their wealth grow by an average 8.1% per year. The top 0.000001% (one person in 100 million, that is, the top 52 billionaires in 2021) saw their wealth increase by 9.3% per year over the period. Another way to present these findings is to show the average wealth growth of each group over the 1995 and 2021 period. This is shown in Figure 4.2.

Extreme growth at the very top

When the growth rate of a group is faster than the growth rate of the average, this group's share of total wealth increases. This is what happened among the wealthiest groups. Figure 4.3a presents the evolution of the global top 0.001% wealth share between 1995 and 2021. This group represents about 51,700 adults in 2021 and to enter

Figure 4.2   *Average annual wealth growth rate, 1995-2021*

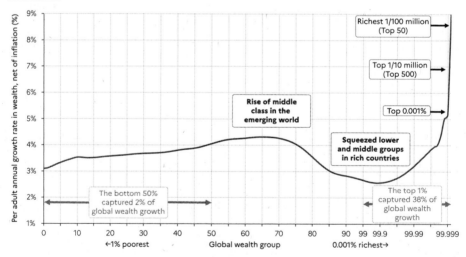

Interpretation: *Growth rates among the poorest half of the population were between 3% and 4% per year, between 1995 and 2021. Since this group started from very low wealth levels, its absolute levels of growth remained very low. The poorest half of the world population has captured only 2.3% of overall wealth growth since 1995. The top 1% benefited from high growth rates (3% to 9% per year). This group captured 38% of total wealth growth between 1995 and 2021. Net household wealth is equal to the sum of financial assets (e.g. equity or bonds) and non-financial assets (e.g. housing or land) owned by individuals, net of their debts* **Sources and series:** *wir2022.wid.world/methodology, Bauluz et al. (2021) and updates.*

it, you need to have amassed wealth of PPP €119 million. If this group owned 100 times the average wealth on earth, then their share in total wealth would be exactly equal to 0.1%. It turns out that their share is just over 6% of global wealth, meaning that their wealth is over 6,000 times higher than the average. Twenty-five years ago, their wealth was very high compared with the average but not as high as that: it was 3,000 times higher than the average, and their share in total wealth was 3%. This represents a substantial increase in extreme wealth inequality over the period. To put this in perspective, the total wealth of the global bottom 50%, a group that is 50,000 more populous than the top 0.001%, is three times smaller. The bottom 50% experienced some growth over several decades (see above), but that growth was much more modest than among the top 0.001%. Figure 4.3b presents the evolution of the wealth of global

billionaires since 1995, as a share of total household wealth.

The evolution of wealth inequality in rich countries

Since the 1980s, rich countries have experienced an increase in wealth inequality after a period of secular decline in top wealth shares. Top 1% wealth shares were very high in Europe and the US at the end of the 19th century, before falling sharply after the military, political and economic shocks of the first half of the 20th century, and it is going back up again today (although generally not to quite as high as in the late 19th century). It is important to note that a series of policies contributed to further reducing top 1% wealth shares and kept wealth inequality in check during the mixed-economy regimes of the 1950s to the 1980s: wars and economic crises do not explain all the reduction of wealth inequality in the 20th century, peace time policies played a crucial role as well.[4]

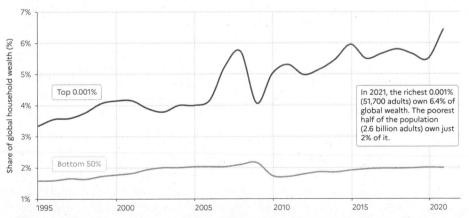

Figure 4.3a   *Extreme wealth inequality: top 0.001% vs. bottom 50% wealth share, 1995-2021*

Share of global household wealth (%)

Top 0.001%

In 2021, the richest 0.001% (51,700 adults) own 6.4% of global wealth. The poorest half of the population (2.6 billion adults) own just 2% of it.

Bottom 50%

Interpretation: *The share of household wealth detained by the richest 0.001% of adults rose from less than 3.5% of total wealth in 1995 to nearly 6.5% today. After a very slight increase, the share of wealth owned by the poorest half of the population has stagnated since the early 2000s at around 2%. Net household wealth is equal to the sum of financial assets (e.g. equity or bonds) and non-financial assets (e.g. housing or land) owned by individuals, net of their debts. **Sources and series:** wir2022.wid.world/methodology, Bauluz et al. (2021) and updates.*

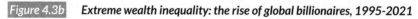

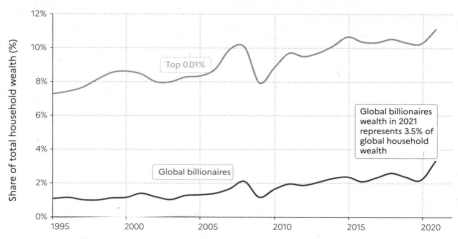

Figure 4.3b   *Extreme wealth inequality: the rise of global billionaires, 1995-2021*

Top 0.01%

Global billionaires wealth in 2021 represents 3.5% of global household wealth

Global billionaires

Share of total household wealth (%)

Interpretation: *The share of wealth detained by the global top 0.01% rose from 7% in 1995 to 11% in 2021. The top 0.01% is composed of 520 000 adults in 2021. The entry threshold of this group rose from €693,000 (PPP) in 1995 to €16,666,000 today. Billionaires correspond to individuals owning at least $1b in nominal terms. The net household wealth is equal to the sum of financial assets (e.g. equity or bonds) and non-financial assets (e.g. housing or land) owned by individuals, net of their debts.* **Sources and series:** *wir2022.wid.world/methodology, Bauluz et al. (2021) and updates.*

Deregulation, privatization and lower progressive taxation contributed to boosting top wealth shares in rich countries after the economic policy turn-around of the 1980s, marked by the election of Margaret Thatcher in the UK in 1979, Ronald Reagan in the US in 1980, and the policies implemented by French President François Mitterrand after 1983. The economic policy mixes implemented in Europe and the US since the 1980s have favored wealth concentration and were successful enough to invert the secular trend observed since the 1910s in rich countries.

Figure 4.4 shows the evolution of the top 1% wealth shares in the US and Western Europe over a century. There are two major take-aways from this graph. First, wealth inequality was very high in the US and Western Europe in the early 20th century. The top 1% wealth owners possessed 43% of all private wealth in the US, and 55% in Western Europe.

Early 20th century inequality levels were similar to those observed during the 19th century in the two regions.[5] This reveals that despite the development of liberal democracies on both sides of the Atlantic, wealth inequality remained high (see our discussion of long-term income inequality in Chapter 2). Indeed, while access to education progressed, there were little or no reforms to spread wealth to lower- and middle-income groups. The development of voting rights was also very limited. First, half of the population—women—was entirely deprived of the vote. It is only in the 1920-40s that women obtained the right to vote in major Western democracies. Second, even among men, voting rights remained unequal at the beginning of the 20th century in several Western countries. In Sweden, for instance, until 1910 only the top 20% of male wealth owners could vote, with significant inequalities within this

Figure 4.4   *Top 1% versus bottom 50% wealth shares in Western Europe and the US, 1910-2020*

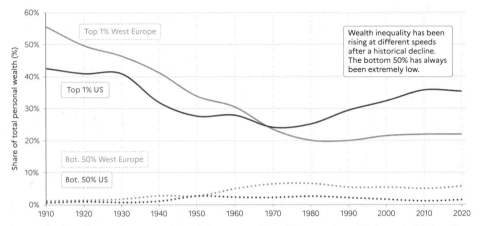

Interpretation: *The graph presents decennial averages of top 1% personal wealth shares in Western Europe and the US. In 1910, the top 1% in Europe owned 55% of wealth, vs. 43% in the U.S. A century later, the US is almost back to its early 20th century level. Net household wealth is equal to the sum of financial assets (e.g. equity or bonds) and non-financial assets (e.g. housing or land) owned by individuals, net of their debts.*
Sources and series: *wir2022.wid.world/methodology, Bauluz et al. (2021) and updates.*

group as well. In the US, it was only after the 1965 Voting Rights Act that African-Americans obtained the right to vote in southern states. The persistence of large political inequalities drastically limited the power of working and middle classes to implement reforms.

The financial crisis of 1929, the military shocks of the First and Second World Wars, as well as independence for Western colonies, significantly affected the wealth positions of the richest. In addition, the development of inheritance taxes, and highly progressive income taxes, as well as series of nationalizations and capital control policies in the Western world, starting in the 1920s and continuing after WWII, further reduced wealth inequality. By 1970, the top 1% wealth shares in Europe and the US had dropped to less than 25%. This reduction of wealth inequality enabled the rise of a patrimonial middle class

(whose wealth is largely composed of housing and retirement savings) on both sides of the Atlantic.

In more recent years, however, top 1% wealth shares have risen again in Europe and especially the US. In the US, the return of top wealth inequality has been particularly dramatic, with the top 1% share nearing 35% in 2020, approaching its Gilded Age level. In Europe, top wealth inequality has also been on the rise since 1980, though significantly less so than in the US. One of the main differences between the two regions is that Europe has so far been able to maintain a relatively strong middle class, while in the US this group has been squeezed by an explosion of debt (particularly housing debt, which triggered the 2008 financial crisis). The middle 40% wealth share in the US dropped from around 34% in 1980 to 28% today, while it remained at around 40% over the period in France. As a result, while Europe was significantly more unequal than the US in the late 19th and early 20th centuries, the reverse is true today. It is impossible to say, however, whether this situation will hold in the coming decades. Significant inequalities in the growth rates of wealth between the top and the middle of the distribution have been observed in Europe in recent decades, which could magnify wealth inequality in the future.

Wealth inequality in emerging countries

We know less about the long-term dynamics of wealth inequality in emerging countries than we know about those in rich ones: most of our series for BRICS (Brazil, Russia, India, China, South Africa) start in the 1990s (Figure 4.5). It is clear, however, that the past three decades have also been marked by an increase in wealth inequality in the emerging world. In some countries (i.e. Russia and China, and to a lesser extent, India) this increase has been particularly strong. These countries were socialist or highly regulated economies until the early 1980s or 1990s, when they went through liberalization and privatization reforms. What is striking when comparing these countries is that the trajectories they followed were very different. In Russia, the rise of the top 1% wealth share was both fast and great. In less than a decade, the top 1% wealth share had doubled, to reach 40%. In India and China, the top 1% wealth share increased very significantly, but is barely over 30% today. This shows that deregulation and privatization can be introduced in many different ways. The path followed by Russia, known as "shock therapy" (characterized by the large-scale sale of public assets, bought at low cost by a handful of wealth-holders), is an extreme case of liberalization.[6] In contrast, liberalization in China was much more contained, and while the housing sector was mostly privatized, the state kept control of large public companies.

Figure 4.5   *Top 1% wealth share in the BRICS, 1995-2021*

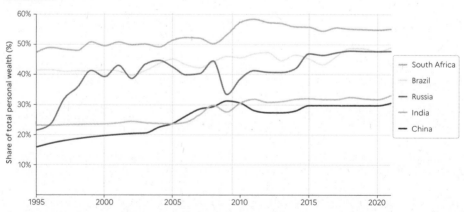

Interpretation: The graph presents the evolution of the share of total personal wealth owned by the richest 1% in emerging countries. This share rose everywhere between 1995 and 2021, with strong increases in Russia, China and India and more moderate increases in Brazil and South Africa where wealth inequality was already extreme at the beginning of the period. Net household wealth is equal to the sum of financial assets (e.g. equity or bonds) and non-financial assets (e.g. housing or land) owned by individuals, net of their debts.
Sources and series: *wir2022.wid.world/methodology, Bauluz et al. (2021) and updates.*

In Brazil and South Africa, the top 1% wealth share was extreme in the 1990s, and is still extreme today. Wealth inequality has slightly risen in these countries. This highlights the persistence of extremely hierarchical economic and social systems that are the modern result of colonial or apartheid societies. While voting rights have been extended to all, the ownership system remains dual. Descendants of slave owners continue to own most of the wealth. In South Africa, for instance, the top 10% wealth group is composed of 60% White South Africans, who represent only 10% or less of the total population.[7] In Brazil, the emergence of the Republic in 1985, after two decades of military dictatorship, enabled the expansion of voting rights. The Workers' Party implemented large-scale transfers to the disadvantaged, and invested in education and healthcare through programs such as the *Bolsa Familia*. These policy reforms were not sufficient, however, to change substantially the structure of ownership in the country.

What is driving global wealth inequality?

As we discussed in Chapter 2, global income dynamics are driven by both inter- and intra-country forces. Wealth inequality involves inter- and intra-country drivers as well. The rise of private wealth has been faster in large emerging economies than in rich countries, a trend driven by high economic growth and large-scale privatization in transition economies. This tends to reduce global wealth inequality between the emerging world and wealthiest nations. The effect was countered, however, by the rise of wealth inequality within countries.

Increasing wealth inequality within countries is due to several factors, including rising income inequality amplified by inequality of savings rates and of rates of return between different wealth groups. Across the world, we typically observe that the wealthy save more than the poor, and also that they benefit from higher rates of return on their investments. This is also known as the snowballing effect of capital accumulation: the more one possesses today, the more one can accumulate tomorrow. However, policies also play a determining role in the evolution of wealth inequality. Public policies such as rent control and regulation contribute to the reduction of rates of returns and limit capital accumulation. Redistribution policies such as wealth taxes and taxes on capital income, limit capital accumulation and generate public resources that can help spread wealth to the worse-off.

How will these forces play out in the future? It is impossible to say which driver will govern wealth dynamics in coming decades. We do know, however, that there was nothing inevitable about the fact that the very top of the global wealth distribution rose so much faster than average world wealth over the past three or four decades. Indeed, the large transfers from public to private wealth that occurred in many countries contributed to this increase. Privatization disproportionately benefited small groups of the population—for example, Russian oligarchs. This helps to explain why top wealth holders' shares rose so fast. It is difficult, however, with the data currently at our disposal, to estimate the precise impact of this factor. There are also cases where privatization has benefited mostly the middle class (for example, of housing in the UK).[8] Whether this channel is likely to be important for the future (in emerging countries, for instance) is another important but uncertain issue.

Another decisive factor behind rising wealth inequality at the top is the financial deregulation and innovation that increased the inequality in rates of return for different sizes of financial portfolios. Some of the most convincing evidence for this effect comes from the observed rates of return on university endowments (such as for Ivy League universities in the United States), which since the 1980s has varied from 4–5% per year for the smallest endowments to as much as 7–9% per year for the largest ones (after deduction of inflation and management costs). The size advantage on rates of returns has persisted for decades and shows no signs of disappearing. It is plausible to think that rates of returns for individuals are also growing even among the very

wealthy. Billionaires often use very sophisticated wealth management strategies that resemble those of the large endowments of non-profit institutions.

One thing is certain: if the rates of inequality observed between wealth groups over the past several decades continues into the future, then global wealth inequality will continue to increase and will eventually reach enormous levels. Figure 4.6 presents the evolution of the top 0.1% and middle 40% wealth shares, assuming that each group grows over the coming decades at the same speed as it has done since 1995. Under this hypothetical scenario, by 2070, the global top 0.1% will capture over a fourth of global wealth. By the end of the century, it will own more than the global middle 40% (30%). Without major economic policy changes or shocks (environmental catastrophes, wars, economic crises), the future is bright for global multimillionaires.

Figure 4.6   *Projections of the top 0.1%, middle 40% and bottom 50% wealth shares, 2000-2100*

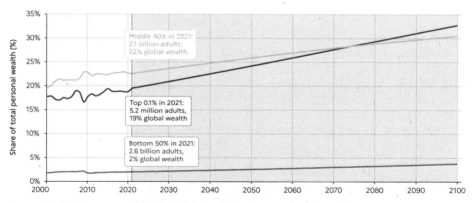

Interpretation: *The graph shows the evolution of the global top 0.1% and middle 40% wealth shares if each group continued to grow at the same speed as they have since 1995; all else being equal. Net household wealth is equal to the sum of financial assets (e.g. equity or bonds) and non-financial assets (e.g. housing or land) owned by individuals, net of their debts.* **Sources and series:** *wir2022.wid.world/methodology, Bauluz et al. (2021) and updates.*

Box 4.1   Who owns what? Breaking down asset ownership by wealth group

Asset portfolios (i.e. the different types of wealth possessed by individuals) vary substantially across the wealth distribution: rich and poor have very different wealth levels, but they also own very different types of wealth. While there can be significant variations across countries, depending on institutions, policies, and level of economic development, there are also relatively strong similarities in asset ownership.

The main form of wealth owned by the very poor (when they have positive net wealth) is cash or bank deposits. Individuals at the bottom of the wealth distribution may own houses and land, but the market value of these assets is typically very small. Middle classes typically own bank deposits as well as real estate, which represent the bulk of their assets. They also own equity and bonds, often in the form of retirement savings, but these represent a relatively small share of their wealth. In the top wealth decile of rich countries, individuals own a non-negligible share of business assets (5-10%), housing assets (30-40%) and financial assets (40-60%). The richer individuals are, the higher the share of financial assets in their wealth. In the very top groups, these can represent 90-95% of all wealth in countries like France or the US. This does not mean that the very wealthy do not own real estate, it means rather that they own very substantial amounts of financial assets.

Box 4.2   How do we measure wealth inequality?

The measurement of wealth inequality is a challenging enterprise given the opacity of the global financial system. In order to measure wealth inequality properly, researchers, the media, and the general public should have access to public information about the number of individuals in different wealth brackets (see Chapter 7). Without such information, inequality scholars have to use imperfect information to track wealth. This includes household surveys, administrative records, national accounts, and rich lists. Household surveys (such as the Household Finance and Consumption Survey in Europe, and the Survey of Consumer Finance in the US) provide essential pieces of the puzzle. However, it is difficult for surveys to capture the top distribution well (the US Survey of Consumer Finances uses income tax data to find its high wealth sample, and is the most sophisticated attempt to capture the very rich in surveys). National accounts provide the value of overall wealth in an economy, and hence help us understand the mismatch between what is reported in surveys and the reality. In order to understand better how wealth is distributed across the population, it is essential to use administrative data, typically obtained from tax departments, which can give a more precise picture of wealth levels among the very top groups. Wealth inequality can be estimated from estate tax data (the so-called estate multiplier method). It can also be estimated using individual income tax data from which we can infer the stock of wealth from the flow of capital income (the capitalization method).

The aim of the WID.world projects is to mobilize all available sources on wealth inequality and to combine them in a systematic and transparent manner, so that anyone can reproduce the different steps of the method and contribute to a better understanding of wealth inequality with more recent raw data or alternative assumptions.

In the case of wealth inequality estimates, our coverage for North America, European countries and the BRICS (Brazil, Russia, India, China, South Africa) is relatively good but our coverage for low-income countries remains poor. For low-income countries with no wealth inequality data, we estimate the level of wealth inequality from the levels of aggregate wealth and income inequality.[9] We discuss issues associated with the measurement of aggregate wealth across the world in Chapter 3. We observe a strong regularity between income inequality levels and wealth inequality levels in countries where we observe both dimensions (**Figure FB4.1**). This relationship is then used to infer wealth inequality levels in countries that have no wealth inequality data at all. Estimates for these countries should be seen as preliminary, but they already offer a plausible level of wealth inequality. The quality of estimates for each country, as well as the complete set of sources used, and methodological documents, are available online on WID.world.

Wealth inequality estimates produced by the systematic combination of surveys, administrative data and national accounts are not supposed to reproduce exactly the number of billionaires observed country by country in rich lists such as those published by Forbes and Bloomberg. Indeed, our aim is to provide wealth levels for the entire distribution, from bottom to top, and to do so, the best way is to start with survey and administrative data, not with rich lists, which cover only a tiny fraction of the distribution. It should be noted too that Forbes' and Bloomberg's methodologies are not perfect: they can miss high net worth individuals in certain countries, and over or under evaluate their true wealth in others. We should also recognize, however, that surveys and administrative data, even properly combined, are not perfect either, especially at the top of the top. We therefore also mobilize Forbes data country by country, to provide series that are closer to theirs. More precisely, top wealth levels observed in WID.world series are corrected to ensure that the billionaire wealth reported for a country is at least as much as is reported in rich lists.[10]

Figure B4.1   *Wealth inequality vs. income inequality across the world*

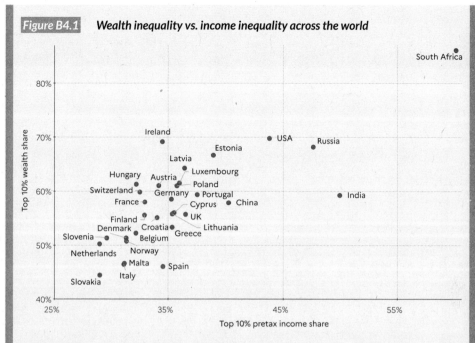

Interpretation: *Each country's data point refers to the average top 10% share over 1995-2021. Income is measured after pension and unemployment payments and benefits received by individuals but before other taxes they pay and transfers they receive. Net household wealth is equal to the sum of financial assets (e.g. equity or bonds) and non-financial assets (e.g. housing or land) owned by individuals, net of their debts. **Sources and series:** wir2022.wid.world/methodology, Bauluz et al. (2021) and updates.*

NOTES

[1] This chapter is based on data from Blanchet, T., L. Bauluz, A. Sodano C. Toledano. (2021). "Estimation of Global Wealth Aggregates in WID. world: Methodology." World Inequality Lab working paper 2021/22; and from Félix Bajard, Lucas Chancel, Rowaida Moshrif, Thomas Piketty, « *Global Wealth Inequality on WID.world: Estimates and Imputations* », WID.world Technical Note, 2021/16

[2] 2021 values are based on estimations.

[3] See Chapter 1 of the Report, Figure 1.1. Numbers may not add up due to rounding

[4] See Alvaredo, F., L. Chancel, T. Piketty, E. Saez, G. Zucman. 2018. *World Inequality Report 2018*, Harvard University Press. See also Piketty T. 2020. *Capital and Ideology*, Cambridge: Harvard University Press.

[5] See Roine J. and D. Waldenstrom (2014), Long-Run Trends in the Distribution of Income and Wealth. IZA Working Paper; Piketty T. 2014. *Capital in the*

21st century. Cambridge: Harvard University Press; Alvaredo et al. *World Inequality Report 2018*.

[6] See Alvaredo et al. World Inequality Report 2018, Section 4.

[7] See Chatterjee, A., L. Czajka, L. and A. Gethin 2020. "Estimating the distribution of household wealth in South Africa" (No. 2020/45). WIDER Working Paper. In South Africa, strong racial inequalities coexist with strong inequalities within ethnic groups. For instance, the Gini index for wealth among Whites is equal to 0.74, compared to 0.98 among Blacks according to the National Income Dynamics Survey.

[8] Alvaredo et al. *World Inequality Report*.

[9] See Blanchet et al. "Estimation of Global Wealth Aggregates".

[10] See Félix Bajard, Lucas Chancel, Rowaida Moshrif, Thomas Piketty, « *Global Wealth Inequality on WID.world: Estimates and Imputations* », WID.world Technical Note, 2021/16

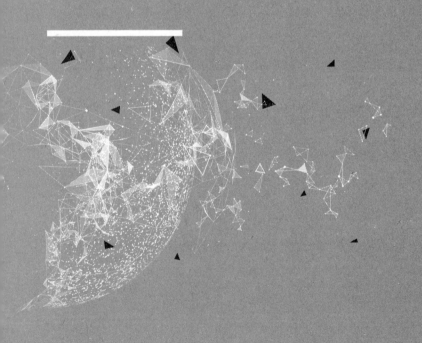

CHAPTER 5

Half the sky? The female labor income share from a global perspective

WORLD
INEQUALITY
REPORT
2022

This chapter is based on "Half the sky? The Female Labor Income Share in a Global Perspective", by T. Neef and A.-S. Robilliard.[1]

The previous chapters of this report focus on the inequality between income and wealth groups, between and within countries. So far, we have not looked at a major dimension of socio-economic inequality – gender. There are many ways to look at gender inequality. Under the umbrella term Gender Economics, a large literature on patterns of gender inequality and its causes has emerged. One key concept developed in this literature is the gender pay gap, as measured by the average gap between men's and women's wages and salaries, before or after controlling for the type of work, the level of qualification or other factors. The unadjusted gender pay gap is the overall gap in remuneration between men and women, while the adjusted gender pay gap controls for differences in education, experience and occupation and thus only compares the pay of men and women with similar observable labor market characteristics.

Certain gender inequality measures have been quite well disseminated in the media over the past years. For instance, activist groups and institutions celebrate "Equal Pay Day" in several countries. This day symbolizes how far into the year the average woman would have to work in order to earn what the average man earned over the previous calendar year. The exact date therefore varies from country to country because the date is typically set based on the gender pay gap measures before

controlling for qualifications or occupation: in the US, Equal Pay Day was celebrated on March 24 in 2021 (because the value of the gap is found to be 18% on average).

These metrics play an important role in informing us about the persistence of large income gender inequalities in both high- and low-income countries. We believe, however, that these analyses should be complemented with other types of indicators which can shed light on broader structural inequalities between women and men but are not fully captured by pay differentials. In fact, gender pay gaps generally do not consider inequalities in employment level. Women continue to have less access to the labor market (and especially to the most rewarding occupations) in many countries and this exacerbates the gender inequality in total earnings. For a clear understanding of where societies stand in terms of gender inequality at work, the relative overall shares of labor income accruing to women and men stands out as an essential indicator, but it has so far been overlooked. We see it as the best metric to consider gender income inequality from a systemic perspective.

The aim of this chapter is therefore to address the following questions: how big is the share of total labor income earned by women across the globe? (The detailed methodology and full set of results are available in Neef and Robilliard's study.)[2] How has women's share of labor income evolved since the 1990s? And how prominent is the under-representation of women at the top of the labor income distribution? Our main income concept, labor income, comprises wage and salaries as well as the labor share of self-employment income. We assume the latter to be 70% of full self-employment income. The female share of total labor income is the national aggregate labor income earned by women relative to the total aggregate of labor income within a country.

The data presented below, collected, harmonized and analyzed by Theresa Neef and Anne-Sophie Robilliard is, to our knowledge, the first data set on female labor income shares covering 180 countries since 1990 (see Box 5.1 on Methodology).

Female labor income share across the world today: regional divides

Figure 5.1 presents a world map of female income shares in 2019 based on the World Inequality Lab's modeled estimates. In a country with perfect equality between women and men, the female labor income share would be equal to 50% (though at the global level, there are very slightly more men than women and the ratio is 50.4%). In practice, we find that the female labor income share is systematically below 50%, with significant variations across countries, ranging from below 10% to 45%.

The former Eastern Bloc is where female labor income shares are the highest, with the average female share near 41%, with values typically ranging around 38-43%. The lowest level is found in Bosnia Herzegovina (34%) and the highest in Moldova (45%). In 15 countries, the share is above the 40% line. In the Russian Federation, the female labor income share stands at 40%.

Western Europe is found to have high labor income shares in comparison with other parts of the world; the average female share is estimated at around 39% and variability across countries appears to be relatively low, with values ranging from 35% in Austria to 44% in Portugal. In the three most populous countries (Germany,

---

Figure 5.1   *Female labor income shares across the world, 2019*

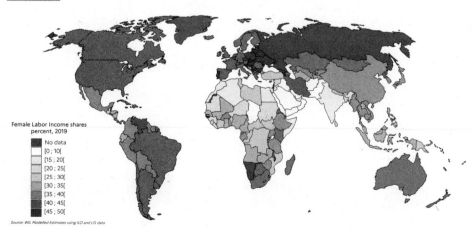

Female Labor Income shares
percent, 2019

- No data
- [0 ; 10[
- [15 ; 20[
- [20 ; 25[
- [25 ; 30[
- [30 ; 35[
- [35 ; 40[
- [40 ; 45[
- [45 ; 50[

Source: WIL Modelled Estimates using ILO and LIS data

Interpretation: *In 2019, the share of labor income earned by women was 41% in France, whereas it is 18% in India.* **Sources and series:** *wir2022.wid.world/methodology and Neef and Robilliard (2021).*

France and the UK), the shares stand at 36-41%. In comparison, North America and Australia have similar but slightly lower shares than those found in Europe: the US and Canada exhibit shares of 38-39%. This means that men capture around 62-64% of total labor income, i.e. more than half as much again as women. This illustrates the magnitude of systemic gender inequality – a simple fact that can be overlooked in indicators on gender gaps that control for the type of job or occupation held by men and women.

Latin American countries appear to be relatively homogeneous. There, the average female labor income share stands at 35% with values ranging from 26% in Guatemala to 42% in Barbados. In the two most populous countries (Brazil and Mexico), the shares are 38% and 33% respectively.

Asian countries exhibit lower shares than Europe and North America, with an average of 27%. There appears to be a strong east-west distinction, with East Asian countries exhibiting much higher shares. Eleven countries have values above 30% while two (Pakistan and Afghanistan) exhibit shares below 10%. The two most heavily populated countries (China and India) exhibit shares of 33% and 18% respectively.

MENA countries (the Middle East and North Africa) exhibit low levels of female labor income share, with an unweighted average of 15%. A majority of them have shares under 20% and five (Yemen, Iraq, Saudi Arabia, Qatar, Oman) are under 10%. Israel stands out with a share of 38%.

Female labor income shares are found to be higher on average in Sub-Saharan Africa, with an average value of 28%. The two countries with the lowest shares (Somalia and Chad) are around 8%. The four countries with the highest shares (Eritrea, Botswana, Namibia, Guinea-Bissau) are around 40%. These values illustrate the wide variation of the female labor income share across the continent.

The regional perspective provides some clues about the levels observed. MENA countries share religious and cultural backgrounds, with social norms that tend to hinder the participation of women in the labor market.[3] In contrast, former Eastern Bloc countries share a history of communist regimes that supported the participation of women in the labor market through law and policy.[4] From that perspective, the case of China raises some questions, given its historically strong policy emphasis on gender equality and high female labor force participation, illustrated by the slogan of the Communist Party of China – "Women hold up half the sky" – proclaimed by Mao Zedong. China's female labor income share has decreased substantially since 1990. While it is still high by Asian standards, it is much lower than in the former Eastern Bloc countries.

Evolution of women's income share across the world

Figure 5.2 presents the level and evolution of women's income share across the regions of the world from 1990 to 2019 in 5-year brackets. The figure confirms the strikingly low position of MENA and Asian countries (excluding China) relative to the other regions.

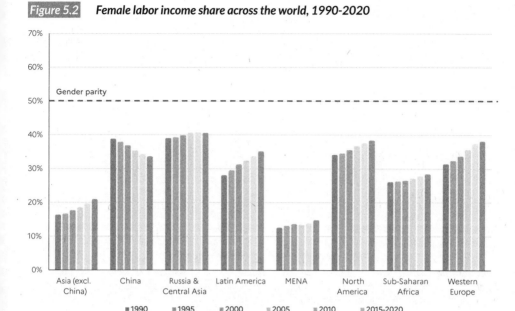

Figure 5.2   *Female labor income share across the world, 1990-2020*

1990 1995 2000 2005 2010 2015-2020

Interpretation: *The female labour income share rose from 34% to 38% in North America between 1990 and 2020.* **Sources and series:** *wir2022.wid.world/methodology and Neef and Robilliard (2021).*

In terms of evolution over time, the female labor income share appears to have increased in all regions except China. The evolution is strongest in Latin America and Western Europe. It is much slower in Asian and MENA countries, Sub-Saharan Africa, Oceania and North America, as well as in former Eastern Bloc countries, where it appears to have stagnated in the last two decades.

The downward trend for China might seem surprising at first. According to our estimates, the female labor income share has declined significantly over the period, from 39% in 1991 to a little more than 33% in 2019. This result is supported by several studies that indicate a declining trend and only slow progress towards gender equality despite historically strong policy emphasis on gender equality and high female labor force participation.[5] According to these studies, the decline could be explained by various factors, including the downsizing of state-owned enterprises (SOEs), which led to a sharper decline in labor force participation among urban women than among urban men, and the relaxation of the One-Child Policy at the end of 2013, among others.

Women earn just a third of labor income across the globe

How do the regional changes translate at the global level? Figure 5.3 provides two different answers. The first metric corresponds to the population-weighted average of country-level values of the female labor income share and delivers a preliminary answer: since 1994, the population-weighted average of labor income paid to women has barely changed, stagnating at around 28%. The second statistic is women's global labor income share, computed by

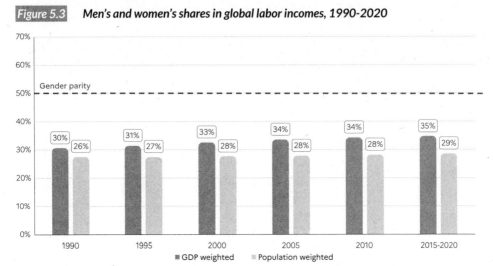

Figure 5.3   *Men's and women's shares in global labor incomes, 1990-2020*

Legend: GDP weighted, Population weighted

Interpretation: *Between 2015 and 2020, women made 35% of global labor incomes. The population-weighted country average female share of labor income is even lower (29%).* **Sources and series:** *wir2022. wid.world/methodology and Neef and Robilliard (2021).*

adding up all female labor income and dividing it by global labor income. According to this metric, women's income share increased from 31% in the 1990-1994 period to 35% in 2015-2019. The higher value of the global share compared with the population-weighted share can be explained by the fact that Western countries are both richer and have on average higher female income shares. These two statistics provide strong evidence that although women hold up half the sky, they only get a third of labor income for it.

Various factors have been suggested to explain gender differences in employment and earnings that result in women earning a smaller share of labor income. Among these is the fact that, according to time-use surveys, women spend substantially more time than men on unpaid care work. As shown by Ferrant, Pesando and Nowacka, this appears to be true across regions, although the female–male ratio of time devoted to unpaid care

work shows great variability across countries.[6] In the MENA region, where the gap tends to be largest, women spend on average more than five hours doing unpaid care work per day, while men spend less than one hour.[7] This higher load of unpaid care work is likely to prevent women from participating in the labor market, and, when they do work, to prevent them from attaining high-paying positions. When paid and unpaid work are combined, women's contribution to work increases substantially and thus makes the female labor income share appear even more unfair (see Neef and Robilliard for specific examples).[8]

The role of pay ratios vs. employment ratios

The labor income share held by women depends on two dimensions: their labor force participation compared with men on the one hand, and the gender earnings ratio on the other hand. In order to understand both the regional differences and the evolution over time of the female labor income share, it is interesting to see how earnings and employment ratios vary across regions and have evolved over time. In this chapter, we use ratios instead of gaps to make it easier to compare the values with the female income shares presented earlier: female labor income shares increase with both ratios. In other words, when both the earnings and employment ratios are high, women's labor income share is high as well. The results are presented on Figure 5.4.

Asia (excluding China) and the Middle East and North Africa, which both exhibit low female income shares, seem to have different underlying determinants. In Asia, the female-to-male employment ratio is higher than in the MENA region, while the female-to-male earnings ratio is comparatively lower. In other words, women participate more in the labor market in Asia than they do in MENA: the employment ratio is close to 50% on average over the period in Asia, as against 28% in MENA. Conversely, when working, women's earnings as a share of male earnings is a little more than 44% in Asia and 59% in MENA. This pattern hints at a particular selection process in the labor market in the MENA region, whereby only high-earning women participate.

Moving to other regions, Sub-Saharan Africa exhibits a very high employment ratio: it stands at 86% on average over the whole period. And yet, the female earnings ratio is much lower, at 46%. Women in this region have broad access to paid work, but are paid much less than men.

As in MENA, results for Latin America are consistent with the selection of higher-earning women into the labor

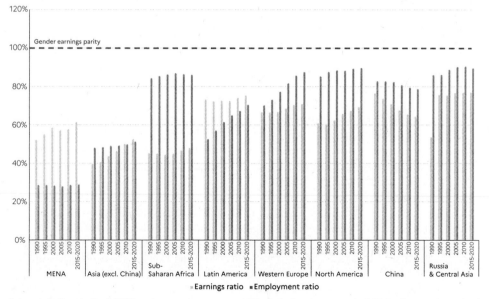

Figure 5.4   *Regional trends in earnings and employment ratios, 1990-2020*

*Interpretation: In the MENA region, a woman earns 61% of what a man earns in 2020, whereas the ratio of employed women to employed men is only 29%. **Sources and series:** wir2022.wid.world/methodology and Neef and Robilliard (2021)*

market: here again the employment ratio is lower than the earnings ratio. However, the employment ratio in Latin America is much higher than in MENA and shows an increase during the 1990-2020 period. This increase in the employment ratio could signal a convergence toward a labor market structure similar to that in Western Europe and North America.

Turning to Western countries, the ratio pattern is similar across Western Europe, North America and Oceania: in all three regions, the employment ratio is high (88-90% in the 2015-2020 period) and has been increasing since 1990. In contrast, the earnings ratio is lower (71% in Western Europe and 69% in North America and 59% in Oceania) and while it has increased in Western Europe and North America, it seems to have decreased in Oceania since 1990.

Finally, China and the former Eastern Bloc countries exhibit a similar pattern to that of Western countries (i.e. employment ratios are higher than earnings ratios). The main difference between China on one side and North America and Europe on the other is the trend in both employment and earnings ratios, which have been declining, as discussed above.

Breaking the glass ceiling: women at the top of the wage distribution

Since women have overtaken men in educational attainment in many countries since the 1990s, the key factors inhibiting the closing of the gender pay gap are linked to the horizontal and vertical segregation of labor markets.[9] This section takes a closer look at the phenomenon of vertical segregation, which is shown empirically in the under-representation of women at the top of the wage distribution. Analyzing the very top of the wage distribution requires high-quality administrative data. Since few countries provide such data at an individual level, from social security records or tax data, this part of the analysis is limited to the US, Spain, Brazil, and France.

Figures 5.5ab present women's representation among wage earners and at the top of the wage distribution in Brazil, Spain, France and the US. All countries show an increasing representation of women at the top of their wage distributions since the 1990s. While the share of women in the top 10% of the US wage distribution rose from 22% in 1995 to 30% in 2019, in the same year, Spanish women increased their share from 19% in 1995 to almost 36% (Figure 5.5a). Similarly, Brazilian women's representation in the top 10% of wage earners grew from 24% in 1996 to about 36% in 2018. Brazil and Spain show a substantially higher representation of women in the top 10% of wage earners than the US or France in recent years.

Women's representation in the top 1% is substantially lower than in the top 10% in all countries, indicating that there is a strong "glass-ceiling" effect, whereby the wage gap increases towards the top of the wage distribution, the main driver of which is the under-representation of women in top-paying positions.[10] The representation of women in the top 1% has been increasing only slowly in the United States, and has been faster in Spain and

Brazil (Figure 5.5b). It is striking that today women are better represented in the top 1% in Spain and Brazil than in the US, which led the way in women's empowerment in the 20th century.

Thus, overall, women are still under-represented at the top of the national wage distributions though to differing degrees and the glass ceiling effect seems particularly pronounced in the US and France, whereas Spain, and Brazil have a relatively high female representation at the top of their wage distributions. The reasons for these cross-country differences are not easily detected. Spain and Brazil have only increased the representation of women among all wage earners in recent years and have not reached parity in the labor market. This could hint at a selection effect – only the more highly-skilled women enter formal wage employment. However, these three countries might also have promoted gender equality by increasing the compatibility

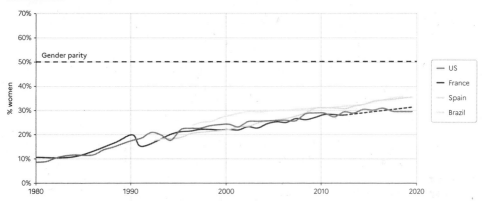

Figure 5.5a *Female representation among top 10% earners, 1980-2020*

Interpretation: *In Spain, 36% of top 10% wage earners were women in 2019.* **Sources and series:** *wir2022. wid.world/methodology, based on Neef and Robilliard (2021).*

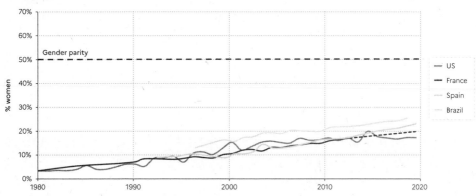

Figure 5.5b *Female representation among top 1% earners, 1980-2020*

Interpretation: *In Brazil, the share of women in the top 1% of wage earners was 25% in 2018.* **Sources and series:** *wir2022.wid.world/methodology, based on Neef and Robilliard (2021).*

of career and family with more generous state-subsidized childcare, or boosted women at the top using quotas and other policies promoting women's job advancements. Yet another reading is possible: Goldin stresses that the last step toward gender equality in the US labor market is the temporal inflexibility of many high-paying jobs, particularly the more than proportional reward for working long hours in executive jobs, which many women cannot do because of childcare and household duties.[11] Thus, the difference between the glass ceiling effects in the US on one side and Brazil and Spain on the other, might also be due to different structures in the high-paying wage sectors. Knowing whether the difference emerges from progressive policies or from the different structure and time inflexibility of jobs at the top of the wage distribution requires further research.

Box 5.1 **Methodology**

The data series used for this chapter represent the largest database on the historical evolution of women's labor income share across the world, spanning from 1990 to the eve of the Covid crisis. They are based on work carried out at the World Inequality Lab that combines different international data sources. The full methodology is detailed in Neef and Robilliard's study.[12] We present below the general methods followed.

Cross-country analyses of gender inequality are inherently difficult due to differing labor income concepts, and whether specific sectors and part-time workers are included or excluded.[13] Neef and Robilliard overcome this difficulty by making use of harmonized survey data from the Luxembourg Income Study (LIS) and the EU-SILC. This allows them to calculate women's share of total labor income directly from survey micro data for 58 countries. Using these LIS and EU-SILC data, they estimate a simple regression model of the female share of total labor income on wage and self-employment shares, which then allows them to impute the female share in labor income for all countries and years using ILO-modeled estimates of wage and self-employment shares – the most globally comprehensive source on labor market participation and earnings indicators. Finally, the LIS-SILC and imputed series are combined. For countries for which LIS or EU-SILC data is available, Neef and Robillard interpolate linearly between data points and extrapolate backward and forward using imputed estimates. For countries with no labor income data, they use imputed estimates. Country-level female labor income shares provided in this chapter should thus be interpreted with caution, but they provide valuable information when considered from a cross-country comparative perspective.

Box 5.2   Gender inequality metrics

Gender inequality has many dimensions and different metrics should be used to properly track its dynamics across the globe. The analysis of labor income shares is an important dimension because it shows how incomes are split between women and men at the level of a society as a whole (rather than in a given sector of the economy or a given position). It offers a more systemic perspective than the income gaps that are typically discussed in public debates. The female labor income share is also straightforward to interpret: since women represent half the population, in a gender equal society they would earn half of all labor income.

Other indicators should also be looked at to grasp the various facets of gender inequality. The United Nations Human Development Programme, for instance, has defined a Gender Inequality Index, which combines various dimensions of inequality.[14] On top of women's participation in labor markets, these dimensions include health and "empowerment". Health indicators combine data on maternal mortality and teenage births. "Empowerment" indicators include gender inequality in access to both higher education and to seats in parliament. These indicators are aggregated into a single index, which has a value of 0 in places where there are no gender inequalities and 1 represents extreme inequality between genders.[15] Table B5.1 presents indicator values for different world regions in 2018. It is striking, for instance, that maternal mortality ratios can vary by a factor of 20 between Europe/Central Asia

and Sub-Saharan Africa, whereas inequality in shares of parliamentary seats varies by a factor of just two between the most unequal and the least unequal regions. It should be stressed that all regions, whether rich or emerging, remain extremely unequal in terms of representation of women in parliament.

On this basis, it is possible to investigate the levels and evolution of women's share of labor income across the world's regions. Further, Neef and Robilliard break down this share into its two main parts: the gender earnings ratio and the gender employment ratio. Finally, drawing on high-quality administrative data for Brazil, Spain, and the US, they explore the representation of women at the top of the wage and salary distribution and illustrate the so-called glass-ceiling effect of a widening gender gap toward the top of the distribution.

Figure B5.1 shows the evolution of the average gender inequality index across the world between 1995 and 2019. It reveals that there has been an overall improvement in gender equality between 1995 and 2010 but a stabilization afterward. Progress before 2010 was mainly due to advances in access to education (with women almost reaching parity in average primary enrollments) and in health. The maternal mortality rate declined by 45% from 2000, but since the late 2000s, progress has been much slower. This overall pattern both complements and contrasts with the trends presented in this chapter. While we observe some progress since 1995, it remains very limited (as we have shown, the GDP-weighted global labor income only slightly increased since 1990 and the population-weighted share has stagnated).

The strength of multidimensional indexes is their ability to summarize complex realities in a single composite indicator. Multidimensional aggregations have inherent limits: the construction of these indicators can be quite complex from a mathematical point of view, and different values are not always straightforward for the average reader (and experts) to interpret. Ultimately, what is interesting is to understand which sub-dimensions are driving the evolution of a composite indicator. Focusing on a single dimension of gender inequality will never suffice to comprehend its drivers and dynamics, but then neither will composite indexes alone.

Figure B5.1   *Global gender inequality index, 1995-2019*

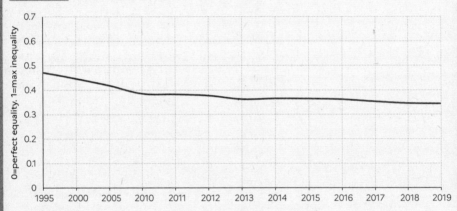

Interpretation: *There are 5-year intervals between 1995 and 2010, then 1-year intervals after that.*
Sources and series: *wir2022.wid.world/methodology based on Human Development Report (2019)*

Table B5.1   *Multidimensional Gender Inequality Indicators across the world*

	UN Gender inequality index	Maternal mortality ratio (deaths per 100.000 live births)	Adolescent birth rate (birth per 1.000 women aged 15-19)	Share of seats in parliament (% held by women)	Population with at least some secondary education (% aged 25 and older)		Labour participation rate (% aged 15 and above)	
					Female	Male	Female	Male
Arab States	0.53	148	47	18	46	55	20	74
East Asia	0.31	62	22	20	69	76	60	77
Europe & Central Asia	0.28	25	28	21	78	86	45	70
Latin America	0.38	68	63	31	60	59	52	77
South Asia	0.51	176	26	17	40	61	26	79
Sub-Saharan Africa	0.57	550	105	24	29	40	64	73

Interpretation: *the UN Gender Inequality Index developed by the UNDP is composed of the different dimensions of gender inequality presented in this table. An index of 0 represents perfect equality while an index of 1 represents maximum inequality.* **Sources and series:** *wir2022.wid.world/methodology. based on Human Development Report (2019).*

Conclusion

To summarize, this chapter shows that income inequalities between men and women remain particularly significant both within countries and at the world level today, not only because of strong inequalities in pay differentials but also because of inequalities in types of occupation.

Most countries have increased women's share of national labor income since the 1990s. Exceptions are China as well as some countries of the former Eastern Bloc (Lithuania, Poland, Russia, Slovenia and Slovakia), wherein the female labor income share decreased from an already high level in international comparisons. The MENA region exhibits the lowest female income share with a value of 15%, while the former Eastern Bloc exhibits the highest at 41%.

Globally, the share of labor income accruing to women stands at slightly under 35% and has shown a positive trend over the past three decades, up from around 31% in 1990. At the same time, the average labor income share across countries, weighted by national population, was stable at around 28% over the period. Both indicators reveal that the female labor income share has remained strikingly low over the past 30 years: men earn approximately twice as much as women across the world, on average. Such indicators are arguably more telling than standard gender pay gap measures because they take into account systemic inequalities beyond pay differentials, such as inequalities in occupational type.

However, the dynamics we observe vary across countries. In Western Europe, North America, Latin America and the Caribbean, the slight increase in the female labor income share was mainly driven by women's increased participation in the labor market. In Asia, we observe that the earnings ratio has been on the rise. The MENA region shows a relatively high female earnings ratio, but low participation rates among women. This suggests that only highly paid women are selected into the labor market there. Sub-Saharan Africa, on the contrary, has a high female employment rate but a relatively low and stagnating earnings ratio.

Furthermore, the data reveal that women have increased their representation at the top of the wage distribution since the 1990s in many countries. Strikingly, while the US and France have a high representation of women among all wage earners, they lag behind in women's representation in top income positions. Brazil and Spain exhibit much higher shares of women in the top 10% and top 1% of wage earners than the US and France.

The persistence of strong inequality in access to good jobs and to good pay, as well as the negative trajectory observed in large countries over the past decades (such as China), explain why, despite some progress at the regional and country levels, the global female labor income share has not grown more rapidly since the 1990s. In the early 2020s, working-age women continue to earn about half as much as men.

NOTES

[1] Neef, T., and A-S. Robilliard. 2021. "Half the Sky? The Female Labor Income Share in a Global Perspective." World Inequality Lab. Working paper 2021/22.

[2] Neef and Robilliard, "Half the Sky."

[3] See Jayachandran, S. 2021. "Social Norms as a Barrier to Women's Employment in Developing Countries." IMF Economic Review, 1-20.

[4] Van der Lippe, T. and L. Van Dijk. 2002. "Comparative Research on Women's Employment." Annual Review of Sociology 28, no. 1: 221-241.

[5] Dasgupta, S., M. Matsumoto and C. Xia. 2015. "Women in the labour market in China." ILO Working Papers 994879663402676, International Labour Organization; Tang Y.& Long W. 2013. "Gender Earnings Disparity and Discrimination in Urban China: Unconditional Quantile Regression." African Journal of Science, Technology, Innovation and Development, 5:3, 202-212.

[6] Ferrant, G., L. M. Pesando, and K. Nowacka. 2014. "Unpaid Care Work: The Missing Link in the Analysis of Gender Gaps in Labour Outcomes." OECD Development Centre.

[7] Ferrant, Pesando and Nowacka, "Unpaid Care Work."

[8] Neef and Robilliard, "Half the Sky."

[9] See Meurs, D. and S. Ponthieux. 2015. "Gender Inequality." In Handbook of Income Distribution vol 2, ed. A.B. Atkinson and F. Bourguignon. Elsevier; and Blau F. D. and L. M. Kahn. 2017. "The Gender Wage Gap: Extent, Trends, and Explanations." Journal of Economic Literature 55, no. 3: 789-865.

[10] Albrecht, J., A. Björklund, S. Vroman, et al. 2003. "Is There a Glass Ceiling in Sweden?" Journal of Labor Economics 21, No.1. January.

[11] Goldin, C. 2014. "The Grand Gender Convergence. Its Last Chapter." American Economic Review 104, no. 4: 1091–1119.

[12] Neef and Robilliard, "Half the Sky."

[13] Meurs and Ponthieux, "Gender Inequality."

[14] United Nations. 2019a. "Beyond Income, Beyond Averages, Beyond Today: Inequalities in Human Development in the 21st Century." Human Development Report. New York.

[15] United Nations. 2019b. "Technical Notes" to "Beyond Income, Beyond Averages, Beyond Today: Inequalities in Human Development in the 21st Century." Human Development Report 2019. New York. 8. http://hdr.undp.org/sites/default/files/hdr2019_technical_notes.pdf

CHAPTER 6

Global carbon inequality

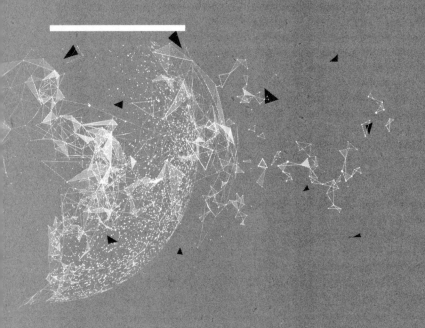

This chapter is based on Chancel (2021) "Global carbon inequality, 1990-2019", World Inequality Lab working Paper 2021/21

The need for better monitoring of global ecological inequalities

The planet is entering its sixth mass extinction of species.[1] Global atmospheric carbon dioxide concentration is at its highest level in millions of years.[2] And the mass of anthropogenic plastic pollution in oceans has multiplied by more than 200 since the 1960s.[3] What do we currently know about the links between these global trends and income and wealth inequality? Not enough.[4]

In the previous chapters of this report, we have focused on the distribution of economic assets, i.e. inequalities that can be measured in monetary units: euros, dollars or yuan, earned and owned by different groups of individuals across the world (between and within countries, and between genders). The distribution of income and economic assets is tightly connected to many forms of social inequality, including inequality in access to health, to education and to power (see Chapter 10). It is because economic inequalities play a central role in the many social injustices that we initially developed the World Inequality Database (see Box 1.2), focusing on income and wealth.

As key advances have been made in our understanding of income and wealth dynamics, we believe that we can now make contributions in other dimensions of global inequality, and in particular, ecological inequalities. Global ecological inequality also takes many forms, including inequality of access to natural resources, inequality of exposure to pollution and to the catastrophes induced by unsustainable use of these resources, and inequality of contribution to environmental degradation. Each

---

Figure 6.1 *Global annual CO2 emissions by world region, 1850-2019*

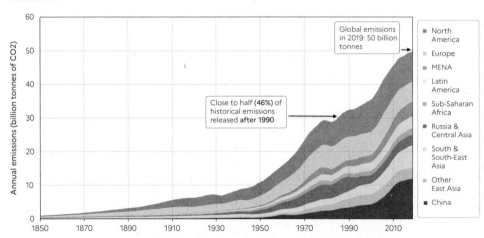

Interpretation: *The graph shows annual global emissions by world regions. After 1990, emissions include carbon and other greenhouse gases embedded in imports/exports of goods and services from/to other regions.* **Sources and series:** *wir2022.wid.world/methodology and Chancel (2021). Historical data from the PRIMAP-hist dataset. Post-1990 data from Global Carbon Budget.*

of these dimensions must be better understood if we are to develop sound and effective environmental policies. It goes beyond the scope of this report to treat all these dimensions, so our goal for this chapter is more modest: we focus on carbon emissions. Our objective is to gain a better understanding of how these emissions are distributed across the world's population.

Bridging the gap between macro data on carbon emissions and individual perceptions

To study global carbon emissions, we start from the same general assumption as when we study income and wealth inequality: that looking at national averages and totals is important, but not sufficient. It is also necessary to navigate between different scales of analysis: the global level and the individual level. To do so we investigate in a systematic way the emissions levels of national and regional societies, as well as how emissions are distributed among different groups of individuals within these societies.

It can sometimes be difficult for anyone to make sense of the magnitude of the climate challenge and how figures about global pollution levels relate to their own lives. In other words, it is sometimes difficult for individuals to understand to what extent they themselves contribute to climate change, and how they can be part of the solution to it. By constructing new data on carbon emissions inequality, we wish to contribute to a better collective understanding of the drivers and dynamics of carbon pollution.

Global carbon inequality: initial insights

Carbon dioxide emissions are the result of the burning of fossil fuels, certain industrial processes (such as cement production), agricultural production (for example, cows emit a lot of greenhouse gases), waste management, and deforestation. These activities generate carbon dioxide (CO_2), as well as other greenhouse gases such as methane (CH_4), and nitrous oxides (NO_x). Each of these gases contributes differently to global warming: one tonne of methane is equivalent to the release of 30 tonnes of CO_2, and one tonne of nitrous oxide equivalent to 280 tonnes of CO_2. The numbers presented below refer to CO_2 equivalents, i.e. they take into account the different GHGs.[5]

In 2021, humans released nearly 50 billion tonnes of CO_2 into the atmosphere, reversing most of the decline observed during the 2020 Covid pandemic. Of these 50 billion tonnes, about three quarters were produced in the burning of fossil fuels for energy purposes, 12% by the agricultural sector, 9% by industry (in cement production among other things) and 4% came from waste.[6] On average, each individual emits just over 6.5 tonnes of CO_2 per annum (see Table 6.1). These averages mask considerable disparities between countries and within them, as we discuss below.

Global emissions have been rising almost continuously since the industrial revolution (Figure 6.1). In 1850, one billion tonnes of carbon dioxide equivalents were emitted overall.[7] By 1900, the number had risen to 4.2 billion tonnes, it reached 11 billion tonnes by 1950, 35 billion tonnes in 2000, and about 50 billion today. Close to half of all emissions since the industrial revolution have been produced since 1990, the year of the first report from the Intergovernmental Panel on Climate Change (IPCC).

Of the total 2,450 billion tonnes of carbon released since 1850 (Figure 6.2), North America is responsible for 27%, Europe 22%, China 11%, South and South-East Asia 9%, Russia and Central Asia 9%, East Asia (including Japan) 6%, Latin America 6%, MENA 6%, and Sub-Saharan Africa 4%. Figure 6.2 compares historical emissions with available carbon budgets intended to limit climate change. According to the latest IPCC report, there are 300 billion tonnes of CO2 left to be emitted if we are to stay below 1.5°C (with an 83% confidence rating) and 900 billion tonnes of CO2 left to stay below 2°C (with the same level of confidence). At current global emissions rates, the 1.5°C budget will be depleted in six years and 2°C budget in 18 years.

Table 6.1   *Global carbon emissions, 1850-2019*

	Global emissions (billion tonnes)	Emissions per capita (tonnes per person)
1850	1.0	0.8
1880	2.5	1.8
1900	4.2	2.7
1920	6.6	3.5
1950	10.9	4.3
1980	30.2	6.8
2000	35.3	5.8
2019	50.1	6.6

Interpretation: *Emissions of carbon dioxyde equivalent (including all gases) from human activites (including deforestation and land-use change).* **Sources and series:** *wir2022.wid. world/methodology and Chancel (2021).*

Figure 6.2   *Historical emissions vs. remaining carbon budget*

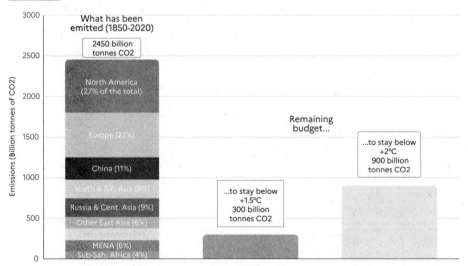

Interpretation: *The graph shows historical emissions by region (left bar) and the remaining global carbon budget (center and right bars) to have 83% chances to stay under 1.5°C and 2°C, according to IPCC AR6 (2021). Regional emissions are net of carbon embedded in imports of goods and services from other regions.* **Sources and series:** *wir2022.wid.world/methodology and Chancel (2021). Historical data from the PRIMAP-hist dataset.*

Global emissions per capita rose from 0.8 tonnes of CO2 per annum in 1850, 2.7 tonnes in 1900, 4.3 tonnes in 1950, and 6.8 tonnes in 1980s, before dropping to 5.8 in 2000 and rising again to 6.6 tonnes today (Table 6.1). The reduction observed between 1975 and 1980 was the result of a combination of factors, including global population growth (population increased faster in regions where emissions were below the global average), and some improvement in energy efficiency following the oil crises of the 1970s.

To understand better the size of the carbon mitigation challenge, we begin by comparing current emissions levels with level of emissions required to stay below an average global warming of 1.5°C and 2°C.[8] The Paris Climate Agreement seeks to stay at a level of warming well below 2°C. Table 6.2 presents the sustainable per capita global carbon budget, i.e. the volume of emissions per individual living between now and 2050 were all remaining CO2 emissions shared equally over the period.

To obtain these numbers, we simply divide the remaining carbon emissions budget by the cumulative global population that will be emitting it over the coming decades. According to the United Nations, there will be 265 billion individual-years between now and 2050. This implies a sustainable per capita budget, compatible with the +2°C temperature limit, of 3.4 tonnes per person per annum between now and 2050. This value is about half of the current global average. The per capita sustainable budget compatible with the 1.5°C limit is 1.1 tonne of CO2 per

annum per person, i.e. about six times less than the current global average.[9] We stress at the onset that these numbers are derived for comparative purposes and should be interpreted with care. These values do not take into account historical responsibilities associated with climate change. Taking historical responsibilities into account implies that high-income nations have no carbon budget left.[10] Let us also note that scenarios consistent with the 2°C target show that overall emissions must decrease progressively to reach zero in 2050 – and cannot be maintained at a certain high level until this date then suddenly drop to zero.

| Table 6.2 | Global per capita carbon budget |

Sustainable emissions level...
(tonnes CO2 per person per year)

... to stay below +1.5°C	... to stay below +2°C	Carbon budget shared before
1.1	3.4	2050
0.4	1.1	2100

Interpretation: *Sharing the remaining carbon budget to have 83% chances to stay below 1.5°C global temperature increase implies an annual per capita emissions level of 1.1 tonnes per person per year between 2021 and 2050 (and zero afterwards). Sharing this same budget between 2021 and 2100 implies a per capita annual emissions of 0.4 tonne. Global carbon budget values from IPCC AR6, 83% confidence.* **Sources and series:** *wir2022.wid.world/ methodology and Chancel (2021).*

Carbon inequalities between regions are large and persistent

Figure 6.3a shows average emissions per capita for world regions, and Table 6.3 expresses these values as a percentage of the world

Figure 6.3a   *Average per capita emissions by world region, 2019*

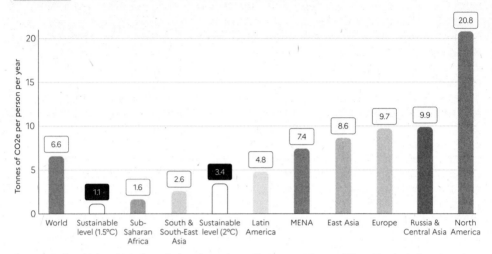

Interpretation: *Values include emissions from domestic consumption, public and private investments as well as imports and exports of carbon embedded in goods and services traded with the rest of the world. Sustainable level correspond to an egalitarian distribution of the remaining carbon budget until 2050.* **Sources and series:** *wir2022.wid.world/methodology and Chancel (2021).*

average. Per capita emissions in Sub-Saharan Africa (1.6 tonnes per person per annum) represent just one quarter of the average global per capita emissions. Thus, average emissions in Sub-Saharan Africa are close to 50% above the 1.5°C sustainable level and about half of the 2°C budget. At the other end of the spectrum, per capita emissions in North America are 21 tonnes per capita (three times the world average and six times higher than the 2°C sustainable level). In between these two extremes stand South and South-East Asia, at 2.6 tonnes per capita (40% of the current world average and 80% of the 2°C budget) and Latin America at 4.8 tonnes (70% of world average, 1.4 times the 2°C budget), followed by MENA, East Asia, Europe, and Russia and Central Asia, whose averages fall in the 7.5-10 tonnes range (between one and 1.5 times the world average, and two to three times more than the 2°C sustainable level).

Figure 6.3b compares historical emissions with current emissions of regional populations. The graph reveals that, while carbon inequalities between regions have declined recently (though China's share in current global emissions is significantly higher than its historical share), inequalities persist and are even more striking when compared with the population share of each region.

Inequalities in average carbon emissions between regions are quite close to the inequality in average incomes between regions (see Figure 1.2a), but with notable differences: US average emissions are 3.2 times the world average, while its average income is three times the world average, and Europe's emissions are less than 1.5 times the world average while the income figure is close to two. There is a close link between per capita income and emissions, but this link is not perfect: certain regions are more effective than others in

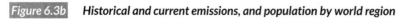

Figure 6.3b   *Historical and current emissions, and population by world region*

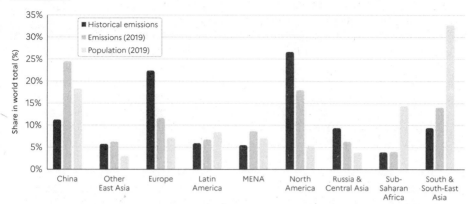

Interpretation: *China's share in world historical emissions since 1850 is 11% whereas its share in current emissions is 24%. Current emissions include carbon embedded in consumption.* **Sources and series:** *wir2022. wid.world/methodology and Chancel (2021).*

limiting emissions associated with a given level of income.

Table 6.3   **Average per capita emissions by world region, 2019**

	(tonnes per capita)	(x global average)	(x 2° budget)
World	**6.6**	**1**	**1.9**
Sub-Saharan Africa	1.6	0.3	0.5
South & South-East Asia	2.6	0.4	0.8
Latin America	4.8	0.7	1.4
MENA	7.4	1.1	2.2
East Asia	8.6	1.3	2.5
Europe	9.7	1.5	2.9
Russia & Central Asia	9.9	1.5	2.9
North America	20.8	3.2	6.1

Interpretation: *Estimates take into account emissions of all greenhouse gases from domestic consumption, public and private investments as well as net imports embedded in goods and services from the rest of the world. The +2°budget corresponds to an egalitarian distribution across the world population, between now and 2050, of all emissions left to limit temperature increase to +2°C. To stay*

below +1.5°C, the equitable per capita budget is 1.1 tonne per person per year. **Sources and series:** *wir2022.wid.world/methodology and Chancel (2021).*

Emissions embedded in goods and services increase carbon inequalities between regions

The emission levels cited above include emissions produced within a country as well as those associated with the import of goods and services from the rest of the world. Put differently, when North Americans import smartphones from East Asia, carbon emissions created in the production, transport and sale of those smartphones are attributed to North Americans and not to East Asians. This is the best way to measure emissions associated with the standard of living of individuals across the world. In this report, we refer to these emissions as "carbon footprints" rather than "territorial emissions", which correspond only to carbon emissions within territorial boundaries, and do not take into account imports and exports of carbon embedded in goods and services. Territorial emissions continue to be used by authorities around the globe when they report progress on emissions reduction or when they discuss international climate agreements. But referring only to territorial emissions obviously presents many problems: high-income countries can reduce their territorial emissions and develop ecological dumping strategies to externalize their carbon-intensive industries to the rest of the world, then import back goods and services produced elsewhere. Factoring in the carbon embedded in goods and services adds the climate change mitigation efforts of high-income countries, in particular in Europe where imports represent a notable share of per capita emissions.

Table 6.4 shows the differences between carbon footprints and territorial emissions by region. In North America, the difference between footprints and territorial emissions expressed in percentage points is relatively low, because Americans import but also export carbon-intensive goods, and they consume very significant quantities of carbon at home. In Europe, the carbon footprint is about 25% higher than territorial emissions. Nearly two tonnes of carbon per person are imported from other regions of the world, largely China. In East Asia, carbon emissions are 8% lower than territorial emissions: nearly one tonne of carbon per person is produced in East Asia to satisfy the needs of individuals in other parts of the world. Factoring in the carbon that is embedded in the consumption of goods and services increases the inequality between high and middle to low income regions, compared with when we count territorial emissions only.

| Table 6.4 | **Carbon footprints vs. territorial emissions across the world, 2019** |

	Footprint inc. consumption (tCO2/capita)	Territorial (tCO2/capita)	% difference footprint vs. territorial
World	6.6	6.6	0%
Sub-Saharan Africa	1.6	2.1	-22%
South & South-East Asia	2.6	2.7	-5%
Latin America	4.8	4.9	-2%
MENA	7.4	8.0	-7%
East Asia	8.6	9.4	-8%
Europe	9.7	7.9	23%
Russia & Central Asia	9.9	11.9	-17%
North America	20.8	19.8	5%

Interpretation: *Carbon footprints include emissions from domestic consumption, public and private investments as well as net imports embedded in goods and services from the rest of the world.* **Sources and series:** *wir2022.wid. world/methodology and Chancel (2021).*

Carbon inequalities within regions are even larger than carbon inequalities between them

Significant inequalities in carbon footprints are observed in every region of the world. Figures 6.4a and 6.4b present the carbon footprints of the poorest 50%, the middle 40% and the richest 10% of the population across the regions. In East Asia, the poorest 50% emit on average around three tonnes per annum, while the middle 40% emit nearly eight tonnes, and the top 10% almost 40 tonnes. This contrasts sharply with North America, where the bottom 50% emit fewer than 10 tonnes, the middle 40% around 22 tonnes, and the top 10% over 70 tonnes of carbon dioxide equivalent.

Figure 6.3a   *Average per capita emissions by world region, 2019*

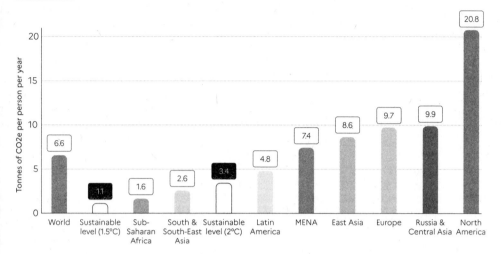

Interpretation: *Values include emissions from domestic consumption, public and private investments as well as imports and exports of carbon embedded in goods and services traded with the rest of the world. Sustainable level correspond to an egalitarian distribution of the remaining carbon budget until 2050.* **Sources and series:** *wir2022.wid.world/methodology and Chancel (2021).*

Figure 6.3b   *Historical and current emissions, and population by world region*

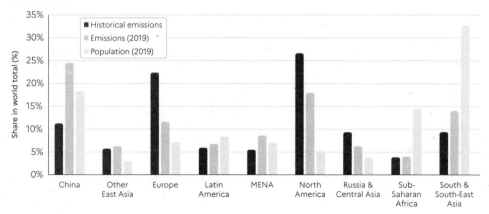

Interpretation: *China's share in world historical emissions since 1850 is 11% whereas its share in current emissions is 24%. Current emissions include carbon embedded in consumption.* **Sources and series:** *wir2022. wid.world/methodology and Chancel (2021).*

This in turn can be contrasted with the emissions in Europe, where the bottom 50% emit nearly five tonnes, the middle 40% around 10.5 tonnes, and the top 10% around 30 tonnes. Emissions levels in South and South-East Asia are significantly lower, from one tonne for the bottom 50% to fewer than 11 tonnes on average for the top 10%.

It is striking that the poorest half of the population in the US has emission levels comparable with the European middle 40%, despite being almost twice as poor.[11] This difference is largely due to the carbon-intensive energy mix in the US, where emissions from electricity are about twice as much as in the European Union. In the US, basic infrastructure consumes much more energy (because of the more widespread use of cars, for example), and devices tend to be less energy efficient (on average, cars are larger and less fuel efficient in the US than in Europe).

Nevertheless, European emissions remain very high by global standards. The European middle class emits significantly more than its counterparts in East Asia (around 10.5 tonnes compared with eight tonnes) and all other regions except North America. Yet it is also remarkable that the richest East Asians and the richest 10% in the Middle East and North Africa emit more than the richest Europeans (39 tonnes, 34 tonnes, and 29 tonnes, respectively). This difference results from the higher income and wealth inequality levels in East Asia and the MENA region than in Europe, and to the fact that investments by wealthy Chinese

are associated with significant volumes of emissions.

Turning to other regions, we find that Russia and Central Asia have an emissions profile close to that of Europe, but with higher top 10% emissions. Sub-Saharan Africa lags behind, with the bottom 50% emissions around 0.5 tonnes and top 10% emissions around 7 tonnes per person per annum. Overall, it stands out that only the poorest 50% of the population in Sub-Saharan Africa and South and South-East Asia come in under the 1.5°C per capita budget. Measuring levels against the 2°C per capita budget, we observe that the bottom half of the population in each region is below or close to the threshold. In fact, it is striking that the bottom 50% in high and middle income regions such as Europe, and Russia and Central Asia emit levels that fall within the 2°C budget. This shows that climate mitigation is largely a distributional issue, not only between countries but also within them.

Figure 6.5a   *Global carbon inequality, 2019: emissions by group*

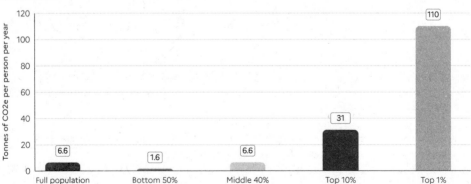

Interpretation: *Personal carbon footprints include emissions from domestic consumption, public and private investments as well as imports and exports of carbon embedded in goods and services traded with the rest of the world. Modeled estimates based on the systematic combination of tax data, household surveys and input-output tables. Emissions split equally within households.* **Sources and series:** *wir2022.wid.world/ methodology and Chancel (2021).*

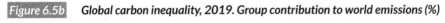

Figure 6.5b   *Global carbon inequality, 2019. Group contribution to world emissions (%)*

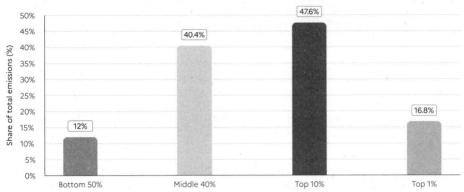

Interpretation: Personal carbon footprints include emissions from domestic consumption, public and private investments as well as imports and exports of carbon embedded in goods and services traded with the rest of the world. Modeled estimates based on the systematic combination of tax data, household surveys and input-output tables. Emissions split equally within households. **Sources and series:** wir2022.wid.world/methodology and Chancel (2021).

Global carbon emissions inequality: one tenth of the population is responsible for close to half of all emissions

Figures 6.5a and 6.5b present the inequality of carbon emissions between individuals at the world level, in the same way as we have done in the previous chapters when looking at income or wealth. The global bottom 50% emit on average 1.6 tonnes per annum and contribute 12% of the total. The middle 40% emit 6.6 tonnes on average, making up 40.4% of the total. The top 10% emit 31 tonnes (47.6% of the total). The top 1% emits 110 tonnes (16.8% of the total). Global carbon emissions inequality thus appears to be very great: close to half of all emissions are due to one tenth of the global population, and just one hundredth of the world population (77 million individuals) emits about 50% more than the entire bottom half of the population (3.8 billion individuals).

Table 6.5 presents more details on the global distribution of carbon emissions. The bottom 20% of the world population (1.5 billion individuals) emit fewer than 0.8 tonne per capita per annum. In fact, about one billion individuals emit less than a tonne per capita. The entry threshold to get in the middle 40% is 3.1 tonnes, and it takes 13 tonnes per capita per annum to get in the top 10%. It takes 130 tonnes to break into the global top 0.1% group of emitters (7.7 million individuals). (Figures 6.9a and 6.9b, discussed below, show how each world region contributes to these different groups of emitters.)

Per capita emissions have risen substantially among the global top 1% since 1990 but decreased for poorer groups in rich countries

How has global emissions inequality changed over the past few decades? A simple way to represent the evolution of carbon emissions inequality is to plot average emissions growth rate by percentile of the global emissions distribution, in the same way as we

Table 6.5   **Carbon emissions per capita, 2019**

	Number of individuals (million)	Average (tonne CO2 per capita)	Threshold (tonne CO2 per capita)	Share (% total)
Full population	7,710	6.6	<0.1	100%
Bottom 50%	3,855	1.6	<0.1	12.0%
incl. Bottom 20%	1,542	0.8	<0.1	2.5%
incl. Bottom 30%	2,313	2.1	1.8	9.5%
Middle 40%	3,084	6.6	3.1	40.4%
Top 10%	771	31	13	47.6%
incl. Top 1%	77.1	110	46	16.8%
incl. Top 0.1%	7.71	467	130	7.1%
incl. Top 0.01%	0.771	2,531	569	3.9%

Interpretation: *Personal carbon footprints include emissions from domestic consumption, public and private investments as well as imports and exports of carbon embedded in goods and services traded with the rest of the world. Modeled estimates based the systematic combination of tax data, household surveys and input-output tables. Emissions split equally within households.* **Sources and series:** *wir2022.wid.world/ methodology and Chancel (2021).*

did in Chapter 2. Global polluters earners are ranked from the least emitters to the highest emitters on the horizontal axis of Figure 6.6, and their per capita emissions growth rate is presented on the vertical axis. Since 1990, average global emissions per capita grew by about 7% (and overall emissions grew by 58%). The per capita emissions of the bottom 50% grew faster than the average (32%), while those of the middle 40% as a whole grew more slowly than the average (4%), and some percentiles of the distribution actually saw a reduction in their emissions of between five and 25%. Per capita emissions of the top 1% emissions grew by 26% and top 0.001% emissions by more than 110%.

Per capita emissions matter, but understanding the contribution of each group to the overall share of total emissions growth is critical. Groups starting with very low per capita emissions levels can increase their emissions substantially over a given period, yet still contribute very little to the overall growth in global emissions. This is in effect what has happened since 1990 (see Table 6.6, last column). The bottom half of the global population contributed only 16% of the growth in emissions observed since then, while the top 1% (77 million individuals) was responsible for 21% of emissions growth. These values are reported in the two boxes of Figure 6.6.

One of the most striking results shown in Figure 6.6 is the reduction in the emissions of about 15-20% of the world population, which largely corresponds to the lower and middle income groups of the rich countries. In these countries, the working and middle classes have reduced their emissions over the past 30 years. To be sure, these reductions are insufficient to meet the goals of the Paris Climate Agreement to limit global warming to 1.5°C or 2°C, but they contrast nevertheless with the emissions of the top 1% in these countries (and at the global level), which have significantly increased. Such a gap in carbon mitigation efforts between the rich and the less well-off in rich countries raises important questions about climate policies. In societies where the standards of living of the wealthy also shape the emissions of other social groups, this can have

Figure 6.6   *Global carbon emissions inequality, 1990-2019: the carbon elephant curve*

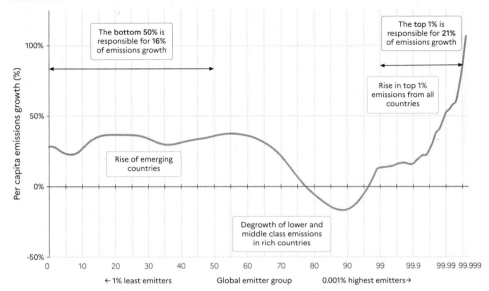

Interpretation: *Emissions of the global bottom 50% rose by around 20-40% between 1990 and 2019. Emissions notably declined among groups above the bottom 80% and below the top 5% of the global distribution, these groups mainly correspond to lower and middle income groups in rich countries. Emissions of the global top 1% and richer groups rose substantially. Personal carbon footprints include emissions from domestic consumption, public and private investments as well as imports and exports of carbon embedded in goods and services traded with the rest of the world. Modeled estimates based on the systematic combination of tax data, household surveys and input-output tables. Emissions split equally within households.*
Sources and series: *wir2022.wid.world/methodology and Chancel (2021).*

Table 6.6   *Emissions growth and inequality, 1990-2019*

	Per capita emissions (tonnes CO2e per capita)		Total emissions (billion tonnes CO2e)		Growth in per capita emissions	Growth in total emissions	Share in emissions growth
	1990	2019	1990	2019	(1990-2019)	(1990-2019)	(1990-2019)
Full population	6.2	6.6	32.0	50.5	7%	58%	100%
Bottom 50%	1.2	1.6	3.1	6.1	32%	96%	16%
Middle 40%	6	6.6	13.3	20.4	4%	54%	39%
Top 10%	30	31	15.7	24.0	4%	54%	45%
Top 1%	87	110	4.5	8.5	26%	87%	21%
Top 0.1%	323	467	1.7	3.6	45%	114%	10%
Top 0.01%	1,397	2,531	0.7	2.0	81%	168%	7%

Interpretation: *Personal carbon footprints include emissions from domestic consumption, public and private investments as well as imports and exports of carbon embedded in goods and services traded with the rest of the world. Growth in total group emissions are different to growth in per capita emissions, due to population growth. Modeled estimates based the systematic combination of tax data, household surveys and input-output tables. Emissions split equally within households. **Sources and series:** wir2022.wid.world/methodology and Chancel (2021).*

consequences for future emissions patterns. These dynamics also fuel criticisms of environmental policies such as carbon taxes, which have been shown to affect working and middle classes disproportionately in several countries (more on this below).

Figure 6.7 presents the evolution of the top 1% and the bottom 50% shares in total emissions between 1990 and 2019. Between 1990 and 2019, the global bottom 50% increased its share of the total, from around 9.5% to 12%, but at the same time, the top 1% share rose from 14% to close to 17%. Put differently, the gap in emissions between the top of the distribution and the bottom remained substantial over the entire period.

Inequalities within countries now represent the bulk of global emissions inequality

What has been driving the dynamics of global carbon inequality over the past decades: the average emission differential between countries, or within them?

Figure 6.8 compares the share of global emissions that is due to within-country differences with the between-country differences. In 1990, most global carbon inequality (63%) was due to differences between countries: then, the average citizen of a rich country polluted unequivocally more than the rest of the world's citizens, and social inequalities within countries were on average lower across the globe than today. The situation has almost entirely reversed in 30 years. Within-country emissions inequalities now account for nearly two thirds of global emissions inequality. This does not mean that there do not remain significant (often huge) inequalities in emissions between countries and world regions (see Figure 6.3a), on the contrary. In fact, it means that on top of the great between-countries inequality

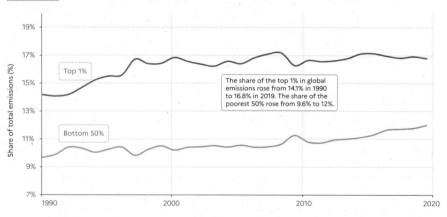

| Figure 6.7 | *Top 1% and bottom 50% shares in global carbon emissions, 1990-2019* |

The share of the top 1% in global emissions rose from 14.1% in 1990 to 16.8% in 2019. The share of the poorest 50% rose from 9.6% to 12%.

Interpretation: *This figure presents the share of global GHG emissions by the top 1% and bottom 50% of the global population between 1990 and 2019. GHG emissions measured correspond to individual footprints, i.e. they include indirect emissions produced abroad and embedded in individual consumption. Modeled estimates based on the systematic combination of tax data, household surveys and input-output tables. Emissions split equally within households. **Sources and series:** wir2022.wid. world/methodology and Chancel (2021).*

Figure 6.8   *Global carbon inequalities are mainly due to inequality within countries (1990-2019)*

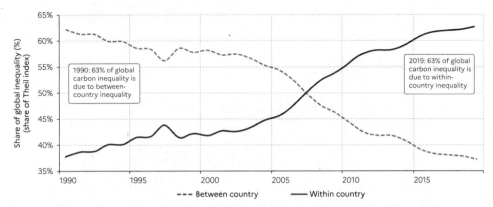

Interpretation: *37% of global carbon inequality between individuals is due differences in emissions levels between countries while 63% is explained by inequality within countries in 2019.* **Sources and series:** *wir2022.wid.world/methodology and Chancel(2021).*

in carbon emissions, there also exist even greater inequalities in emissions between individuals. This has major implications for global debate on climate policies.

Figure 6.9a shows the geographical breakdown of each group of emitters. More precisely, the graph tells us about the share of population of each region in each percentile of the global carbon distribution. It shows, for example, that China, Latin America, and MENA are well represented among the low emitters as well as among the high emitter groups. This reflects the dual nature of these societies, where extreme polluters live close to very low polluters. Europe and North America are essentially represented in the top half of the global distribution (right hand side of the graph). The representation gap between Europe and North America among the very top of the distribution is clear in this graph, as is the large representation of Chinese among the highest polluters.

Figure 6.9b provides another representation of the global carbon distribution. Each color wedge is proportional to the population of a region, and the total colored area represents the global population. The graph summarizes the main insights into the global distribution of carbon emissions presented above.

Addressing the climate challenge in unequal societies

Social movements in rich and emerging countries in 2018-2019 (including waves of protests against hikes in fuel and transport prices in Ecuador or Chile in 2019, and the Yellow Vest movements in Europe one year earlier) showed that policy reforms which do not properly factor in the degree of inequality in a country, and the winners and losers of these reforms, are unlikely to be publicly supported and are likely to fail. This is particularly so for environmental policies. A clear illustration of this is the so-called Yellow Vest movement in France. In 2018, the French

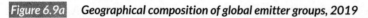

Figure 6.9a   *Geographical composition of global emitter groups, 2019*

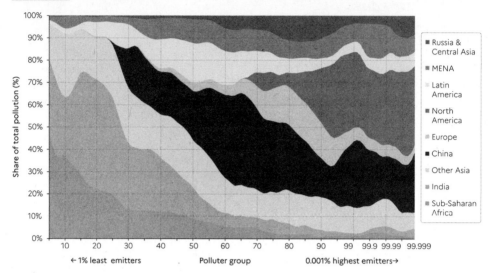

Interpretation: *The graph shows the share of world regions in each group of global emitters, from the bottom 1% to the top 0.001%.*
Sources and series: *wir2022.wid.world/methodology and Chancel (2021).*

Figure 6.9b   *The distribution of global carbon emissions in 2019*

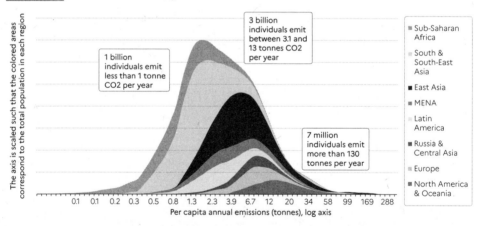

Interpretation: *The graph shows the global distribution of emitters in 2019. GHG emissions measured correspond to individual footprints, i.e. they include indirect emissions produced abroad and embedded in individual consumption.* **Sources and series:** *wir2022.wid.world/methodology and Chancel (2021).*

government implemented a hike in the carbon tax (which projected about 4 billion euros in additional carbon tax revenues). While the tax was presented as a way of reducing carbon emissions, it was not accompanied by significant compensatory measures for low and middle income households.

The reform was introduced at the same time as a suppression of the progressive wealth tax on financial assets and capital incomes (which would create around 3-4 billion euros of tax cuts, essentially concentrated among the top 1-2% of the wealth distribution). This reform was immediately opposed by the majority of the population. Many low and middle income households had to pay the carbon tax every day in order to go to work, having no alternative to using their cars, while tax cuts were given to the very rich, living in cities, with low-carbon transport options, who also benefit from very low energy tax rates when they travel by plane. This situation triggered a wave of social protests (which eventually spread to other European countries) and eventually led to the abandonment of the carbon tax.

In principle, a carbon tax can be a powerful tool to reduce emissions. In some countries, it has been implemented successfully and has contributed to limiting carbon emissions. However, the French example shows that when carbon policies are improperly designed and do not consider the socio-economic context in which they are implemented, they can easily fail and generate mistrust, making environmental policies look unfair. Let us be clear: the scale of transformation required to cut greenhouse gas emissions drastically in rich countries cannot be attained if environmental and social inequalities are not integrated into the very design of environmental policies. We discuss options to properly address carbon inequalities within and between countries below.

The first way to address carbon inequality is to properly track individual emissions within countries. Most governments do not publish aggregate carbon footprint estimates (they publish territorial emissions but, as discussed earlier, this is not sufficient to assess the actual environmental impact of policies). Governments also fail to properly track and publish estimates of the inequality in carbon footprints, meaning they that cannot properly foresee the distributional consequences of their climate policies. The estimates presented in this chapter provide a sound basis for these discussions to take place. But let us be clear: a lot of progress still needs to be done by governments in order to properly account individual emissions levels, in a timely and systematic manner.

Figures 6.10abcd present our best estimates of the carbon emissions of different population groups in the US, India, China, and France. The figures also present countries' climate targets for 2030. These countries are chosen as representatives of a wider set of countries (the US for Canada, Australia, and New Zealand, which have similar carbon inequality levels), France for European countries, and India and China for low income and emerging countries.[12]

The carbon emission commitments displayed in Figures 6.10abcd are the pledges that states made at the Paris Agreement (or have made since then).[13] Pledges are typically expressed in aggregate emissions percentage reductions from a base year. Using population growth forecasts, these pledges can be expressed in terms of emissions per capita at a certain time, to make better sense of what they imply. In emerging countries (India and

Figure 6.10abcd **Per capita emissions by income group and reduction requirements to meet Paris Agreement targets in the US, France, India, and China**

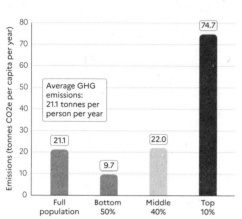

Per capita emissions by income group in the US, 2019 estimates

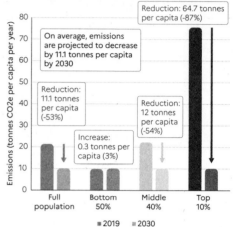

Emissions reduction requirement to meet Paris Agreement 2030 targets in the US

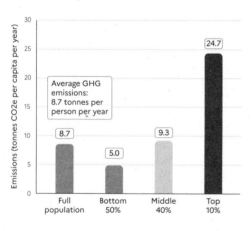

Per capita emissions by income group in France, 2019 estimates

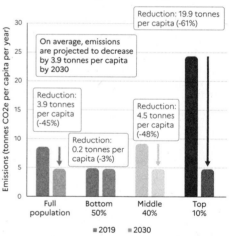

Emissions reduction requirement to meet Paris Agreement 2030 targets in France

China, for example), targets are set on the basis of the carbon intensity of GDP. In these cases, it is possible to estimate the actual number of aggregate emissions implied by an estimated GDP level to be reached in 2030, and to express this number in per capita values, as is done in Figures 6.10abcd.

Note that these targets do not represent what should be done from a climate perspective in order to keep emissions below 1.5 or 2°C. So far, the official commitments do not add up to meeting the 2°C objective, much less to meeting the 1.5°C target. Rather, these numbers represent our best knowledge of what countries have pledged to achieve. In the US, we find that pledges amount to a 53% reduction by 2030 of the late 2019 per capita

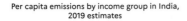

Per capita emissions by income group in India,
2019 estimates

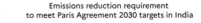

Emissions reduction requirement
to meet Paris Agreement 2030 targets in India

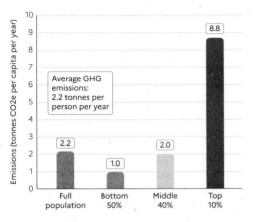

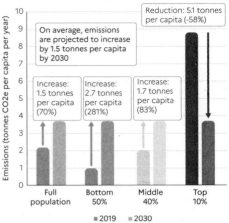

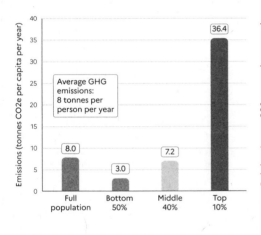

Per capita emissions by income group in China,
2019 estimates

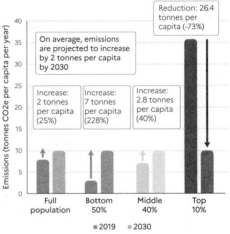

Emissions reduction requirement
to meet Paris Agreement 2030 targets in China

Interpretation: Individual carbon footprints include emissions from all greenhouse gases stemming from domestic consumption, public and private investments as well as imports and exports of carbon embedded in goods and services traded with the rest of the world. Modeled estimates based on the systematic combination of national accounts, tax and survey data, input-output models and energy datasets. Emissions are split equally within households. The 2030 target corresponds to the overal emissions budget annouced by governments for 2030, divided by the total population of the country in 2030. **Sources and series:** *wir2022.wid.world/ methodology and Chancel (2021).*

emissions (which are close to mid-2021 emissions levels). In France, the pledge amounts to a 45% reduction. In India, emissions per capita are projected to increase by 70% between now and 2030, and also in China, by 25%.

The bottom half of the population in rich countries already nears 2030 targets

Two main results stand out from these figures. First, in rich countries, the bottom 50% is already below the 2030 per capita target (in the US, for example), or very close to it (France). It follows that all emissions reductions efforts are to be made by the top half of the distribution. In the US, the top 10% must cut its emissions by close to 90% in order to reach the 2030 per capita target, and the middle 40% by around 50%. The degree of efforts required from the top 10% and middle 40% in France is similar. Second, it appears that in emerging countries, not all groups should increase their emissions levels. While the bottom and middle of the distribution are currently below the 2030 target, the top 10% is significantly above it. Indeed, in China, the top 10% must cut its emissions by more than 70% to meet the sustainable target. The value is also significant in India (-58%).

A new approach to climate policymaking

There are many ways to meet the 2030 pledges and there is no single ready-made solution or magic formula to implement just carbon policies. What is paramount is to factor in the large levels of carbon inequalities in the design of climate policy. As a matter of fact, different types of policy instruments (whether regulations, taxes, incentives or investments) have different types of impacts on socio-economic groups.

One of the key conclusions of this chapter is that if countries wish to deviate from the egalitarian perspective presented above (e.g. by demanding relatively less emissions reduction efforts from richer groups), then this will inevitably mean demanding more reductions from low income groups, who have

fewer resources to reduce their own carbon footprints. Such strategies raise the question of financial compensation mechanisms for low-income groups and of the just financing of these efforts.

Table 6.7 presents a schematic framework of climate policies and their potential impacts on different types of the distribution of income (bottom, middle and top income groups).[14] Climate policies are broken down into three categories: decarbonizing energy supply, decarbonizing energy access, decarbonizing existing energy end-uses (such as existing transport systems). The table is non-exhaustive and illustrates the variety of climate-energy policies available for policymakers and the set of possible impacts on different social groups. We argue that an inequality reality check of climate policies should become center stage of climate policy-making.

Examples of climate policies that effectively address inequality exist across the world. In British Columbia (Canada), a carbon tax was implemented along with a significant package of transfers to low- and middle-income households, which ensured the social viability of the reform.[15] In Indonesia, energy subsidies reforms were coupled with substantial investments in the public health system, largely financed by increased revenues from energy taxes. In Sweden, decades of large-scale public investments in low-carbon infrastructure made it possible for low-income groups to access affordable, clean energy sources. When a carbon tax was eventually introduced, low-income groups had the choice between greener and fossil options.[16]

Table 6.7   *An inequality reality check for climate policies*

		What kind of climate policy?		
		Increase green energy supply	Increase green energy access	Switch in energy end-uses (building, transport, industry)
Which social group is targetted?	Bottom 50%	Industrial policy: public investments in renewables (off or on-gridd); Social protection: increase transfers to workers in industries affected by the transition	Public investments in green energy access (e.g. clean cookstoves; construction of new zero carbon social housing)	Develop public transport systems: low-carbon bus, rail, car-sharing strategies; energy retrofitting in social housing; cash-transfers to compensate increase in fossil energy prices
	Middle 40%	Same as above + Financial incentives to encourage middle-class investments in green energy. Bans on new fossil investments	Subsidies for green housing construction; Buildings regulations; penalty and bans on sales of inefficient housing	Same as above; Stricter regulations & taxes on polluting purchases (SUVs, air tickets); Subsidies on green alternatives (elec. vehicles)
	Top 10 % & Top 1%	Wealth or corporate taxes with pollution top-up to finance the above & accelerate divestment from fossils; Bans on new fossil investments	Wealth or corporate taxes with pollution top-up (see left); Fossil fuel subsidy removal*	Strict regulations on polluting purchases (SUVs, air tickets); Wealth or corporate taxes with pollution top-up (see left); Carbon cards to track high personal carbon footprints & cap them

Interpretation: *The table presents a non-exhaustive list of different types of climate policies and of their potential impacts on social groups. *Fossil fuel subsidies typically benefit wealthy groups more than poorer groups in rich and developing countries.* **Sources and series:** *Table adapted from Voituriez and Chancel (2020) and Rodrik and Stantcheva (2021).*

One dimension which has been largely left aside by climate policies around the globe is addressing the large carbon footprints of the very wealthy. Given the huge responsibility of wealthy groups in overall emissions levels (within countries and at the global level), this lack of focus is questionable. So far, the standard way to think about carbon taxation has been in the context of uniform tax rate across individuals, i.e. whether rich or poor, individuals should pay the same carbon tax rate. In unequal societies, this de facto means giving more polluting rights to wealthy individuals, who are less affected by an increase in carbon prices than low-income individuals. To accelerate carbon emissions reductions among the wealthiest, progressive carbon taxes can become a useful instrument. Progressive carbon taxation means that the rate of a carbon tax increases with the level of emissions or the level of wealth of individuals. Chancel and Piketty made proposals along these lines, and also proposed specific taxes on luxury carbon-intensive consumption items.[17] These can include business class tickets, yachts, etc. Indeed, progressive carbon taxes cannot suffice: stricter regulations (i.e. bans) on the consumption of expensive carbon goods or services should also be implemented: for example on the purchase of SUVs.

Shifting the focus from consumers to asset owners

Finally, we argue that climate policy instruments focusing on the regulation and taxation of asset portfolio (rather than on the consumption of goods and services) should deserve more attention. Carbon consumers, especially from low and middle income groups are often constrained in their energy choices, because they are locked-in carbon intensive infrastructures systems. On the contrary, investors who opt for investments in fossil industries do so while they have many alternative options to invest their wealth in. Therefore, the purchase of stock in fossil companies which continue to develop new extraction projects, should be highly regulated. Such moves can be accompanied, for a short period of time (before effective bans), by steeply progressive tax rates on polluting stock ownership.

In Table 6.8, we provide estimates of a global progressive wealth tax on global multimillionaires, including a pollution top-up. Revenue estimates are based on those presented in Chapter 7, and include an additional tax component, based on the ownership of stock in the world's leading oil and gas majors. A discount is applied when fossil fuel companies invest in renewable energy. If companies shifted all their operations to renewable energy supply, then their shareholders would not face the pollution wealth tax top-up anymore. Currently, though, this is far from being the case: only 2% of oil major investments are made in renewable energy activities.[18] Radical investment decision changes would therefore need to be made in order to avoid the wealth tax pollution top-up.

Applying a 10% tax rate on the value of carbon assets owned by global multimillionaires would generate at least $100bn in a year. This value is non-negligeable: it represents about 1.5 times the current estimated annual costs of adaptation to global warming in developing countries (about $70bn per year in 2020). Yet, compared to current additional investment requirements in energy systems globally, this value remains small. It is estimated that 2% of GDP in additional annual

Table 6.8   *Revenues from a progressive wealth tax with a pollution top-up*

Wealth group ($)	Number of adults (million)	Total group wealth ($ bn)	Avg. group wealth ($ m)	Wealth tax revenues from group ($bn)	Revenues from fossil assets top-up ($bn)	Total tax revenues (% global income)
All above 1m	62.2	174,200	2.8	1695	100	1.7%
1m - 10m	60.3	111,100	1.8	684	64	0.7%
10m - 100m	1.8	33,600	19	432	19	0.5%
+100m	0.1	29,570	387	579	17	0.6%

Interpretation: *The table presents revenues from a global progressive wealth tax with a pollution top-up. The wealth tax rates range from 1% for individuals with net wealth between $1m-$10m, 1.5% between $10m-$100m, 2% between $100m-$1bn, 2.5% between $1bn-$10bn, 3% between $10bn-$100bn, 3.5% above $100bn. On top of this wealth tax, we apply a tax on the ownership of assets in oil, gas and coal majors. The rate ranges from 10% to 15%, with a discount proportional to these firms' green energy production (which is currently extremely low for oil majors, around 2% only of capital investments in renewables).* **Sources:** *Chancel (2021)* investments are required (i.e. about $2,000bn). As a matter of fact, the very large additional investments in infrastructures required to meet the energy transition challenge needs considerable new sources of financing and these will hardly be met by taxes on highly polluting assets alone. Progressive taxes based on both carbon and non-carbon assets will be essential instruments to ensure that sufficient amounts of investments are made, in a timely manner by governments. In Chapter 7, we present different progressive wealth tax strategies to raise several percentage points of global GDP from global multimillionaires.

Box 6.1   **Measuring carbon inequality between individuals**

Measuring carbon inequality between individuals across the globe is an even more challenging task than measuring it for income and wealth. In this report, our emissions estimates are based on observed national carbon footprints across different sectors of the economy, inequalities in private consumption, wealth inequality, and levels of government spending. The novelty of our approach is to combine systematically the new data sets on global income and wealth inequality produced by the WID.world project with international carbon data series, known as environment input–output tables.[19]

Environmental input–output (IO) tables are based on the pioneering work of Nobel prize winner Wassily Leontief, who systematized the work of one of the first economists of the 18th century, François Quesnay, and extended it, to study the relationship between production and the consumption of environmental inputs.[20] Environmental IO tables make it possible to measure the carbon content associated with the production of an economic sector, taking into account all the emissions used in the intermediary production process of the goods produced by this sector. Intermediary emissions include both those made on a territory and those made abroad by foreign suppliers. This is particularly useful for measuring carbon footprints rather than only territorial emissions (see above). The strength of Environmental IO methodology is also its systematicity: it ensures that one tonne of carbon used in the production of a good is never counted twice. The problem of double counting arises in other methods of measuring carbon footprints, known as Life Cycle Analyses, which allow more detailed estimates for a specific product, but cannot provide systematic and coherent macro-level statistics. The two approaches are complementary, but when we are investigating global emissions inequality, we prefer the IO approach.

From Environmental IO tables, we can reconstruct, country by country, and sector by sector, the volume of emissions associated with household consumption, the government sector, and private investments in an economy. With this information, we can distribute each component to income groups within countries. We distribute emissions to private consumption on the basis of observed regularities in the relationship between individual (carbon) consumption and income. Typically, micro-level household surveys find that carbon emissions increase with income, but less than proportionally.[21] We then add emissions associated with government spending. Our assumption is both simple and conservative (i.e. it uses a low limit to emission inequality), as we assume that emissions associated with government spending are distributed as a lump sum to individuals. We also take into account emissions associated with investments, based on the distribution of assets across the population. For instance, if a group is responsible for 25% of all private investments, then this group is attributed 25% of the emissions associated with those investments. Our method is adaptable: it will be refined as more elaborate data sources on carbon emissions associated with private consumption and wealth are developed.[22] While it is urgent to improve the quality of the public monitoring of carbon inequalities, we believe that we can already produce reliable statistics that are consistent with carbon inequality levels produced by more detailed micro-level studies.

Box 6.2   **Carbon footprints of the very wealthy**

How much CO2 do the wealthiest individuals on earth emit? Our estimates show that emissions can reach extreme levels: the global top 1% of individuals emits around 110 tonnes on average, the top 0.1% 467 tonnes, the top 0.01% 2,530 tonnes per person per annum. These emissions stem both from individual consumption and from the investments they make. There are variations within each group: certain very wealthy individuals invest in less carbon-intensive activities than others and consume fewer carbon-intensive goods. On average, however, the answer is quite clear: extreme wealth comes with extreme pollution.[23] Our estimates should be interpreted with care, given the difficulty of properly assessing the carbon content of wealth and the carbon embedded in consumption, but our approach is rather conservative: we tend to underestimate the carbon footprint associated with extreme wealth rather than overestimate it.

Perhaps the most conspicuous illustration of extreme pollution associated with wealth inequality in recent years is the development of space travel. Space travel is expected to cost from several thousand dollars to several dozen million dollars per trip. An 11-minute flight emits no fewer than 75 tonnes of carbon per passenger once indirect emissions are taken into account (and more likely, in the 250-1,000 tonnes range).[24] At the other end of the distribution, about one billion individuals emit less than one tonne per person per year. Over their lifetime, this group of one billion individuals does not emit more than 75 tonnes of carbon per person. It therefore takes a few minutes in space travel to emit at least as much carbon as an individual from the bottom billion will emit in her entire lifetime[25]. This example shows that there is scarcely any limit to the carbon emissions of the ultra-wealthy.

NOTES

[1] The rate of extinction of species is 100 times the "normal rate" of extinction of our geological times. See Ceballos and Ehrlich (2018) The misunderstood sixth mass extinction, Science 360(6393).

[2] Global atmospheric CO2 concentration is at its highest level in 14 million years.

[3] Lebreton, L., M. Egger, and B. Slat. 2019. "A Global Mass Budget for Positively Buoyant Macroplastic Debris in the Ocean." Sci Rep 9, 12922. https://doi.org/10.1038/s41598-019-49413-5.

[4] This chapter is based on Lucas Chancel. 2021. "Global Carbon Inequality,1990-2019." World Inequality Lab working paper 2021/21.

[5] In that sense, the term CO2 is interchangeable with the use of "CO2-equivalent" or "CO2e". We prefer to use CO2 in this chapter for simplicity and readability.

[6] It is estimated than an additional 5–7 billion tonnes are associated with deforestation and land-use, land-use change, and forestry (LULUCF). Because these emissions are harder to take into account country by country, we do not include them in the national and regional figures presented in this chapter. Including deforestation, per capita emissions could reach around seven tonnes CO2 per capita.

[7] Estimates of deforestation indicate an additional 1.5 billion tonnes due to deforestation in 1850; see PRIMAP historical data set: https://www.pik-potsdam.de/paris-reality-check/primap-hist/.

[8] We should also note that the Paris Climate Agreement seeks to stay below 2°C.

[9] Logically, these budgets would decrease should we decide to split them between now and 2100 (rather than between now and 2050). Doing so would reduce the 2°C sustainable level to 1.1 tonnes per person per annum. The equivalent figure for the 1.5°C compatible budget drops to 0.4 tonne per person per annum.

[10] For discussions on climate justice principles and applications to different carbon budget sharing strategies, see Grasso, M. & Roberts, T. (2014). A compromise to break the climate impasse. Nat. Clim. Change 4, 543–549; Fuglestvedt, J. S. & Kallbekken, S. (2015) Climate responsibility: Fair shares? Nat. Clim. Change; Matthews, H. D. (2015) Quantifying historical carbon and climate debts among nations. Nat. Clim. Change; Raupach, M. R. et al. (2014) Sharing a quota on cumulative carbon emissions. Nat. Clim. Change 4, 873–879; Landis, F. & Bernauer, T. (2012) Transfer payments in global climate policy. Nat. Clim. Change 2, 628–633.

[11] The middle 40% of Europeans earn on average €38,500 per annum and per adult after all taxes and transfers, whereas the bottom 50% the US distribution earn €20,000 per annum and per adult after all taxes and transfers are taken into account.

[12] There are variations in carbon emissions levels across European countries (France has a slightly lower carbon footprint than many of its neighbors), but these differences are minor compared with differences with the US on the one hand, and China and India on the other.

[13] We report pledges announced up to the last semester 2020.

[14] The table is adapted from Voituriez and Chancel (2020) "How do governments' responses to the coronavirus crisis address inequality and the environment?", in Human Development Report 2020, United Nations Development Programme, Human Development Report 2020. For a version focusing on redistribution and predistribution policies, see Rodrik and Stantcheva (2021) "A policy-matrix for inclusive prosperity"NBER Working Paper No. 28736, April 2021.

[15] See Chancel (2020), Unsustainable inequalities: social justice and the environment. Harvard University Press.

[16] See Chancel (2020).

[17] See Chancel and Piketty (2015) Carbon and inequality: from Kyoto to Paris. Paris School of Economics Study.

[18] See Financial Times, https://www.ft.com/content/95efca74-4299-11ea-a43a-c4b328d9061c.

[19] For more details, see Chancel (2021) "Global Carbon Inequality, 1990-2019", World Inequality Lab working paper. See also Chancel and Piketty (2015) and Kartha et al. (2020) The Carbon Inequality Era, Joint Research Report, SEI and Oxfam, September 2020.

[20] Leontief, W. 1966. Input–Output Economics. Oxford: Oxford University Press and Leontief, W. 1970.

[21] Using country-level micro studies, we assume a central elasticity of 0.6 between income and emissions from private consumption, meaning that when income increases by 10%, emissions rise by 6%.

[22] See Rehm, Y. (2021). Measuring and Taxing the Carbon Content of Wealth, PSE dissertation.

[23] See also [DOI: 10.1038/s41558-019-0402-3, Gössling (2019), Celebrities, air travel, and social norms, Annals of Tourism Research vol. 79.

[24] See Chancel (2021).

[25] One billion people emitting less than one tonne per annum and whose life expectancy is less than 75 years.

CHAPTER 7

The road to redistributing wealth

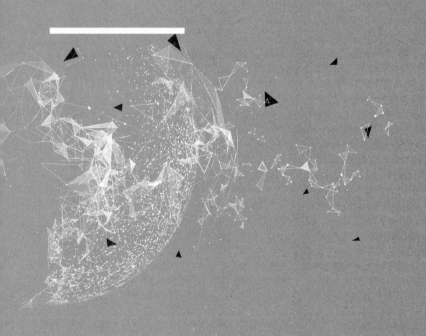

WORLD
INEQUALITY
REPORT
2022

Why tax wealth?

The past few years have been marked by a renewal of debates about progressive wealth taxation. While progressive wealth taxes have been on the decline in rich countries, they still exist in varying forms in several countries, such as the Netherlands, Norway, Spain or Switzerland. More recently, some countries have discussed or voted in favor of the introduction of new wealth taxes (such as Argentina). In several other countries, there have been discussions about wealth taxes based on detailed proposals (such as in the USA, Germany, the UK or Chile). This renewed interest in progressive wealth taxation has been stirred by two factors: the surge in aggregate private wealth relative to national income (Chapter 3) and the increase in wealth concentration (Chapter 4). This phenomenon was accelerated during the COVID crisis: while national income fell, the value of private wealth increased, and this increase was particularly extreme among billionaires.

While the debate on progressive wealth taxation is gaining momentum, progressive wealth taxes remain an exception to the rule rather than the norm across the world nowadays. However, most countries in the world already tax individual wealth with property and inheritance taxes. You may recall that overall tax revenue accounts for 30-50% of national income in rich countries, 15-30% in emerging countries and less than 10% in low-income countries. Wealth taxes on individuals– including property and inheritance taxes- typically generate 2-3% of national income in rich countries,

1% in middle income countries and 0.5% in low-income and emerging countries: they represent non negligeable fractions of total tax revenue.

Property taxes–and their equivalent in various countries, such as *taxe foncière* in France–are by far the largest component of total wealth tax revenue: they typically account for 80-100% of total tax revenue on individual wealth. Property taxes generally take the form of taxes on real estate and land, which have been levied in many countries for centuries. In pre-modern societies, where land and housing assets represented the bulk of wealth, property taxes were a means to collect revenue by taxing those who could afford to pay. Today, in most countries, property taxes are flat, i.e. proportional to value: whether an individual owns a €10 million mansion or a € 50,000 flat, they will pay the same tax rate. Furthermore, property taxes are due regardless of whether the owner has any mortgage debt on the property.

In contrast to previous property taxes, wealth and income taxation in the 20th century were characterized by the introduction of progressivity. With a progressive tax, the tax rate rises as taxpayers' income or wealth increases. This progressivity was particularly steep in some countries in the 20th century. In the USA, the UK, Germany or Japan, top income tax rates reached 80% (or more) a few decades back, while rates remained much lower for bottom income earners. In the USA, very high income tax rates were no one-time anomaly: Between 1936 and 1980 the top income tax rate was consistently 70% or more. While most countries have reduced top income tax rates since 1980, progressive taxation remains the defining principle of modern income taxation: the higher the income or the wealth, the higher the tax rate.

Therefore, the flat rate on property tax stands in sharp contrast to modern progressive income and wealth taxes. Let us be clear: there is no real economic justification to flat property tax rates in the world today. This is the continuation of archaic tax regimes in modern times, which could have been acceptable in pre-modern societies but which are at odds with basic democratic conceptions of tax justice today. In many ways, today's situation regarding wealth taxation is comparable to the situation prevailing in the early 20th century before the introduction of modern progressive income taxes. The existing wealth tax system is archaic and disconnected from the current socio-economic reality, but many economic interests and political forces are still supporting the status quo.

Modernizing personal wealth taxation

The best way to modernize property tax would be to extend its base to all forms of wealth, rather than just real estate, and to shift from flat rates to progressive tax schedules. In actual fact, this amounts to transforming flat property taxes into modern, progressive taxes on wealth. There is a widespread misunderstanding in the contemporary debate about progressive wealth taxation: some commentators, opposed to personal wealth taxation, have argued that wealth should not be taxed at all, but they generally forget the fact that personal wealth in the form of housing–the main asset of the middle class–is already taxed, albeit in a regressive manner. Today, the wealthiest mostly own financial assets, rather than real estate and land (see Chapter 4), which in real terms means that the property tax represents a much smaller fraction of the total wealth for multimillionaires and billionaires than for the middle class. Transforming property taxes into modern progressive taxes, encompassing all forms of assets, would be a major step towards a more coherent and integrated tax system.

Relatively low tax rates on wealth can yield substantial tax revenue, contribute to spreading wealth better, hence increasing the wealth-generation potential of billions of citizens entirely deprived of capital. Progressive wealth taxes also contribute to containing the rise of extreme wealth inequality, and therefore help to mitigate the potentially negative impact of extreme wealth concentration, such as the rise of monopolies or the risks of political capture by financial interests.

But wouldn't wealth taxes harm the economy? The first answer is that personal wealth is already taxed almost everywhere (with property taxes) in a regressive way. The second answer is that we now have a relatively good understanding of what works and what doesn't in terms of personal wealth taxation, thanks to a wide range of historical and contemporary examples of personal wealth taxes. In a nutshell, given the enormous increase in the aggregate value and concentration of private wealth in recent decades, it would be completely unreasonable not to ask more to top wealth-holders in the future, especially in light of the social, developmental and environmental challenges ahead.

Estimates for a global progressive wealth tax

Below is a focus on the revenue potential from global progressive wealth taxes on millionaires and billionaires. These taxes could be implemented as a way to modernize and replace existing flat property taxes or be added on top of these. Our basic rationale, which we will further develop in **Chapters 8 and 9,** is that there is no sound economic justification for flat taxes on personal wealth when countries introduce progressive taxes on income – and even less so when they already implement personal

wealth taxes. Here, we suggest three scenarios of progressive wealth taxation (low, significant and very high, see **Table 7.2**).

Table 7.1 presents the number of individuals in different wealth brackets in 2021, along with their total net wealth and the taxes they should pay according to three global wealth taxation scenarios. At the global level, there are 62 million individuals owning more than a million dollars at market exchange rates. This represents the top 1.2% of the global adult population. There are a little less than 1.8 million individuals owning more than $10 million (top 0.04%), 76,500 owning more than $100 million (top 0.001%) and 2,750 owning more than a billion dollars (top 0.00005%). Pooled together, global billionaires own more than $13 trillion, which amounts to 3.5% of global wealth.

Table 7.1   *Global millionaires and billionaires, 2021*

Wealth group ($)	Number of adults	Total wealth ($ bn)	Average wealth ($ m)	Tax scenario 1		Tax scenario 2		Tax scenario 3	
				Effective wealth tax rate (%)	Total revenues (% global income)	Effective wealth tax rate (%)	Revenues (% global income)	Effective wealth tax rate (%)	Revenues from group (% global income)
All above 1m	62,165,160	174,200	2,8	1.0	1.6	1.2	2.1	3.2	5.3
1m - 10m	60,319,510	111,100	1,8	0.6	0.6	0.6	0.6	0.6	0.6
10m - 100m	1,769,200	33,600	19	1.3	0.4	1.1	0.4	1.3	0.4
100m - 1b	73,710	16,500	220	1.5	0.2	2.4	0.4	5.2	0.8
1b - 10b	2,582	7,580	2,940	2.3	0.2	4.5	0.3	12.9	0.9
10b - 100b	159	4,170	26,210	2.8	0.1	6.4	0.3	40.1	1.6
Over 100b	9	1,320	146,780	3.2	0.04	8.3	0.1	66.6	0.9

Interpretation: *In 2021, 62.2 million people in the world owned more than $1 million (at MER). Their average wealth was $ 2.8 million, representing a total of $174 trillion. In our Tax scenario 2, a global progressive wealth tax would yield 2.1% of global income, taking into account capital depreciation and evasion.* **Note:** *Numbers of millionaires are rounded to the nearest ten.* **Sources and series:** *wir2022.wid.world/methodology.*

Table 7.2 details the three tax scenarios we are considering. The rates presented are marginal rates, i.e. they apply to the fraction of wealth possessed between two thresholds and not to total wealth. The first scenario is a modest wealth tax proposal: between $1 million and $10 million, the rate is 1% and it rises progressively up to 3.5% for individuals owning more than $100 billion. This scenario generates 1.6% of global income in tax revenue after taking into account possible tax evasion and capital depreciation (see more below). Our estimates are relatively conservative, meaning that tax evasion could in practice be lower and consequently revenues higher (reaching up to 2.1% in this scenario).

In the second scenario (high wealth tax), the rate applied to individuals owning between $1 million and $10 million is also 1%, but it increases more steeply than in scenario 1. The tax rate is 5% between $1 billion and $10 billion and rises to 7% in the $10-100 billion bracket. On wealth over $100 billion, the rate is 10%. These rates should be compared with the average annual rate of billionaires' increasing wealth over the entire 1995-2021 period: 7-8% (see Chapter 4). This means in real terms that wealth would have increased by 1-2% per year for billionaires in the $1-10 billion bracket even after paying for the wealth tax. This scenario generates a wealth tax equivalent of 2.1% of global income, even when factoring in a fair amount of tax evasion.

In the third scenario, the rate applied on millionaires in the $1-10 million category remains unchanged but

tax progressivity is even steeper than in scenario 2. Rates reach 50% over $10 billion and 90% over $100 billion. This would in effect ban wealth accumulation over $10 billion. The revenue generated in this scenario is equivalent to 5.3% of global income after tax evasion. Naturally, such a wealth tax scenario cannot raise such revenue for ever as it effectively prevents decabillionaires and especially centibillionaires from keeping their wealth.

Table 7.2   *Wealth tax scenarios*

Wealth group ($)	Scenario 1	Scenario 2	Scenario 3
	(Tax rate, % bracket wealth)		
1m - 10m	1.0%	1.0%	1.0%
10m - 100m	1.5%	1.5%	1.5%
100m - 1000m	2%	3.0%	7.0%
1bn - 10bn	2.5%	5.0%	15.0%
10b - 100b	3.0%	7.0%	50.0%
Over 100bn	3.5%	10.0%	90.0%

Interpretation: *The table presents marginal wealth tax rates applicable to wealth brackets according to three tax scenarios. In Scenario 1, a person who owns $20 million is taxed at 1% on $9 million (10m-1m=9m) and at 1.5% on the remaining 10 million (20m-10m=10m). The total annual wealth tax in this case is $240k (9m x 1%=90k + 10m x 1.5%=150k).* **Sources and series:** *wir2022.wid.world/methodology.*

Regional wealth tax estimates

Tables 7.3a-h present regional wealth tax revenue estimates. In East Asia, 13 million individuals own more than $1 million. Under Scenario 1, wealth tax revenue accounts for 1.3% of regional income and is close to 1.7% in Scenario 2. In Europe, there are 16 million individuals owning more than $1 million and

499 billionaires. Total revenue under Scenario 1 would be 1.5% of European total income and 1.8% in scenario 2. In North America, there are 29 million people owning more than $1 million and 835 billionaires. Total tax revenue under scenario 1 accounts for about 2.8% of total income and revenue in scenario 2 accounts for 3.5% of total income. In Sub-Saharan Africa, there are 240,000 people owning more than $1 million and 11 billionaires. Total tax revenue under scenario 1 accounts for about 0.3% of total income and revenue in scenario 2 accounts for 0.4% of total income. In South and South-East Asia, there are 850,000 people owning more than $1 million and 260 billionaires. Total tax revenue under scenario 1 accounts for about 0.7% of total income and revenues in scenario 2 accounts for 1.0% of total income. In Latin America, there are 1.9 million people owning more than $1 million and 105 billionaires. Total tax revenue under scenario 1 accounts for about 1.1% of total income and revenue in scenario 2 accounts for 1.3% of total income. In the Middle East and North Africa, there are 915,000 people owning more than $1 million and 75 billionaires. Total tax revenue under scenario 1 accounts for about 0.5% of total income and revenue in scenario 2 accounts for 0.6% of total income. In Russia and Central Asia, there are 230,000 people owning more than $1 million and 133 billionaires. Total tax revenue under scenario 1 accounts for about 0.8% of total income, and total tax revenue under scenario 2 accounts for 1.4% of total income.

Let us stress the fact that tax revenue in each of our scenarios here is quite substantial. In scenario 1, 0.5-3% of national income is generated by tax depending on the region. This is considerable given that such a tax would not raise taxes for 98-99% of the global population in each region and considering that, in scenario 1, wealth would continue to grow significantly at the top of the distribution (tax rates are significantly below the average wealth growth rates observed for the groups over the past decades). In fact, there are only very few taxes which can generate significant revenue, while impacting such as small fraction of the population.

Factoring-in behavioral responses to wealth taxation

The estimates presented above include basic tax evasion with two parameters: a tax evasion rate and a capital stock depreciation or appreciation rate. Our tax evasion parameter defines the expected share of unreported taxable wealth due to the multiple forms of tax evasion (underreporting, offshoring, fraud, etc.). An evasion rate of 10% means that 10% of the net value of taxable wealth will not be reported and therefore that revenue will be 10% lower than what it could be, absent tax evasion. The stock depreciation or appreciation parameter helps to anticipate the potentially negative or positive impacts of wealth taxation on asset prices. Assuming a depreciation parameter of 15% amounts to assuming that the market value of financial and non-financial assets declines by 15% following the introduction of a wealth tax. The benchmark estimates presented above take into account tax evasion and depreciation (respectively 10% and 15%).

Assuming an evasion of 0% and a capital depreciation of 0%

generates 2.1%, 2.7%, 7.0% of global income as wealth tax revenue for scenarios 1, 2 and 3 respectively. Assuming an evasion rate of 40% and a capital depreciation rate of 10% generates 1.2%, 1.5% and 3.8% of wealth tax revenue respectively.

In North America, even in the most conservative scenario, both in terms of taxation rates and evasion and capital depreciation, revenue generated still amounts to 2% of national income. On the other hand, it could reach 11% of

Table 7.3a **Multimillionaires and billionaires in Europe, 2021**

Wealth group ($)	Number of adults	Total wealth ($ bn)	Average wealth ($ m)	Tax scenario 1		Tax scenario 2		Tax scenario 3	
				Effective wealth tax rate (%)	Total revenues (% global income)	Effective wealth tax rate (%)	Revenues (% global income)	Effective wealth tax rate (%)	Revenues from group (% global income)
All above 1m	16,040,560	38,325	2	0.9	1.5	1.1	1.8	2.4	4.1
1m - 10m	15,721,680	28,348	2	0.6	0.8	0.6	0.8	0.6	0.8
10m - 100m	310,710	5,425	17	1.3	0.3	1.1	0.3	1.3	0.3
100m - 1b	7,680	2,134	278	1.5	0.1	2.5	0.2	5.6	0.5
1b - 10b	474	1,671	3,525	2.3	0.2	4.6	0.3	13.2	1.0
10b - 100b	24	558	23,250	2.8	0.1	6.3	0.2	39.2	1.0
Over 100b	1	189	189,000	3.2	0.03	8.1	0.1	63.7	0.5

Interpretation: *The graph presents summary statistics related to wealth tax scenarios defined in Table 7.2. Wealth measured at MER. See additional tables for alternative assumptions.* **Note:** *Numbers of millionaires are rounded to the nearest ten.* **Sources and series:** *wir2022.wid.world/methodology.*

Table 7.3b **Multimillionaires and billionaires in North America, 2021**

Wealth group ($)	Number of adults	Total wealth ($ bn)	Average wealth ($ m)	Tax scenario 1		Tax scenario 2		Tax scenario 3	
				Effective wealth tax rate (%)	Total revenues (% global income)	Effective wealth tax rate (%)	Revenues (% global income)	Effective wealth tax rate (%)	Revenues from group (% global income)
All above 1m	29,249,990	85,370	3	0.9	2.8	1.2	3.5	2.9	8.4
1m - 10m	28,273,730	54,365	2	0.6	1.2	0.6	1.2	0.6	1.2
10m - 100m	936,830	17,454	19	1.3	0.8	1.1	0.7	1.3	0.8
100m - 1b	38,600	8,729	226	1.5	0.4	2.4	0.7	5.2	1.5
1b - 10b	768	2,429	3,163	2.3	0.2	4.5	0.4	13.0	1.1
10b - 100b	62	1,777	28,661	2.8	0.2	6.4	0.4	41.0	2.5
Over 100b	5	616	123,200	3.2	0.1	8.4	0.2	68.2	1.4

Interpretation: *The graph presents summary statistics related to wealth tax scenarios defined in Table 7.2. Wealth measured at MER.* **Note:** *Numbers of millionaires are rounded to the neares ten.* **Sources and series:** *wir2022.wid.world/methodology.*

national income under the third tax scenario, and absent evasion and depreciation. Let us stress that behavioral responses to wealth taxation obey no law of nature–they are governed by tax policy choices (or lack thereof). The impact of wealth taxation on the overall stock of wealth also depends on how revenue is used. When recycled to improve access to basic education and healthcare, this revenue can provide an economy with a chance to improve its productive potential and helps to appreciate the stock of wealth. In chapters 8

Table 7.3c **Multimillionaires and billionaires in East Asia, 2021**

Wealth group ($)	Number of adults	Total wealth ($ bn)	Average wealth ($ m)	Tax scenario 1		Tax scenario 2		Tax scenario 3	
				Effective wealth tax rate (%)	Total revenues (% global income)	Effective wealth tax rate (%)	Revenues (% global income)	Effective wealth tax rate (%)	Revenues from group (% global income)
All above 1m	12,705,850	35,718	3	1.0	1.3	1.4	1.7	3.9	5.0
1m - 10m	12,330,520	20,589	2	0.6	0.4	0.6	0.4	0.6	0.4
10m - 100m	353,100	7,652	22	1.3	0.3	1.1	0.3	1.3	0.3
100m - 1b	21,390	4,031	188	1.5	0.2	2.3	0.3	4.9	0.7
1b - 10b	789	1,784	2,261	2.2	0.1	4.3	0.3	12.3	0.8
10b - 100b	46	1,300	28,261	2.8	0.1	6.4	0.3	40.8	1.9
Over 100b	3	362	120,667	3.2	0.0	8.4	0.1	67.7	0.9

Interpretation: The graph presents summary statistics related to wealth tax scenarios defined in Table 7.2. Wealth measured at MER. Note: Numbers of millionaires are rounded to the neares ten. Sources and series: wir2022.wid.world/methodology.

Table 7.3d **Multimillionaires and billionaires in South and South-East Asia, 2021**

Wealth group ($)	Number of adults	Total wealth ($ bn)	Average wealth ($ m)	Tax scenario 1		Tax scenario 2		Tax scenario 3	
				Effective wealth tax rate (%)	Total revenues (% global income)	Effective wealth tax rate (%)	Revenues (% global income)	Effective wealth tax rate (%)	Revenues from group (% global income)
All above 1m	848,940	3,905	5	1.3	0.7	2.1	1.0	6.2	3.1
1m - 10m	809,380	1,551	2	0.6	0.1	0.6	0.1	0.6	0.1
10m - 100m	37,390	739	20	1.3	0.1	1.1	0.1	1.3	0.1
100m - 1b	1,910	540	282	1.5	0.1	2.5	0.2	5.6	0.4
1b - 10b	245	713	2,910	2.3	0.2	4.5	0.4	12.9	1.2
10b - 100b	15	278	18,533	2.8	0.1	6.2	0.2	36.4	1.3

Interpretation: The graph presents summary statistics related to wealth tax scenarios defined in Table 7.2. Wealth measured at MER. Note: Numbers of millionaires are rounded to the neares ten. Sources and series: wir2022.wid.world/methodology.

and 9, we discuss policy options to reduce tax evasion and enhance the productive potential of wealth taxes. Chapter 10 discusses options on how to use wealth tax revenue.

Table 7.3e   *Multimillionaires and billionaires in Latin America, 2021*

Wealth group ($)	Number of adults	Total wealth ($ bn)	Average wealth ($ m)	Tax scenario 1		Tax scenario 2		Tax scenario 3	
				Effective wealth tax rate (%)	Total revenues (% global income)	Effective wealth tax rate (%)	Revenues (% global income)	Effective wealth tax rate (%)	Revenues from group (% global income)
All above 1m	1,930,730	5,815	3	1.0	1.1	1.2	1.3	2.6	2.9
1m - 10m	1 859 370	3,614	2	0.6	0.4	0.6	0.4	0.6	0.4
10m - 100m	69,450	1,240	18	1.3	0.3	1.1	0.3	1.3	0.3
100m - 1b	1,810	518	287	1.5	0.1	2.5	0.3	5.6	0.6
1b - 10b	99	303	3,061	2.3	0.1	4.5	0.3	13.0	0.7
10b - 100b	6	116	19,333	2.8	0.1	6.3	0.1	38.1	0.8

Interpretation: *The graph presents summary statistics related to wealth tax scenarios defined in Table 7.2. Wealth measured at MER.* **Note:** *Numbers of millionaires are rounded to the neares ten.*
Sources and series: *wir2022.wid.world/methodology.*

Table 7.3f   *Multimillionaires and billionaires in Sub-Saharan Africa, 2021*

Wealth group ($)	Number of adults	Total wealth ($ bn)	Average wealth ($ m)	Tax scenario 1		Tax scenario 2		Tax scenario 3	
				Effective wealth tax rate (%)	Total revenues (% global income)	Effective wealth tax rate (%)	Revenues (% global income)	Effective wealth tax rate (%)	Revenues from group (% global income)
All above 1m	243,220	726	3	1.0	0.3	1.2	0.4	2.2	0.7
1m - 10m	234,730	448	2	0.6	0.1	0.6	0.1	0.6	0.1
10m - 100m	8,200	155	19	1.3	0.1	1.1	0.1	1.3	0.1
100m - 1b	288	70	243	1.5	0.1	2.5	0.1	5.3	0.2
1b - 10b	11	52	4,727	2.4	0.1	4.7	0.1	13.8	0.3

Interpretation: *The graph presents summary statistics related to wealth tax scenarios defined in Table 7.2. Wealth measured at MER.* **Note:** *Numbers of millionaires are rounded to the neares ten.*
Sources and series: *wir2022.wid.world/methodology.*

Table 7.3g   *Multimillionaires and billionaires in MENA, 2021*

Wealth group ($)	Number of adults	Total wealth ($ bn)	Average wealth ($ m)	Tax scenario 1		Tax scenario 2		Tax scenario 3	
				Effective wealth tax rate (%)	Total revenues (% global income)	Effective wealth tax rate (%)	Revenues (% global income)	Effective wealth tax rate (%)	Revenues from group (% global income)
All above 1m	915,050	2,978	3	1.0	0.5	1.2	0.6	2.3	1.2
1m - 10m	873,940	1,701	2	0.6	0.2	0.6	0.2	0.6	0.2
10m - 100m	39,730	756	19	1.3	0.2	1.1	0.2	1.3	0.2
100m - 1b	1,300	339	261	1.5	0.1	2.5	0.2	5.5	0.3
1b - 10b	72	145	2,014	2.1	0.1	4.2	0.1	11.9	0.3
10b - 100b	3	37	12,333	2.6	0.0	5.7	0.0	30.0	0.2

Interpretation: *The graph presents summary statistics related to wealth tax scenarios defined in Table 7.2. Wealth measured at MER.* **Note:** *Numbers of millionaires are rounded to the neares ten.*
Sources and series: *wir2022.wid.world/methodology.*

Table 7.3h: *Multimillionaires and billionaires in Russia and Central Asia, 2021*

Wealth group ($)	Number of adults	Total wealth ($ bn)	Average wealth ($ m)	Tax scenario 1		Tax scenario 2		Tax scenario 3	
				Effective wealth tax rate (%)	Total revenues (% global income)	Effective wealth tax rate (%)	Revenues (% global income)	Effective wealth tax rate (%)	Revenues from group (% global income)
All above 1m	230,830	1,378	6	1.5	0.8	2.6	1.4	8.3	4.6
1m - 10m	216,170	443	2	0.6	0.1	0.6	0.1	0.6	0.1
10m - 100m	13,790	166	12	1.1	0.1	1.0	0.1	1.1	0.1
100m - 1b	739	139	188	1.5	0.1	2.3	0.1	4.9	0.3
1b - 10b	127	483	3,803	2.3	0.4	4.6	0.9	13.4	2.6
10b - 100b	6	103	17,167	2.8	0.1	6.2	0.3	37.1	1.5

Interpretation: *The graph presents summary statistics related to wealth tax scenarios defined in Table 7.2. Wealth measured at MER.* **Note:** *Numbers of millionaires are rounded to the neares ten.*
Sources and series: *wir2022.wid.world/methodology.*

| Box 7.1 | Learning from past and current examples of progressive wealth taxation |

Most European countries have abolished progressive wealth taxation in recent decades. This specific form of wealth taxation applied in a number of European countries had three main weaknesses. Firstly, there was tax competition (for example the French wealth tax was immediately cancelled out when moving from Paris to London) and offshore evasion (until recently there had been no cross-border information sharing). Secondly, European wealth taxes had low exemption thresholds, causing liquidity problems for some moderately wealthy taxpayers with few liquid assets and limited cash income. Thirdly, European wealth taxes, many of which had been designed in the early 20th century, had not been modernized, perhaps reflecting ideological and political opposition to wealth taxation in recent decades. These wealth taxes relied on self-assessments rather than systematic information reporting. These three weaknesses led to reforms that gradually undermined the integrity of the wealth tax: the exemption of some asset classes such as business assets or real estate, tax limits based on reported income, or the repeal of wealth taxation altogether.

A modern wealth tax can overcome these three weaknesses. First, offshore tax evasion can be fought more effectively today than in the past, thanks to a recent breakthrough in cross-border information exchange. Besides, wealth taxes could apply to expatriates (for a few years at least), alleviating concerns about tax competition. Second, a comprehensive wealth tax base with a high exemption threshold and no preferential treatment for any asset classes can dramatically reduce avoidance possibilities and apply to the truly wealthy class who by definition do not face liquidity issues. Third, by leveraging modern information technology, tax authorities have the opportunity to collect data on the market value of most forms of household wealth and use this information to pre-populate wealth tax returns, reducing evasion possibilities to a minimum. As a matter of fact, the recent wealth tax proposals made in the United States have a high exemption threshold ($50 million instead of $1 million or less for European wealth taxation), a comprehensive tax base with no exemptions, and aggressive tax enforcement.

NOTES

<> On top of the 2,750 billionaires in the WID.world dataset, there are 5 billionaires in the Forbes' rich list residing in very small jurisdictions not available as countries on WID.world.

<> Saez, E. and G. Zucman. Fall 2019. "Progressive Wealth Taxation." Brookings Papers on Economic Activity, 437-511

<> The weaknesses of existing progressive wealth taxes are described in detail and how to remedy them.

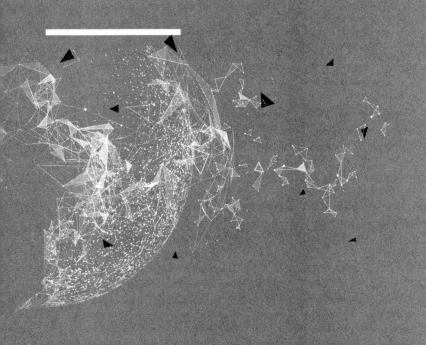

CHAPTER 8

Taxing multinationals or taxing wealthy individuals?

The role of corporate tax in the progressivity of the tax system

Along with the wealth tax, the taxation of multinationals has attracted a lot of attention in recent years. This is hardly surprising: billionaires and multinationals are the most powerful economic actors globally, and have become even more prosperous in the post-Covid world. So much so that it is hard to think of changing the global economic system without a major reform of taxation for both high wealth individuals and large multinational corporations. Unfortunately, these two discussions are often dealt with separately. We believe that it is important to link them up in a more systematic manner than what is usually done.

Generally speaking, corporate tax contributes to the progressivity of the tax system because it is a tax on corporate profits, and corporate profits tend to be concentrated at the top of the income distribution. As such, increasing the corporate income tax rate can increase the progressivity of the overall tax system. To think about this more accurately, several considerations need to be taken into account.

Firstly, corporate tax is a relatively blunt instrument to increase tax progressivity, because it is typically levied at a flat rate. In other words, a profit of €1 billion is taxed at the same rate as a profit of €1 million. In theory, corporate profits could be subject to a progressive tax rate schedule, with higher rates applying to larger profits. The main practical obstacle to this policy is that this would incentivize corporations to split in order to avoid the higher tax brackets. Furthermore, owners of very large businesses are not always richer than owners of smaller businesses. For example, pension funds for the middle-class own parts of the largest businesses whose shares are publicly traded, while smaller start-ups are privately owned by very wealthy founders or venture capitalists. For that reason, although some countries apply lower rates to small corporations, in many countries all corporate profits are subject to the same rate.

Secondly, not all business profits are subject to corporate tax. Some businesses are taxed at the individual level: their profits, exempt from corporate tax, are allocated to shareholders and subject to the progressive personal income tax schedule. This is the case for partnerships and S-corporations in the United States and for business partnerships in Germany, for example. The more profits are taxed at the individual level, the less powerful corporate tax, as an instrument for affecting the progressivity of the tax system, becomes (while personal income tax becomes a more powerful instrument).

Thirdly, the current progressivity of corporate tax system depends on the concentration of equity wealth, which varies across countries and over time depending on the development of wealth inequality. More wealth inequality is typically associated with more concentrated equity ownership. For a given level of overall wealth inequality, equity wealth can be less concentrated in countries with broad-based pension funds than in countries with pay-as-you-go pension systems.

Figure 8.1 illustrates the overall tax progressivity in the United States between 1910 and 2020. It shows that the effective tax rate of the top 1% and top 0,01% of individuals rose steeply between 1910 and 1940 and remained significantly above that of other groups of the population until the 1970s-1980s and dropped significantly afterwards. Over the course of the 20th century, total taxes paid by poorer groups increased. Today, the effective tax rates of the working class, the middle class and top 1% are very close. As a matter of fact, the decline of corporate taxation played an important role in the strong decline of overall tax progressivity in the US.

Figure 8.2 illustrates the progressivity of the corporate tax system in the United States. Let us note that the US is one of the very few countries in which estimates for the joint distribution of income and equity wealth are available[1]. Adults in the top 1% in the highest pre-tax income bracket earned 19% of total U.S. pre-tax income in 2019. They also owned about 30% of the equity wealth of corporations subject to corporate tax, including equities held through pension funds. Therefore, corporate tax, although levied at a flat rate, was progressive. Moreover, as shown by

Figure 8.1   *Total taxes paid by income group in the US. 1910-2020*

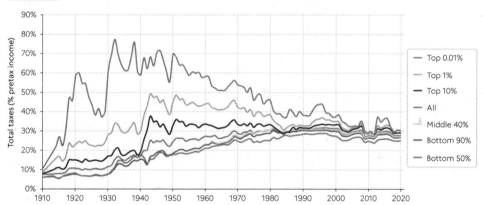

Sources and series: wir2022.wid.world/methodology and Piketty, Saez and Zucman (2018).

Figure 8.2   *Share of the top 1% pre-tax income vs share of corporate tax paid by the top 1% in the US. 1960-2019*

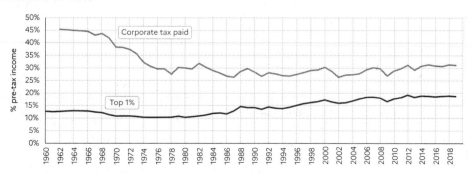

Sources and series: wir2022.wid.world/methodology.

Saez and Zucman[2], corporate taxes are on average more progressive than other U.S. taxes. While the top 1% paid about 30% of the corporate tax, they paid around 21% of all taxes (federal, state, and local) in 2020. This means that an increase in the taxation of corporate profits would introduce greater progressivity in the U.S. tax system.

Figure 8.2 also shows that the U.S. corporate tax was more progressive in the 1960s, when equity wealth was even more concentrated than it actually is today, before the rise in pension funds somewhat broadened equity ownership.

Finally—and perhaps most importantly— corporate tax matters for the progressivity of the tax system as it prevents wealthy individuals from avoiding paying progressive personal income tax. Progressive personal income tax cannot function properly when corporate tax rates are too low: in such case, high-income people can incorporate to report their income through their personal companies (subject to low corporate tax rate) rather than in their individual capacity (subject to high personal income tax rate). This is the reason why in most high-income countries, corporate income tax was born around the same time as personal income tax, in most cases just before or during World War I[3], Although it also comes to serve other purposes—for instance, ensuring that companies contribute to funding the infrastructure they benefit from — corporate tax is consequently fundamentally a backstop: it prevents wealthy individuals from shielding their income from taxation by pretending this income has been earned by a firm.

In sum, corporate tax and personal income tax are supplements. It is hard to have a highly progressive income tax system without a high enough corporate tax. "Taxing corporations" is not a substitute for "taxing wealthy individuals", but a requirement to do so effectively.

The decline in corporate taxation since the 1980s

One of the most striking developments in global tax policy since the 1980s has been the decline in corporate income tax rates. Between 1985 and 2018, the global average statutory corporate tax rate fell by more than half, from 49% to 24%[4]. This trend shows no sign of abating. Since 2013, Japan has cut its rate from 40% to 31%; the United States from 35% to 21%; Italy from 31% to 24%; Hungary from 19% to 9%; a number of Eastern European states are following suit.

Effective corporate income tax rates have also declined, albeit slightly less so. According to recent estimates[5], the global effective average corporate tax rate fell from close to 30% in the 1960s to about 25% in the 1980s and 18% in 2020. The decline was less dramatic than the fall in statutory rates, because of the decline in interest payments (which are deductible from the corporate tax base) and other changes in the tax base. The decline was concentrated in high-income countries. In the United States, for example, the U.S. (federal plus state) effective corporate tax rate on U.S. corporations' profits (for corporations subject to corporate income tax) was halved between 1980 (28%) and 2020 (14%).

This development raises issues. Firstly, it reduces government revenue at a time of growing public deficits and declining public wealth. Secondly, it erodes the progressivity of the tax system. Thirdly, and most importantly, it undermines the sustainability of progressive income taxation. With the decline in corporate tax rates, incorporating is becoming more valuable for high-income individuals[6]. Once they operate as corporations, high-income individuals can shift income from personal income tax to corporate tax. Examples of such shifting abound throughout the world, from Israel to Sweden. Norway or Finland.[7,8,9,10]

The main difference between available historical record and today's situation is that until recently, governments were often careful to limit the gap between top income tax rates and corporate taxes. With the accelerated decline of corporate taxation globally, this gap is increasing and putting new pressure on the personal income tax system. If policymakers want to maintain progressive income taxation, it is essential to stop the 'race to the bottom' regarding corporate tax rates and increase effective taxation of corporate profits.

The promises and pitfalls of minimum taxation

In June 2021, more than 130 countries and jurisdictions agreed that multinational profits would be subject to a minimum tax of 15%.[11]

Such an agreement—whose details have not yet been finalized—would mark a milestone, because it would be the first international agreement establishing a limit on how low tax rates can go. Since the end of the 1990s and under the auspices of the OECD, high-income countries have signed agreements to harmonize their tax bases. The Base Erosion and Profit Shifting (BEPS) process, launched in 2015, tries to achieve a harmonized definition and allocation of taxable profits across countries to prevent some forms of corporate tax avoidance, such as breaching double tax treaties (and inconsistencies therein). But countries face no limits in how they set rates. Any rate, even 0%, is acceptable.

An agreement on minimum taxation would change such situation. Countries in which multinational companies are headquartered could collect a tax on profits made by their subsidiaries to ensure that profits are taxed at an effective rate of at least 15% on a country-by-country basis. For example, if the Irish subsidiary of a French multinational has an effective tax rate of 10% in Ireland, then France could collect a tax of 5% to reach a rate of 15%; if a subsidiary has an effective rate of 0% in Bermuda. France could collect a tax of 15% on the profits booked in Bermuda. Other countries could proceed similarly with their own multinationals. Estimates of such minimum tax levied by countries were produced for the US[12] and European Union countries.[13]

If well implemented, a minimum tax of this kind would remove incentives for countries to offer rates lower than 15%, since these low rates would be offset by additional taxes owed in the parent country. This would alleviate some of the most extreme forms of tax competition such as some countries choosing to offer zero statutory rates and zero effective tax rates Existing estimates suggest that about 36% of multinational profits are transfered to tax havens each year.[14]

However, the agreement is also flawed in several key aspects. Firstly, the rate—15%—is lower than what working-class and middle-class people typically pay in high-income countries. It is also lower than the average statutory rate that corporations face in those places. There is a risk that such a low reference point might trigger an additional reduction in statutory corporate tax rates in the countries that currently apply higher rates, thus reinforcing the 'race to the bottom' with corporate taxation observed since the 1980s. A higher rate (of 25%, for example) would reduce the risk of such a counterproductive outcome.

Secondly, the draft agreement includes carve-outs allowing corporations with sufficient activity in low-tax countries to be exempt from the minimum tax. Specifically, the proposed agreement allows multinationals to reduce profits subject to the minimum tax by an amount equal to 5% of the value of their assets and labor costs in each country. In theory, a minimum tax with no substance carve-out means that some tax rates are considered too low by the international community. A minimum tax with carve-outs, by contrast, reflects a different perspective. With such a tax, a company that owns €1 billion in assets in a country with a 0% corporate tax rate, and makes €50 million in profit in the afore-mentioned country, could still be exempt from taxes. Thus, a minimum tax with carve-outs for capital and employment does not address the 'race to the bottom' in corporate taxation. Worse still, it

incentivizes firms to move capital and employment to places where tax rates are very low, to avoid paying the minimum tax.[15]

Thirdly, the agreement includes a provision that allows corporations to challenge the determination with which countries say they should pay taxes through a secretive arbitration system[16]. Decades of investment arbitrations have demonstrated that "who decide" can be even more important than the written rules themselves. Arbitrators, acting out of the public eye and paid on a case-by-case basis, will have incentives to interpret the new rules in ways that favor corporations and generate future cases for them to arbitrate. If it is deemed necessary to have some type of legal mechanism to resolve international tax disputes, it is preferable to build on the international public law system with tenured judges in the fields of trade and human rights.

Some of these flaws could be addressed by increasing the minimum tax rate and simplifying the proposal, so that it applies to all profits (with no exemption for substance or any other reasons). Table 8.1 shows simulations of how much revenue each EU country and several non-EU countries (including large developing countries such as China) could collect for two minimum tax rates (15% vs. 25%), with and without carve-outs for substance.[17] Among the countries considered, a 25% minimum tax without carve-out could generate four times more revenue than the current OECD-led proposal of 15% with carve-outs: €479 billion per year, as opposed to €111 billion. The table also shows the negative effects of carve-outs introduction, especially as one considers higher rates than 15%. A 25% minimum tax with carve-outs generates 21% less revenue than the same tax without carve-outs.

Big multinational companies—and their shareholders—have been the main winners from globalization: their profits have boomed thanks to the ever-closer integration of world markets. As their activity rose, so did their power and influence; for some of the largest multinationals, this power now rivals that of nation-states. Asking multinational firms to pay €128 billion more in taxes annually when they could pay €479 billion more (with a 25% rate, which would remain low from a historical perspective) is a policy and a political choice which need to be democratically and transparently debated.

Table 8.1　*Revenues of a global minimum tax of 15% and 25%. 2021*

Headquarter country	Revenue gains at a 15% minimum tax in billion €		Revenue gains at a 25% minimum tax in billion €	
	Without carve-out	With carve-out of 5%	Without carve-out	With carve-out of 5%
Austria	3.0	2.2	7.0	5.1
Belgium	10.5	9.7	19.0	17.4
Cyprus	0.3	0.2	0.9	0.8
Czech Republic	0.1	0.1	1.1	0.7
Germany	5.7	4.8	29.1	22.0
Denmark	0.7	0.6	3.5	3.0
Estonia	0.1	0.1	0.4	0.2
Spain	0.7	0.6	12.4	8.6
Finland	1.7	1.5	4.7	4.0
France	4.3	3.8	26.1	20.7
Greece	0.1	0.1	1.6	1.1
Hungary	0.6	0.4	1.9	1.3
Ireland	7.2	6.5	14.0	12.6
Italy	2.7	2.4	11.1	9.1
Luxembourg	4.1	3.4	7.9	6.4
Latvia	0.1	0.1	0.5	0.3
Malta	0.1	0.1	0.3	0.2
Netherlands	0.9	0.7	9.3	6.6
Poland	3.7	2.5	11.0	7.4
Portugal	0.1	0.1	0.6	0.4
Sweden	1.5	1.3	5.3	4.2
Slovenia	0.0	0.0	0.1	0.0
Slovakia	0.0	0.0	0.0	0.0
EU total	48.3	40.9	167.7	132.3
Impact in %		-15.2%		-21.1%

Headquarter country	Revenue gains at a 15% minimum tax in billion €		Revenue gains at a 25% minimum tax in billion €	
	Without carve-out	With carve-out of 5%	Without carve-out	With carve-out of 5%
Australia	2.3	1.9	11.7	8.9
Bermuda	6.2	5.8	14.1	12.4
Brazil	0.9	0.8	7.4	5.7
Canada	16.0	11.6	34.7	24.9
Chile	0.2	0.1	1.2	0.7
China	4.5	3.5	30.2	13.1
Indonesia	0.1	0.0	0.9	0.5
India	0.5	0.4	1.4	1.2
Japan	6.0	5.1	28.7	23.2
Korea	0.0	0.0	6.2	3.8
Mexico	0.5	0.4	1.3	1.1
Norway	0.5	0.4	3.3	2.5
Singapore	0.6	0.6	1.9	1.7
United States	40.7	38.8	165.4	142.5
South Africa	0.6	0.4	3.0	2.3
CbC reporting countries	114.8	100.6	414.3	329.4
Decrease in %		-12.3%		-20.5%
Full sample	127.8	110.8	479.3	376.8
Decrease in %		-13.3%		-21.4%

Sources and series: wir2022.wid.world/methodology, based on Barake et al 2021b, Table 1.

NOTES

[1] Piketty. T.. E. Saez and G. Zucman. 2018. "Distributional National Accounts: Methods and Estimates for the United States." Quarterly Journal of Economics. 133(2). 553–609.

[2] Saez. E. and G. Zucman. 2021. "A Wealth Tax on Corporations' Stock". working paper.

[3] Zucman. G. 2014. "Taxing across borders: Tracking personal wealth and corporate profits." Journal of economic perspectives 28. no. 4: 121-48.

[4] Tørsløv. T. R.. L. S. Wier. and G. Zucman. 2018. "The missing profits of nations." National Bureau of Economic Research. No. w24701.

[5] Bachas. P.. A. Jensen. M. Fisher-Post and G. Zucman. 2021. "Globalization and Factor Income Taxation." working paper.

[6] Saez. E. and G. Zucman. 2019. The Triumph of Injustice: How the Rich Dodge Taxes and How to Make them Pay. New York: W. W. Norton.

[7] Romanov. D. 2006. "The Corporation as a Tax Shelter: Evidence from Recent Israeli Tax Changes." Journal of Public Economics 90. no. 10–11: 1939–1954.

[8] Edmark. K. and R H. Gordon. 2013. "The Choice of Organizational Form by Closely-Held Firms in Sweden: Tax Versus Non-Tax Determinants." Industrial and Corporate Change 22. no. 1: 219–243.

[9] Alstadsæter. A. 2010. "Small Corporations Income Shifting Through Choice of Ownership Structure—A Norwegian Case." Finnish Economic Papers 23. no. 2: 73–87.

[10] Pirttilä. J.. and H. Selin. 2011. "Income Shifting within a Dual Income Tax System: Evidence from the Finnish Tax Reform of 1993." Scandinavian Journal of Economics 113. no. 1: 120–144.

[11] OECD. 2021. "Statement on a Two-Pillar Solution to Address the Tax Challenges Arising From the Digitalisation of the Economy". https://www.oecd.org/tax/beps/statement-on-a-two-pillar-solution-to-address-the-tax-challenges-arising-from-the-digitalisation-of-the-economy-july-2021.pdf

[12] Clausing. K.. E. Saez. and G. Zucman. 2021. "Ending Corporate Tax Avoidance and Tax Competition: A Plan to Collect the Tax Deficit of Multinationals." working paper. UC Berkeley and UCLA.

[13] Baraké. M.. P.-E. Chouc. T. Neef and G. Zucman. 2021a. "Collecting the Tax Deficit of Multinational Companies: Simulations for the European Union." EU Tax Observatory Report nº1.

[14] Tørsløv. Wier. and Zucman. "The missing profits of nations."

[15] Baraké. M.. P.-E. Chouc. T. Neef and G. Zucman. 2021b. "Minimizing the Minimum Tax? The Critical Effect of Substance Carve-Outs." EU Tax Observatory Note.

[16] Tucker. T. N.. J. E. Stiglitz and G. Zucman. September 2021. "Ending the Race to the Bottom". Foreign Affairs.

[17] The table is taken from Baraké. Chouc. Neef and Zucman. "Minimizing the Minimum Tax?

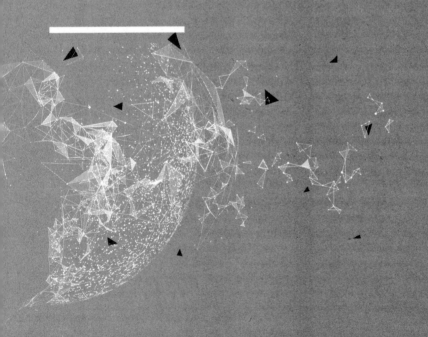

CHAPTER 9
Global vs unilateral perspectives on tax justice

To regulate inequality and address the revenue needs arising from the Covid-19 pandemic, climate change, and public investment (in healthcare, education, and infrastructure), international cooperation is paramount. Over the last decade, there has been progress in some areas of international tax cooperation: more information sharing among countries, and steps towards a fight against the most aggressive forms of tax competition (see Chapter 8) have been taken. However, more ambitious measures—such as a minimum tax on multinational profits, a transnational tax on the very wealthy, or a global carbon tax—may take a long time to materialize. In that context, it is useful to ask what can be done unilaterally by individual countries and how useful such unilateral initiatives can be. It is also critical to design better indicators in order to be able to assess progress in favor of tax justice (or the lack thereof).

Usefulness of unilateral approaches: the case of FATCA

A good example of how useful unilateral approaches can be is given by the Foreign Account Tax Compliance Act (FATCA). For a long time, the notion that offshore tax evasion could be dealt with effectively was viewed with caution. If some countries want to apply strict bank secrecy rules, aren't they entitled to do so, and what could make them review their policies? This changed in 2010, when the United States unilaterally enacted FATCA, which imposes an automatic exchange of data between foreign banks and the US tax authority. Financial institutions throughout the world must identify who, among their clients, are American taxpayers and tell the Internal Revenue Services (IRS) what each person has on their bank accounts and what their income earned is. Failure to take part in this program carries stiff economic sanctions: a 30% tax on all dividends and interest income paid to the uncooperative financial institutions, collected by the US.[1]

This threat has proven effective in securing (formal) cooperation from most of the world's tax havens and financial institutions. Countries such as Switzerland which had refused for decades to send bank information to foreign tax authorities quickly started to do so. Almost overnight, bank secrecy, which had been depicted as immortal, was abolished – at least partly. Some large countries were initially skeptical and there are still some visible cracks in the system nowadays, but by and large, the 30% withholding tax has served as a sufficiently powerful deterrent.

This U.S. initiative paved the way for key developments in tax information sharing across the globe. In 2011, the European Union adopted its own version of FATCA, known as DAC (Directive on Administrative Co-operation). Most importantly, the OECD developed the Common Reporting Standards (CRS) in 2014. The CRS sets out guidelines and procedures for countries to share financial and tax information in a standardized and automatic manner. This is the key novelty of the CRS: an exchange of information between countries absent prior suspicion of fraud by tax administrations. Automatically accessing standardized tax data from other countries is essential for tax authorities, as international requests can otherwise take up to several months or years to be processed—when processed at all. Under CRS, participants must automatically provide information, such as taxpayers' identification, account numbers, account value, and income earned.

The CRS was adopted by more than 100 countries and started to be implemented in 2017 and 2018. Main tax havens, including Luxembourg, Singapore, and the Cayman Islands, are now part of this new form of cooperation. Automatic sharing of bank information has therefore become an global standard. in that respect, unilateral action from one large country eventually led to the emergence of a new form of international cooperation while it was still regarded as a utopian idea ten years ago.

As detailed below, this framework still has loopholes. The lack of information provided by countries makes it impossible to provide a thorough assessment of the CRS effectiveness so far. Furthermore, there is a lack of controls and sanctions for non-compliant financial institutions. It would be naïve to believe that the same institutions, which facilitated tax fraud for decades—sometimes taking extreme steps such as smuggling diamonds in toothpaste tubes or handing out bank statements concealed in sports magazines[2]—are now in all honestly cooperating with global tax authorities. There is also an incentive problem: facilitating tax evasion can generate substantial revenue for some legal and financial intermediaries. Besides, there is also an information problem. Due to financial opacity, it has become easy for wealthy tax evaders to disconnect themselves from their assets, by using trusts, foundations, shell companies, and other intermediaries. Although the CRS mandates financial institutions to look into these intermediaries to identify beneficial owners and forward that information to the relevant tax authority, it remains unclear whether these rules are well applied in practice.

Notwithstanding these limitations, the automatic exchange of bank information marks a major positive break with earlier practices. Before the Great Recession of 2008-2009, hardly any data was exchanged between banks in tax havens and other countries' tax authorities. Hiding wealth abroad, in that context, was easy. Doing so nowadays requires a higher degree of sophistication and determination. The experience of FATCA suggests that unilateral action can make transformative forms of coordination emerge in a relatively short time span.

Estimates of unilateral vs. multilateral tax deficit collection

Could the experience of FATCA be replicated to address corporate profit shift to tax havens? Saez and Zucman[3] discuss how a country can unilaterally collect multinational tax deficit—defined as the difference between what this multinational currently pays in taxes, and what it would have to pay if it were subject to minimum effective taxation in each country where it operates. Baraké and co-authors[4] discuss various ways for EU countries to collect multinational tax deficit, ranging from a perfect international tax cooperation to unilateral action. The following, adapted from Baraké and co-authors[5], clarifies the implications of such scenarios within the EU framework.

To start with, Baraké and co-authors[6] consider a global agreement on a minimum tax of the sort, as currently being discussed by the OECD (see Chapter 8). In this scenario, each EU country collects its own multinationals' tax deficit. For instance, if the internationally agreed minimum tax rate is 25% and a German company has an effective tax rate of 10% on the profits it records in Singapore, Germany would then impose an additional tax of 15% on such profits to reach an effective rate of 25%. More generally, Germany would collect extra taxes so that its multinationals pay at least 25% in taxes on the profits they book in each country. Other nations would proceed similarly. Such a minimum tax of 25% would have increased corporate income tax revenue in the European Union by about €170 billion in 2021. This sum accounts for more than half of the total corporate tax revenue currently collected in the European Union and 12% of total EU healthcare spending.

Secondly, Baraké and co-authors[7] posit an incomplete international agreement in which only EU countries apply a minimum tax, while non-EU countries do not change their tax policies. In this scenario, each EU country collects its own multinationals' tax deficit (like in the first scenario), as well as a portion of the tax deficit of multinationals incorporated outside of the European Union,

based on the destination of sales. For example, if a British company makes 20% of its sales in Germany, Germany would then collect 20% of this company's tax deficit. In such a scenario, using a 25% rate to compute each multinational's tax deficit would mean that the European Union would increase its corporate tax revenues by about €200 billion. Out of this total, €170 billion would come from collecting EU multinationals tax deficit; an additional €30 billion would come from collecting a portion of non-EU multinationals tax deficit.

Lastly, Baraké and co-authors[8] estimate how much revenue each EU country could unilaterally collect, assuming all other countries keep their current tax policy unchanged. This corresponds to a "first mover" scenario, in which one country alone decides to collect multinational companies' tax deficit. The first mover would collect the full tax deficit of its own multinationals, plus a portion (proportional to the destination of sales) of the tax deficit of all foreign multinationals, based on a reference rate of 25%. A first mover in the European Union would increase corporate tax revenue by close to 70% compared to current corporate tax collection. Acting as a "first mover" can yield substantial tax revenue. Of course, a unilateral approach would incentivize existing companies to change nationality— so-called corporate inversions. However, countries have a considerable degree of discretion when defining corporate nationality. A unilateral move would need to go hand in hand with a tightening of regulations to prevent companies from changing nationality.

This analysis has two major implications. First of all, although international coordination is always preferable, a unilateral move from a single state (or a group of states) would push other EU countries to also collect multinationals' tax deficit—since not doing so would be tantamount to leaving tax revenue on the table for first movers to grab. This could pave the way for an ambitious agreement on a high minimum tax within the European Union, and then globally. Unilateral action can play a transformative role, by triggering a "race to the top" in which more and more countries act as "last resort tax collectors" and collect multinational companies tax deficit. A similar approach could be developed to collect billionaires' tax deficit, combining bold transparency requirements and high wealth taxes.

Secondly, refusing international coordination is unlikely to be a sustainable solution, because other countries can always choose to collect taxes that tax havens choose not to collect. This means that the development strategy of tax havens, predicated on low-tax rates, may be unstable. Tax competition is a political choice. Since high-tax countries tend to lose tax revenue, capital, and employment because of tax competition, it is not impossible that some of these countries may try to make different choices—such as unilaterally taxing profits booked in tax havens— in the future. This would make it less financially rewarding for multinational companies to book profits in tax havens, making it in turn less beneficial to tax havens themselves to offer low rates.

What this requires, however, is a stronger political will to curb tax evasion and promote tax justice than what has been observed until now. In particular, individual countries in Europe would need to take unilateral actions, while also recommending an ambitious framework for international cooperation with other countries. Without unilateral action, it is hard to see how the European Union (and the world) will be able to escape the "unanimity trap" which was put in place in the past.

Anti-tax evasion schemes contain many loopholes and cannot be assessed

Together with multinationals' taxation, there has been ample discussion in recent years about global tax evasion and the lack of financial transparency around cross-border financial assets. Following the 2008 financial crisis and the subsequent high profile tax evasion "stories", governments around the world and international organizations claimed that they had made significant progress in the fight against tax evasion. Before the financial crisis of 2008, tax havens typically refused to share any information with foreign tax authorities. Since then, several reforms have been initiated and contributed to changing the rules of the game as regards to the transfer of information between countries. They either took the form of unilateral processes (eg. FATCA) or multilateral ones (eg. CRS, see above).

By 2020, 107 countries took part in the CRS, including notable tax havens (such as Switzerland). The total amount of assets reported in 2019 reached $11.2 trillion, with 84 million accounts reported. As a comparison, the estimated amount of missing portfolio liabilities was $4.5 trillion in the early 2010s.[9] These developments have led the OECD and several news organizations worldwide to trumpet the "end of bank secrecy".[10] Unfortunately, the reality is not as bright.

Today, tax evaders can bypass the CRS in at least three different ways: investing in non-participatory countries, investing in countries with a low rate of CRS enforcement, or investing in bodies that are not subject to reporting.

Firstly, not all countries have agreed to the CRS. As of now, most African countries as well as the USA are not part of this exchange of information . It is worth mentioning that the USA, despite having cracked down on other tax havens over the past few years, and despite FATCA, ranks second in the Financial Secrecy Index[11] (after the Cayman Islands and ahead of Switzerland). As a matter of fact, the USA hosts tax havens, such as Delaware, Nevada and Wyoming. Recent research has shown that the CRS is likely to have increased the level of cross-border deposits in the USA compared to other countries. A possible explanation is that the use of shell companies incorporated in the USA has increased after the CRS[12] was introduced.[13]

Secondly, several countries, which have signed the CRS, are poorly equipped to properly enforce it and to make sure that banks and financial institutions properly report information to tax authorities. Overall, non-compliance with CRS standards remains difficult to monitor nowadays and threats of sanctions appear to be limited.

Thirdly, some institutions or assets are still not subject to reporting requirements. This mechanism has been improved since 2014 to fill some of the loopholes, but participating countries can still decide to exclude certain institutions from the list (if these are not likely to participate in tax evasion, but this assessment largely depends on the country's commitment to seriously do so). Bearing these limitations in mind, we would like to stress that the CRS does represent an improvement from the pre-2010 situation and shows that multilateral cooperation is possible in tax matters. The main issue with the CRS is that it is impossible for independent observers to assess how large or how small these improvements have been, because tax authorities do not disclose the information required to properly track basic progress towards tax justice.

Properly assessing the road towards tax transparency: publishing basic information

If the exchange of information across countries as per the CRS or FATCA were effective, tax authorities across the globe should then be in a position to release key information about their residents' wealth, as well as the amount of (both on-shore and offshore) taxes they pay. Nonetheless, such basic information is not published by countries participating in the CRS. This situation is particularly problematic in terms of governments' accountability and of public policy assessment. No government could claim victory over unemployment, without publishing detailed employment statistics by sector.

To properly assess progress in the fight against tax evasion, governments across the world should publicly release annual data on how many taxpayers there are in each income and wealth tax bracket and how much taxes they pay. Should the CRS work effectively, such information would be easily available. Table 9.1AB below shows the case of wealth (a similar table should be published for income), with different wealth and income tax brackets. For each of these brackets, tax authorities should publish information related to the number of individuals and the breakdown of their income, wealth and other taxes.

Towards a global asset register

Publishing basic information regarding tax transparency will certainly contribute to assessing the effectiveness of CRS or FATCA initiatives and can help to improve them. Putting an end to tax evasion across the world will however require more than the CRS or FATCA.

As a matter of fact, many tax havens and offshore financial institutions do not have incentives to provide accurate information, as they do not face large enough sanctions for non- or poor compliance. In addition, a large and growing fraction of offshore wealth is held by intertwined shell companies, trusts, and foundations, which disconnect assets from their actual owners. This makes it easy for offshore banks to falsely claim that they do not have any European,

American, or Asian clients—while in fact such individuals are the beneficial owners of the assets held by the very same shell companies. Therefore, the best way to end tax evasion across the world is to establish a global financial register. It would allow tax and regulatory agencies to check if taxpayers properly report assets and capital income regardless of whatever information offshore financial institutions are willing to provide tax authorities. It would also allow governments to close corporate tax loopholes by enforcing a fair distribution of tax revenue globally for corporations with increasingly complex overseas operations. A global financial register could also serve as the informational basis for creating of a global wealth tax. Establishing such a register would not, however, mean that asset ownership would be disclosed to the general public. Such information could remain confidential in the same way as current income tax data is kept confidential.

Drawing up a global financial register would in fact be facilitated by the above-mentioned CRS and FATCA. It would however also provide additional sources of crucial financial information, gathered by (mostly private) financial institutions known as Central Securities Depositories (CSD). CSDs are the bookkeepers of equities and bonds issued by corporations and governments. They can maintain accounts as end-investor segregated accounts—which is the most transparent model, as it connects an individual to an asset. Or they can maintain omnibus accounts—a less transparent model, given that assets held by different investors are lumped into a single account under the name of a financial intermediary, making it difficult to identify end-investors. (See Box 9.1)

One key issue with using CSDs as the building block of a global financial register is that omnibus accounts prevail in most large western markets. (The Depository Trust Company in the United States and Clearstream in Europe, for instance, operate with omnibus accounts.) However, technical solutions facilitated by developments in information technologies already exist to allow for the identification of end asset holders in large western CSDs. Moreover, in certain countries such as Norway, or large emerging markets such as China and South Africa, CSDs operate through systems which allow for the identification of end asset owners. In short, creating a global financial register is not facing any insuperable technical problems, and groups of countries such as the European Union (and possibly the United States) could initiate the creation of such a register. The European Commission has recently launched a ·feasibility study for establishing such a register.

Properly assessing the road towards tax transparency: publishing basic information

Table 9.1a   *Number of individuals, Wealth and Taxes paid by wealth bracket*

Net wealth bracket (€)	Number of individuals	incl. number of residents	incl. number of non-residents	Total net wealth	incl. residents	incl. non-residents	Wealth taxes				Income taxes		
							Total wealth taxes	incl. wealth and property tax	incl. capital gains tax	incl. inheritance & estate tax	Total income taxes	incl. personal income tax	incl. corp. income taxes
0-10k													
10k-100k													
100k-1m													
1m-10m													
10m-100m				*Data to be systematically published by governments*									
100m-1bn													
1bn-5bn													
5bn-10bn													
10bn+													

Table 9.1b   *Wealth and income composition by wealth bracket*

Net wealth bracket (€)	Wealth										Income		
	Total wealth	incl. currency & deposits	incl. bonds & loans	incl. equities & fund shares	incl. pension funds & life insur.	incl. real estate	incl. business & other non-fin. assets	incl. debt	incl. total domestic assets	incl. total foreign assets	Total income	incl. capital income	incl. labor income
0-10k													
10k-100k													
100k-1m													
1m-10m													
10m-100m					*Data to be systematically*								
100m-1bn					*published by governments*								
1bn-5bn													
5bn-10bn													
10bn+													

Summary: In order to track inequality, progress toward global financial transparency and tax justice, all countries should commit to publish on an annual basis the following tables. This applies in particular to the countries participating to the various international discussion groups on these issues, in particular those coordinated by OECD on CRS (Common Reporting Standards on cross-border financial assets) and BEPS (Base Erosion and Profit Shifting on corporate taxation).
Net wealth: total assets (real estate, business, financial, etc.), net of debt. For coutry residents, all domestic and foreign assets should be included. For non-residents, all domestic assets should be included (in particuler real estate assets located in the country, as well as all financial assets related to firms and economic activites conducted in the country). To the extent possible, their foreign assets should also be included.

Box 9.1   Central Security Depositories as building blocks for a global financial register

This box draws upon Nougayrède's work, the World Inequality Report 2018 and the World Inequality Database recent updates[14,15,16].

In the modern financial system, shares and bonds issued by corporations no longer are paper certificates but electronic account entries. Holding chains are no longer direct—that is, they do not connect issuers directly with investors, but involve several intermediaries, often located in different countries. Central Securities Depositories (CSDs) are at the top of the chain, immediately after issuers.

Their role is to record ownership of financial securities and sometimes handle transaction settlement. CSD clients are domestic financial institutions in the issuer country, foreign financial institutions, and other CSDs. After CSD participants, there are several other layers of financial intermediaries, and at the end of the chain comes a final intermediary; often a bank, which has a relationship with the investors in question.

Because so many intermediaries are involved, issuers of financial securities are disconnected from end-investors; public companies that issue securities no longer know who their shareholders or bondholders are. CSDs, as a part of the chain of financial intermediation, both enable and blur this relationship. The system was not intentionally designed for anonymity, but it has evolved in this way over the years because of how complex regulations are cross-border securities trading. The evolution towards non-transparency has also been fostered by the fact that this is a highly technical topic and that it has drawn limited attention among the media or public opinion over the past few years.

Non-transparent accounts prevail in most western CSDs.

There are two broad types of accounts in the CSD world. "Segregated accounts" allow one to hold securities in distinct accounts, opened in the name of the individual end-investors. Consequently, this model allows for transparency. The opposite model is that of "omnibus accounts" (or in the USA, "street name registration") where securities belonging to several investors are pooled together into one account under the name of a single account-holder, usually a financial intermediary, thereby blurring end-investors' identity.

One of the key issues for drawing up a global financial register is that non-transparent accounting (that is, "omnibus accounts") prevails in most western markets. For instance, the US CSD, the Depository Trust Company (DTC), uses omnibus accounts. In its books, the DTC only identifies brokerage firms and other intermediaries, but not the end owners of US stocks and bonds. "Omnibus accounts" also prevail in most European countries—in particular, within Euroclear and Clearstream CSDs. This makes it difficult to compile a global financial register based on existing western CSDs.

However, more transparency is possible.

More transparency within western CSDs can however be envisioned. The current system creates a number of risks for the financial industry, of which it is very much aware. In 2014, Clearstream Banking in Luxembourg agreed upon a $152 million settlement with the US Treasury, following allegations that it held $2.8 billion in US securities in an omnibus account for the benefit of the Central Bank of Iran, which was subject to US sanctions. As a result, the securities industry has been discussing a number of options which could be put in place to allow for greater transparency of information on end-investors. These might include discontinuing the use of omnibus accounts and introducing new information transfer standards (as is done in the payments industry) or ex-post audit trails, which would enable information on the identity of the end beneficiary of financial transactions to circulate throughout the chain. New technologies (such as blockchain) could also enhance traceability.

In fact, transparent market infrastructures already exist today in both high income and emerging countries. In Norway, the CSD lists all individual shareholders in domestic companies, acts as formal corporate registrar, and reports back directly to tax authorities while protecting them. In China, the China Securities Depository Clearing Corporation Limited ("Chinaclear") operates a fully transparent system for shares issued by Chinese companies and held by domestic Chinese investors. At the end of 2015, it held $8 trillion worth of securities in custody, roughly the size of the CSDs in France, Germany, and the UK, and maintained securities accounts for 99 million end-investors. Some segregation functionalities already exist within some of the larger western CSDs (like DTC or Euroclear), and could be expanded. Many believe that segregated CSD accounting would push for better corporate governance by giving a greater voice to small investors. All of this suggests that more could be done in large western CSDs to introduce greater investor transparency.

NOTES

[1] Zucman, G. 2015. "The Hidden Wealth of Nations: The Scourge of Tax Havens," The University of Chicago Press.

[2] Zucman, G. 2014. "Taxing across borders: Tracking personal wealth and corporate profits." Journal of economic perspectives 28, no. 4: 121-48.

[3] Saez, E. and G. Zucman. 2019. "The Triumph of Injustice: How the Rich Dodge Taxes and How to Make them Pay." New York: W. W. Norton.

[4] Baraké, Mona, P.-E. Chouc, T. Neef and G. Zucman. 2021. "Collecting the Tax Deficit of Multinational Companies: Simulations for the European Union." EU Tax Observatory Report n°1.

[5] Baraké et al. "Collecting the Tax Deficit of Multinational Companies".

[6] Baraké et al. "Collecting the Tax Deficit of Multinational Companies"

[7] Baraké et al. "Collecting the Tax Deficit of Multinational Companies"

[8] Baraké et al. "Collecting the Tax Deficit of Multinational Companies"

[9] Chiochetti, A. 2020. "The effect of automatic exchange of information on evaded wealth", PSE Master Thesis, 2020;

Zucman, G. 2013. "The Missing Wealth of Nations", The Quarterly Journal of Economics.

[10] See for e.g. Michel, A. 7 June 2019. "L'OCDE constate une importante décrue des dépôts bancaires dans les paradis fiscaux". Le Monde: They noted an "important reduction of bank deposits in tax havens". Unfortunately, deposits only represent a small fraction (5-10%) of assets held in tax havens, and a reduction in deposits can mask an increase in other forms of assets.

[11] The Financial Secrecy Index is available here https://fsi.taxjustice.net/en/. It is published by the Tax Justice Network and complements the Inequality Transparency Index published by the World Inequality Lab on WID.world.

[12] Casi-Eberhard, E., C. Spengel and B. Stage. 2019. Cross-Border Tax Evasion after the Common Reporting Standard: Game Over? ZEW-Centre for European Economic Research Discussion Paper, 18-036.

[13] To address this issue, the OECD took steps in 2017 to counter asset shifting to US banks, by including in reporting FIs entities which advise their clients to open a bank account in non-reporting jurisdictions, and continue to do so.

[14] Nougayrède, D. 2017. "Towards Global Financial Register? The Case for End Investor Transparency in Central Securities Depositories". Journal of Financial Regulation; See Alvaredo, F., L. Chancel, T. Piketty, E. Saez, G. Zucman. 2018. World Inequality Report 2018, Cambridge: Harvard University Press.

[15] See Alvaredo et al. World Inequality Report 2018.

[16] See World Inequality Database: www.wid.world

CHAPTER 10
Emancipation, redistribution and sustainability

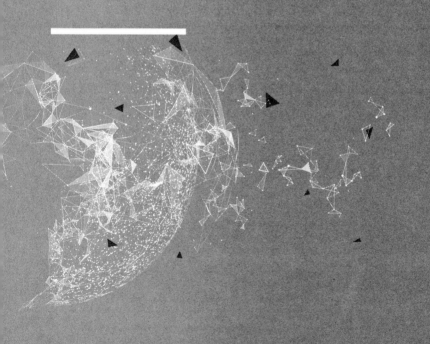

WORLD
INEQUALITY
REPORT
2022

Parts of this chapter are adapted from T. Piketty "A brief history of inequality" (2022), Harvard University Press

The 20th century was marked by a remarkable increase in social progress, redistribution, and economic emancipation policies in high-income countries. This vast movement both benefited from and contributed to the "Golden age of growth" in the West observed between 1950 and 1980. Since the early 1980s, the rise of the Welfare State has come to a halt in rich countries while inequality has been increasing in most countries. In developing and emerging countries, the rise of social spending and redistribution was relatively slow over the past forty years. While hundreds of millions of people were lifted out of extreme poverty, hundreds of millions of individuals still struggle to earn subsistence income levels.[1] The weakness of the Welfare State in many parts of the world raises significant issues at a time when important healthcare, education or infrastructure investments are needed to face the challenges of the 21st century.

The rise of the Welfare State in rich countries (1910-1980)

To better understand the policy levers needed to tackle economic, social, healthcare or environmental inequalities, let us first briefly discuss what we mean by "Welfare State". Welfare States are essentially an invention of the past century. Indeed, at the beginning of the 20th century, total government revenue in rich countries amounted to 5-10% of national income. Revenue was mostly used to fund police, military and administrative functions of governments. Public social spending (on healthcare, education or other forms of support for the worse-off) barely existed. Today, total government revenue account for 30-50% of national income in rich countries and a significant part is allocated to social expenditures (see below). Put differently, a third to a half of all incomes are taxed by governments in rich countries, and a large part of these taxes finds its way back into the economy in the form of social spending.

As a matter of fact, the remarkable increase in tax revenue was coupled with a considerable rise in public education, retirement, and healthcare spending. Public education spending accounted for just 1.2% of national income in 1910 and rose to 6% in 1980 in European countries (Figure 10.1) whereas healthcare spending accounted for 0.2% of national income in 1910 and rose to 7-9% by 1980.

Retirement and disability pensions grew from almost nothing in 1910 to about 11% of national income in 2020. Other social spending (including unemployment insurance benefits, family benefits, housing support) were almost inexistent in 1910 and reached 6-7% of national income in 1980. Since 1980, the progress of the Welfare State has halted. There were some moderate increases in healthcare and retirement spending, but considerably lower than those observed before 1980. In North America, if certain social programs were developed or enhanced over the past decades, overall government tax revenue actually declined between 1980 and the eve of the Covid-crisis.

What drove such an increase in taxes and social spending between 1910 and 1980 and why did it stop thereafter? One of the most powerful drives behind this increase has been the historical ground gained by universal suffrage in the West (first extended to all adult males, then to women and minorities) and the development of new political and social mobilization strategies. In the United Kingdom, the Labor Party won an absolute majority of seats in the 1945 elections and set up the NHS (National Healthcare Service) and a far-reaching system of social insurance. The most aristocratic country in Europe, which until the constitutional crisis of 1909 had been ruled by an aristocratic elite sitting in the House of Lords, became the one country in Europe where profound social reforms were implemented by a workers' party. When Sweden, a country where voting rights used to be based on wealth ownership in the 19th and early 20th centuries, introduced

universal suffrage, workers brought the Social Democrats to power almost continuously from 1932. In France, the Popular Front set up paid holidays in 1936, and due to the strong presence of Communists and Socialists in Parliament and in the government, Social Security was imposed in 1945. In the United States, a popular coalition brought the Democrats to power in 1932 with the New Deal, thereby challenging existing laissez-faire dogmas and the power of the elite.

Two observations should be made on the social revolution which happened in rich countries between 1910-1980. To begin with, for the first time in history at this scale, the state escaped the exclusive control of the ruling classes. This laid the foundations of universal suffrage, parliamentary and representative democracy, electoral processes and political alternance, spurred by an independent press and the trade union movement. This democratic revolution was indeed

Figure 10.1 *The rise of the Welfare State in European countries, 1870-2020*

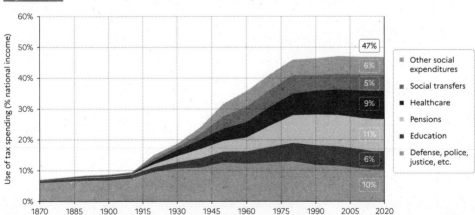

Interpretation: *In 2020, tax revenue represented 47% of national income in Western Europe, on average. 10% of resources were spent on defense, police & justice, 6% on education, 11% on pensions, 9% on healthcare, 5% on social transfers and 6% on other social spending (housing, etc.). Before 1914, defense, police and justice represented the vast majority of government spending. **Sources and series:** wir2022.wid.world/methodology and Piketty (2021).*

highly imperfect: it is not until the 1950s-1960s that women and minorities got the right to vote in all western democracies, and neither did the colonies. It was nonetheless a radical break from the late 19th and early 20th centuries.

Secondly, it shows that modern societies can escape the generalized commodification of goods, lands and human beings[2]. Vast sectors of the economy, starting with education and healthcare, and partly housing, transport, and energy, were organized independent of market logic, with various systems of public employment, mutual or non-profit structures, subsidies and tax-financed investments. Not only did it work, but it worked much more efficiently than the capitalist private sector. Even though some lobbyists continue to claim the opposite (for obvious reasons, and sometimes effectively to a certain extent), evidence shows

that European-style public systems are both less costly and more efficient in terms of well-being and life expectancy than private companies in the United States[3]. In the education sector, hardly anyone offered to replace schools, colleges or universities with companies governed only answering to purely capitalist logic. Whatever the disputes and legitimate debates on improvements to be made in these sectors, no major political movement in the West suggested to return to the pre-1914 situation, when tax revenue accounted for less than 10% of national income and public social spending was almost nonexistent.

The limited rise of tax revenue and public spending in emerging countries since 1980

Let us now turn to tax revenue and spending in low-income countries. In many emerging countries, taxes

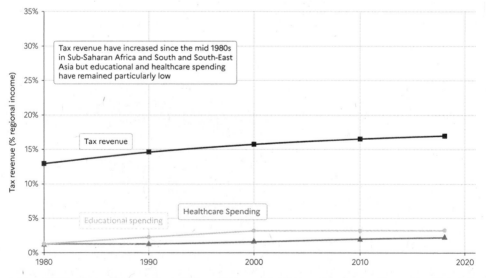

Figure 10.2a   *Tax revenue and public spending on healthcare and education in Sub-Saharan Africa and South and South East Asia 1980-2018*

Interpretation: *The graph shows the evolution of taxes and public spending on education and health in Sub-Saharan African and South and South East Asia.* **Sources and series:** *wir2022.wid.world/methodology.*

and spending have been increasing over the past forty years, but to a much lesser extent than in the West in the 20th century–for that matter in many low-income countries, government revenue even stagnated or declined.

Government revenue in India and China accounted for 10-15% of national income in 1980, i.e. the same level as in rich countries about 60 years before. Since 1980, government tax revenue in these countries has risen to 15-20% of national income. While this represents a significant increase, it has been much slower than the increase observed in rich countries between 1920 and 1960 (where government revenue rose from 10-15% to 30-35% of national income). In Russia and Central Asia, revenue declined from 35% in the mid-1990s, after the collapse of the Soviet Block, to 30% today. In Sub Saharan Africa, tax revenue decreased over the same period, from a little less than 19% to 15%.

Spending on healthcare and education generally follow the overall pattern of tax revenue: an increase in tax revenue means an increase spending in these areas. Public spending increased in emerging countries, such China and Brazil, between 1980 and 2020 (from around 1% to 4% of national income). This increase certainly contributed to combatting extreme poverty, containing inequality and generating new income growth opportunities in these countries.[4] Over the same period of time, spending also increased in the rest of Latin America, but was much more limited in South East Asia. In India, it went from slightly below 1% to slightly over 1% of national

income and increased from 1% to 1.8% in Indonesia. Overall, since 2000, public healthcare spending has decreased in low-income countries, from around 1.3% to 1% of national income.[5]

The stagnation of global tax revenue and social expenditure (1980-2020)

At the global level, tax revenue has barely evolved since 1980, fluctuating around 25% of global income between 1980 and today. Global public spending on education has stagnated (at around 5% of global income) and public spending on healthcare has only slightly increased (from 3% in 1980 to about 5% of global income today) (Figure 10.2b). The trend in global social spending over the past four decades is now markedly different from the one observed between 1950 and 1980 and even more so between 1920 and 1980, when global tax revenue and social spending rose substantially, driven by the vast expansion of high-income countries.[6]

Lessons from failed trickle-down economics

Why has global tax revenue stagnated – and why has spending on education and increased ever so slightly since the 1980s? One of the main reasons for limiting tax revenue is that taxes curb economic growth. Taxation, it is argued, distorts economic incentives, which therefore prevents markets from functioning properly and reaching their full potential. Obviously, some taxation levels hamper economic activity. However, evidence shows that periods of tax expansion in high-

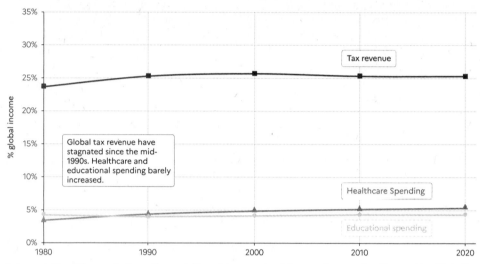

Figure 10.2b   *Global tax revenue and global public spending on healthcare and education (1980-2020)*

*Interpretation: The graph shows the evolution of taxes and public spending on education and health in the world. **Sources and series:** wir2022.wid.world/methodology.*

income countries have not harmed economic growth. As a matter of fact, periods of tax expansion and high progressive taxation boosted Europe and the USA in terms of growth and employment more than periods of low tax progressivity or tax stagnation.

Tax expansion and social spending in the West was accompanied by steep increases in progressive taxes. Progressive tax rates (whether on income or capital) allowed economic actors to be taxed based on their capabilities, thereby generating a significant amount of revenue. Progressive taxation also helps to ensure that tax systems appear fair to taxpayers. Historically, legislators across the world have coupled the general rise of government revenue with highly progressive taxes. Between 1950 and 1980, the average top marginal income tax rate in high-income countries amounted to 72%. In the USA, this average reached 92% between

1951 and 1963, and the top estate tax rate averaged 80% between the early 1940s and the mid-1970s. High rates were also observed in the UK, Germany, Japan, as well as in France and in other high-income or emerging countries (see Figure 10.3).

Figure 10.4 shows that after the USA's top income earners saw their taxes reduced substantially in the 1980s, GDP growth has not increased. Incidentally, growth has been significantly lower after these sizeable tax cuts rather than before them. Many factors, other than tax rates (educational expenses, labor regulations, industrial policy, etc.), impact macroeconomic growth rates, but the large-scale, real-life tax experiments carried out over the 1980-2020 period suggest that trickle-down economics has not lived up to its promises. The lack of clear linkages between tax cuts for the wealthy and positive effects on growth and employment has also been demonstrated in recent

Figure 10.3   *Progressive income tax rates across the world, 1900-2021*

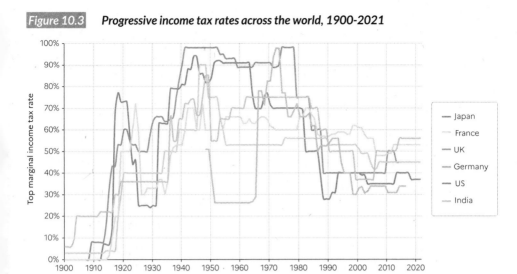

Interpretation: The graph shows the evolution of the top marginal income tax rate across various countries.
Sources and series: wir2022.wid.world/methodology.

Figure 10.4   *Progressive income taxation and growth, 1870-2020*

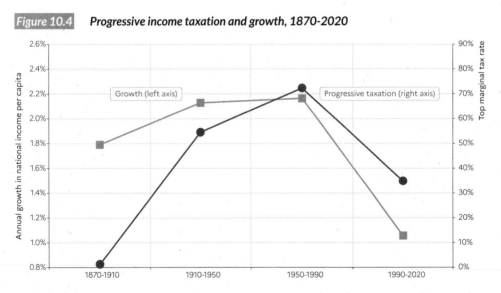

*Interpretation: In the US, growth in national income per capita went from 2.2% per annum)from 1950 to 1990, to 1.1% per annum between 1990 and 2020, while the top marginal income tax rate was reduced from 72% to 35% in the same period. The boost in growth that was promised at the time of the cuts to the top marginal tax rate did not occur. **Sources and series:** wir2022.wid.world/methodology and Piketty (2021).*

theoretical and empirical studies carried out in many countries.[7]

Drawing on the lessons learned from the failure of trickle-down economics suggests adopting a much more pragmatic approach to taxation, based on a sound and transparent empirical analysis of taxation.

The 1980-2020s have been marked by a rise of tax evasion, further undermining tax progressivity

Another reason explaining why social expenditures recorded a sluggish growth across the world is the rise of tax evasion, which has undermined tax progressivity as well as overall support for taxation. Some wondered: "If certain taxpayers can evade taxes, why should we pay any?". The ascent of tax evasion has been facilitated by the rise of financial globalization and the liberalization of cross-border capital flows (with no tax,

social or regulatory counterparts). Between 1995 and 2020, global financial assets rose from 540% to 960% of global income and increased faster than aggregate wealth.[8] In other words, the global economy is increasingly financialized. This rise occurred with little or no government control over financial flows and paved the way for tax evasion from wealthy individuals and multinationals.[9]

Nowadays, global household wealth held in tax havens is estimated at around 10% of global GDP. While there is limited empirical data to prove this, available evidence suggests that global offshore wealth has significantly increased since the 1980s. In 1980, less than 2% of US equity market capitalization was booked in tax havens and this percentage rose close to 10% in the early 2010s.[10]

While governments have been extremely slow to recognize the scale of the challenge–and in many cases encouraged offshore tax evasion–civil society has been

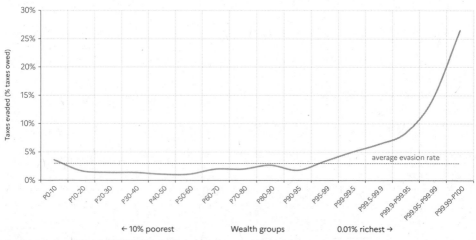

Figure 10.5   *Taxes evaded as a percentage of payable taxes in Scandinavian countries, 2000-2006*

← 10% poorest   Wealth groups   0.01% richest →

Sources and series: *wir2022.wid.world/methodology and Alstadsæter, Johannesen and Zucman (2017).*

working relentlessly to measure and better understand tax evasion. Offshore tax evasion has been drawing a lot of attention in recent years, partly thanks to international media and research consortiums, which released a series of leaked information about tax evasion (the "Panama papers", "HSBC leaks", "LuxLeaks", etc.). Recent research, drawing resources from these leaks, has demonstrated that tax evasion has undermined tax progressivity across the world. Most of the population in advanced economies does not evade much tax—because most of its income derives from wages and pensions, which are automatically reported to the tax authorities. On the contrary, leaked data shows pervasive tax evasion at the very top of the distribution. The top 0.01% of Scandinavian income earners avoid paying 25% to 30% of their personal income taxes, which is significantly higher than the average evasion rate of about 3% (See Figure 10.5).[11] Because Scandinavian countries rank among the countries with the highest social trust, the lowest level of corruption, and the strongest respect for the rule of law, this suggests that evasion among the wealthy may be even higher elsewhere.

Using 21st-century progressive tax revenue to invest in education, healthcare and the environment

Looking back at the decades of global tax revenue stagnating and factoring in the various challenges faced by contemporary societies (in particular in matters of healthcare, education, environment), there appears to have sufficient room for strengthening social states across the world, primarily in low-income and emerging countries, but also in high-income countries which have significant investment needs.

The wealth taxes suggested in Chapter 7 can provide the necessary resources to increase public spending. At the global level, our first wealth tax scenario could increase global public healthcare spending by 25%–this represents a substantial increase in healthcare spending even with moderate wealth tax rates. A combination of personal wealth taxes and taxes on corporate income could multiply healthcare spending by 1.5-2.

Sectors such as education and the green transition (low-carbon transport, energy and production infrastructures) will also require significant public investments across the world in the decades to come (See Chapter 6). Each country should choose how to use wealth taxation to their benefit. The bottom line is that governments should set measurable additional investment targets in terms of education, healthcare and green transition. Progressive wealth taxes are critical instruments to reach these objectives.

Box 10.1   **One-off wealth taxes: a window of opportunity?**

On top of recurrent wealth taxes, governments can also implement one-off wealth taxes. In 2020 alone, global billionaires' wealth increased by more than €3,600 billion (€3.6 trillion). Had a global tax been applied on excess wealth for 2020, global billionaires would still be as rich today as they were on the eve of the pandemics and would almost double global healthcare spending in a year (**Figure B10.1**). Excess wealth taxes were implemented in the past in the aftermath of economic or political shocks to help societies recover and invest in the future. For instance, Germany and Austria implemented exceptional taxes on property in the 1920s for reconstruction after World War I, and Japan did so after World War II.

Figure B10.1   *Global billionaires' wealth growth and healthcare spending*

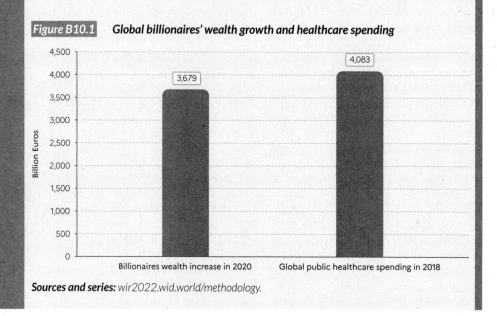

Sources and series: *wir2022.wid.world/methodology.*

Global redistribution: moving beyond development aid

In emerging and developing countries, a lot of focus has been placed on development aid (be it by foreign countries or philanthropists), as a means to increase access to healthcare and education. Too often though, foreign aid has come at the expense of sustainable tax revenue for poor countries. Global development aid currently accounts for less than 0.2% of global GDP today (and a mere 0.03% for emergency aid). To put these values into perspective, climate change impacts in poor countries (mostly caused by the Global North so far) amount to several percentage points of GDP. It should also be noted that in most countries receiving development aid, be it in Africa, South Asia or other regions, money outflows, taking the form of multinational profits, are by far superior to public aid inflows. According to official data, capital income flowing from African countries to the rest of the world represented on average three times the amount of international aid flowing into African countries between 1970 and 2012, and the situation has not significantly changed since then[12]. In other words: rich countries pretend to help poor nations, but all things considered they actually benefit from how economic flows are organized between the "center" and the "periphery".

When considering issues such as international aid and global development, it appears critical to take into account the various dimensions of the problem. Focusing solely on public (or private) development aid and disregarding important capital flows prevents a proper understanding of the global economic system. Let us add that aid is always conditional on the will of a donor country and transferred via its own development agencies or NGOs. While modest overall, development aid can represent substantial amounts in certain countries, particularly when compared with tax revenue. In many countries, the work of development agencies and NGOs have contributed to weaken the State-building process. This was particularly the case in the Sahel region in the 1950-60s, where government actors were never fully recognized and accepted by local actors following independence. Development aid in the form of new tax resources could probably contribute to strengthening government actors, but foreign aid given in the context of a weakening

of governments can hardly be of help to them[13].

Ending center-periphery imbalances

To put an end to large imbalances in capital and income flows between the Global North and the Global South, it is necessary to reassess the basic principles of globalization. It is not unreasonable to assume that each country in the world should have equal rights to development, in the sense that each human being should have equal access to basic education and healthcare services to start with. The question of how to fund such basic services is entirely political, thereby depending on the set of rules and institutions put in place by societies across the world. Starting from these basic principles and recognizing the need to fund access to basic resources, it appears logical that resources derived from the wealth taxes posited in Chapter 7 could be partly allocated to the Global South. The prosperity of the world's most performing economic actors over the past decades has entirely depended on the fact that they were operating in international markets and therefore on the international division of labor. This is a strong argument in favor of a global distribution of their gains.

In the least ambitious wealth tax scenario in Chapter 7, about 2% of global GDP would be raised, that is already 10 times more than all development aid flows accruing to low-income and emerging countries. On top of a share of wealth tax revenue, it is also possible to allocate to low-income countries a share of the revenue generated by multinationals' taxation (See Chapters 8-9). To prevent any form of fraud and corruption with funds used, much more resources should be dedicated to the fight against tax evasion, both in the South and in the North, focusing on public actors as well as private actors.[14] In case of corruption, there is typically a corruptor, or actors directly or indirectly benefitting from tax evasion. These actors are often located in the North.

International aid could then continue to be transferred to low-income countries. But this would be in addition to important additional tax revenue collected by emerging countries. Perhaps one of the main problems with current international aid is that it is assumed that the international economic order is fundamentally fair, in other words that each country is the legitimate owner of the resources it has produced. In Chapter 2, we saw that the rise of the Western world since the Industrial Revolution has been conditional to the international division of labor and the large-scale exploitation of natural resources all over the world. More broadly, rich countries would not exist without poor countries and global environmental resources. This applies both for Western powers and for Asian powers today. After slaves, cotton, wood and coal in the 18th and 19th centuries, economic development in the 20th and 21st century is still based on the depletion of global resources and the use of extensive, cheap manpower in low-income countries.

Chapter 2 also revealed the widespread idea according to which each country (or each individual within each country) is individually responsible for its production (and therefore its income), and outlined that wealth does not make much historical sense. For a start, resources do not belong to any country or individual. Private property is established (or should be established) only insofar as it serves the general interest, within the framework of a balanced set of institutions and rights limiting individual build-up of wealth and achieving a better distribution of wealth.

The fear of not knowing where to stop in such a political process is understandable, especially at the transnational level. At such a level, there is often considerable prejudice and the social groups involved do not know each other well. They may consequently have difficulty properly considering each other's values and respective situations, which makes the search for a common standard of justice even more complex, uncertain, and as fragile as it is essential. The trade-offs and mechanisms that will be found, such as reparations or the global taxes mentioned here, will always be imperfect and temporary. But alternatives, such as making sacrosanct the market and the absolute respect of property rights acquired in the past (whatever their scale or origin), are only inconsistent arrangements aimed at perpetuating injustices and unfounded positions of power, ultimately only preparing for new crises.

| Box 10.2 | Unequal access to healthcare: how the Covid crisis revealed and exacerbated healthcare inequalities between countries[15] |

A survey carried out in seven developing countries (Afghanistan, Bangladesh, · the Democratic Republic of Congo (DRC), Haiti, Nepal, Senegal and Tanzania) strikingly estimated that less than a third of clinics and healthcare centers in Bangladesh, the DRC, Nepal and Tanzania had access to face masks at the onset of the Covid crisis in 2020.[15] While the US had about 33 intensive care unit (ICU) beds per 100,000 population when the pandemic broke out, the ratio was at around 2 per 100,000 in India, Pakistan and Bangladesh in South Asia. In Sub-Saharan Africa, the situation was even worse: Zambia for instance had 0.6 ICU beds per 100,000, Gambia 0.4, and Uganda 0.1.[16] In 43 African countries, the total number of ICU beds was at about 5 per million, against 4,000 per million in Europe.[17] Ventilators barely reached 2,000 in all 41 African countries as of mid-April. 10 African countries had no ventilators at all, compared with 170,000 respirators in the USA in mid-March[18]. There were blatant inequalities in healthcare systems, with 0.2 physicians and 1.0 nurse per thousand people in low-income countries, compared to 3.0 and 8.8 respectively in high-income countries[19].

General government healthcare expenditures expressed as a share of GDP actually shrunk in low-income countries between the pre-financial crisis (2006-2008) situation and the pre-covid crisis (2016-2018). The opposite occurred in OECD countries and middle-income countries. The financial crisis of 2008-2009 exacerbated the long-run discrepancy in public healthcare expenditure between rich and poor countries even though such discrepancy might also occur within the middle and high-income groups. A comparison with total healthcare expenditures (including expenditures funded by private sources) reveals that out-of-pocket spending increased in low-income countries to compensate for the decline in public expenditures in relation to GDP. The decline was even sharper among vulnerable and conflict-affected countries.

The reasons behind developing countries' weak healthcare systems have long been debated. The lack of public resources in the context of imbalanced international flows is part of the equation. The IMF and World Bank's structural adjustment programs in developing countries have also been called into question. In certain places, it has arguably led to underinvestment in systems, which in turn undermined their capacity to respond to the Ebola epidemic[20].

Public finance has followed a different course. In high-income countries, government revenue (including taxes, non-tax revenue, grants and social contributions, expressed as a share of GDP) grew by 1.7% between 2006-2008 and 2016-2018. Low-income countries government revenue remained twice as low, at around 19%. Middle-income countries governments saw their revenue decrease by more than 3% over the same period. These discrepancies hide regional differences. Revenue receded by 14% in the Middle East and North Africa and by 13.5% in Sub-Saharan Africa. Before the Covid crisis hit, general government revenue was below 20% of GDP in Western Central and Eastern Africa, reducing the room for maneuver in the face of emergency spending.

NOTES

[1] The number of global extreme poor (living with less than $1.9 per day) decreased from 1.9 billion in 1990 to 730 million in 2020 according to the World Bank.

[2] Esping-Andersen, G. 1990. The Three Worlds of Welfare Capitalism, Cambridge: Polity Press; Polanyi, K. 1944. The Great Transformation. New-York: Farrar & Rinehart.

[3] Michaud, P.C. et al. 2011. "Differences in Health Between Americans and Western Europeans", Social Science & Medicine; Roser, M. 2017. "Link Between Healthcare Spending and Life Expectancy: US is an Outlier", OurWorldInData; Case, A. and A. Deaton. 2020. Deaths of Despair and the Future of Capitalism, Princeton: Princeton University Press.

[4] For more in depth discussion of inequality dynamics in China and Brazil, see Alvaredo, F., L. Chancel, T. Piketty, E. Saez, G. Zucman. 2018. World Inequality Report 2018, Cambridge: Harvard University Press.

[5] Low-income countries as per World Bank definition, i.e. per capita Gross national income less than $1,045.

[6] We estimate global tax revenues at around 5% of global income in 1900, 20% in 1950 and 25-27% in 1980.

[7] Diamond, P. and E. Saez. 2011. "The Case for a Progressive Tax: From Basic Research to Policy Recommendations." Journal of Economic Perspectives, 25 (4): 165-90. France Stratégie. 2020, Comité d'évaluation des réformes de la fiscalité du capital.

[8] Global financial assets represented 145% of global wealth in 1995 and 180% in 2020.

[9] See Pistor, K. 2019. The code of capital. How the Law Creates Wealth and Inequality. Princeton: Princeton University Press; Piketty, T. 2020. Capital and Ideology, Cambridge: Harvard University Press.

[10] Alstadsæter, A., Johannesen, N., and G. Zucman. 2018. "Who owns the wealth in tax havens? Macro

evidence and implications for global inequality". Journal of Public Economics, 162, 89-100; Zucman, G. 2013. "The missing wealth of nations: Are Europe and the US net debtors or net creditors?". The Quarterly journal of economics, 128(3), 1321-1364.

[11] Alstadsæter, Johannesen, and Zucman. "Who owns the wealth in tax havens?"; Zucman. "The missing wealth of nations".

[12] Piketty, T. 2014. Capital in the 21st century. Cambridge: Harvard University Press.

[13] Mann, G. 2015. From Empires to NGOs in the West African Sahel: The Road to Nongovernmentality. Cambridge: Cambridge University Press.

[14] Recent developments in the fight against tax evasion (with facilitated exchanges between the tax authorities) go in the right direction. However, absent detailed information on tax rates paid by various individuals within countries it is impossible to demonstrate that there are effectives changes.

[15] Gage, A., and S. Bauhoff. 31 March 2020. "Healthcare systems in low-income countries will struggle to protect healthcare workers from covid-19". Center for Global Development.

[16] See Voituriez and Chancel. "Developing countries in times of COVID".

[17] Chowdhury, A. Z., and K. S Jomo. 2020. "Responding to the COVID-19 pandemic in developing countries: Lessons from selected countries of the global South". Development, 63(2), 162-171.

[18] For references, see also Voituriez and Chancel. "Developing countries in times of COVID".

[19] See Gage and Bauhoff. Healthcare systems in low-income countries.

[20] For references, see also Voituriez and Chancel. "Developing countries in times of COVID".

COUNTRY
SHEETS

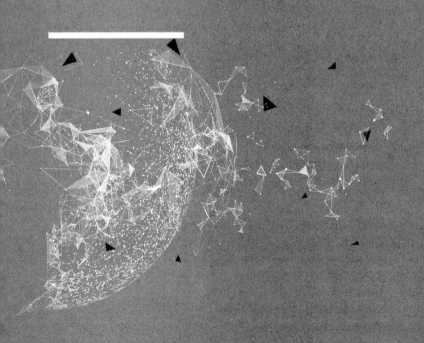

Glossary

- Income inequality levels refer to income measured before income taxes and after operations related to pension and unemployment insurance systems. This means that the income inequality levels reported in this appendix are mostly cash redistribution transfers. For a discussion of other income concepts used in this report, readers can refer to Chapters 1 and 2, which show that factoring in all redistribution does not significantly alter the relative positions of countries.

- When referring to wealth inequality below, we report net household wealth. Net household wealth is equal to the sum of financial assets (e.g. equity or bonds) and non-financial assets (e.g. housing or land) owned by individuals, net of their debts. Total household wealth adds up to the total wealth of the non-profit sector (e.g. foundations, universities) and total public wealth (the wealth owned by the government) to make total national wealth.

- The bottom 50% share is the share of income/wealth accruing to the bottom 50% of the population, i.e. that part of the population whose income/wealth lies below the median.

- The middle 40% share is the share of income/wealth accruing to the middle 40% of the population, i.e. the population whose income/wealth lies above the median and below the top 10% income threshold.

- The top 10% share is the share of income/wealth accruing to the 10% highest incomes/wealth in the country.

- The top 10% to bottom 50% average income gap is the ratio between the income shares of the top 10% and the bottom 50%. It measures the average income difference between the poorest half and the highest earners within a population. The higher the ratio, the higher the inequality.

- In this appendix, we use Purchasing Power Parity (PPP) to compare incomes and wealth levels across the world. Measuring income and wealth at purchasing power parities makes it possible to account for cost-of-living differences across countries (see Chapter 1 for an explanation of these concepts). Values are also converted into local currencies.

- The female labor income share refers to the share of total labor income earned by women. If earnings were distributed equally between males and females then the indicator would be 50%. A ratio of 0% would mean that women have no labor income. The higher the ratio between 0% and 50%, the closer to gender equality.

- Personal GHG footprint refers to the annual greenhouse gas emissions of the average individual. Footprints take into account all emissions, those stemming from direct energy use (e.g. fuel burnt by a car) as well as indirect energy use (CO_2 emitted to produce the goods and services to sustain a lifestyle). Estimates also take into account imports and exports of carbon embedded in goods and services imported or exported to other countries.

- Personal GHG footprints are expressed in CO2-equivalent (or CO2e). This unit includes greenhouse gas emissions from carbon dioxide (CO_2) as well as from other greenhouse gases such methane (CH_4) and nitrogen oxides (NOx).

- For each country in this appendix, we report on Inequality data transparency. This index produced by the World Inequality Lab in partnership with the United Nations Development Program, measures the level of availability and quality of economic inequality data. The index ranges from 0 to 20.

Keep up to date

Each country page displays a QR code. You can flash this code with your phone to access more data about a country and to check recent updates. The country data presented on these pages reflect the best of our knowledge as of late 2021. Our project is collaborative and cumulative: as soon as we access better inequality data about a country, the data is published online on the World Inequality Database. Using QR codes is a way to have the latest information at hand and to check on other inequality indicators than those presented in this summary.

ALGERIA

(POP. 44,617,000 (2021))

Income inequality in Algeria

The average national income per adult in Algeria is equal to €PPP11,630 (DZD666,620).1 This puts the average income in Algeria at a similar level as in Indonesia (€PPP11,700) and above neighboring Morocco (€PPP7,800). The top 10% of Algerians make on average €PPP44,300 (DZD2,538,490), 10 times more than the bottom 50% of the population (€PPP4,400 or DZD253,540). The top 10% captures 38% of national income whereas the bottom 50% captures 19% of it. While the bottom 50% income share is relatively high by historical standards (see below), the bottom 50% incomes have stagnated for almost 15 years at very low levels, fueling concerns about redistribution and social justice in the country.

Income inequality in the long run

Income inequality data for Algeria is scarce: the country's transparency index is 1/20, one of the lowest in the world. Available data based on top incomes suggests, however, that current inequality levels are lower than a century ago. Between 1900 and 1940, the top 10% income share was very probably higher than 60% and then declined to 50% after independence in 1962. The top 10% income share shrank in the 1990s, in the context of the civil war (1991-2002), which led to a general decline in average living standards.

1: 1 PPP = $PPP 1.4 = DZD 57.3

Table 1: *Inequality outlook*

	Income		Wealth	
	Avg. Income (PPP €)	Share of total (%)	Avg. Wealth (PPP €)	Share of total (%)
Full population	11,630	100%	19,131	100%
Bottom 50%	4,424	19%	2,254	5.9%
Middle 40%	12,473	42.9%	17,749	37.1%
Top 10%	44,287	38%	109,047	57.0%
Top 1%	115,253	9.9%	474,449	24.8%
Top 10% to Bot. 50% Income gap	1 to 10			
Female labor share	13%			
GHG footprint	3 tCO2e / capita			
Transparency index	1/20			

Interpretation: *See glossary for definitions of concepts and indicators.*
Sources and series: *wir2022.wid.world/methodology.*

Figure 1: *Top 10% and bottom 50% income shares in Algeria, 1980-2021*

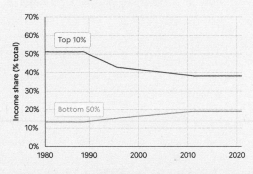

Interpretation: *The Top 10% income share is equal to 38% in 2021. Income is measured after the operation of pensions and unemployment insurance systems and before income tax. Sources and series: see wir2022.wid. world/methodology.*

Wealth inequality in Algeria

Average household wealth in Algeria is equal to €PPP19,100 (DZD1,096,530), similar to Morocco and about 10 times lower than in Western European countries. The top 10% own 57% of total wealth (they own on average €PPP109,000 or DZD6,286,360) whereas the bottom 50% own less than 6% of the total (they own on average less than €PPP2,300 or DZD129,150). Available data suggests that the past decade showed no clear sign of a reduction in wealth inequality.

Gender inequality

Algeria stands out as one of the countries with the lowest female share of total labor incomes, where only 12.5% of labor incomes accrue to women. The share is similar to that in Morocco (14%), lower than in Nigeria (28%) and significantly lower than in Latin America (35%), North America (38%) and Europe (38%-40%).

Carbon inequality

Average greenhouse gas emissions in Algeria are 3.2 tCO2e/capita. This level is similar in other North African countries and South Asian countries such as Indonesia, and slightly above the level in sub-Saharan Africa (2 tonnes). The top 10% emit over nine tonnes on average, whereas the bottom 50% emit fewer than two tonnes. Average emissions have declined over the past 20 years in the context of a drop in average incomes.

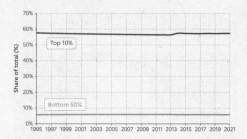

Figure 2: **Wealth distribution in Algeria, 1995-2021**

Interpretation: In 2021, the wealthiest 10% of the population own 57% of total household wealth. Household wealth is the sum of all financial assets (e.g. stock, bonds) and non-financial assets (e.g. housing), net of debts. Sources and series: wir2022.wid.world/methodology

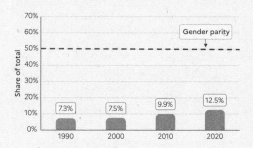

Figure 2: **Female labor income share in Algeria, 1990-2020**

Interpretation: The share of total labor income accruing to women in 2020 is close to 13%. Source and series: wir2022.wid.world/methodology

Table 2: **Carbon table**

	Avg. GHG footprint (tCO2e/capita)
Full population	3.2
Top 1%	26.1
Top 10%	9.4
Middle 40%	3.5
Bottom 50%	1.7

Interpretation: *The table presents average CO2 emissions of different groups of the population in 2019. Emissions take into account carbon embedded in consumption and investment portfolios.*
Sources and series: *wir2022.wid.world/methodology.*

ARGENTINA

(POP. 45,606,000 (2021))

Income inequality in Argentina

In Argentina, the average national income of the adult population is €PPP17,200 (ARS1,133,860).[2] While the bottom 50% earns €PPP5,600 (ARS368,050), the top 10% earns on average 13 times more (€PPP73,500 or ARS4,850,920). Though inequalities in Argentina are lower than the average in Latin America, they remain, overall, particularly high. In 2021, the top 10% earn around more than 40% of total national income (the share rises to more than 55% for Latin America as a whole). This is lower than in neighboring countries, including Brazil and Chile (59%), but significantly greater than in European countries (30-35%).

Inequality in the long run

Available estimates suggest that inequality in Argentina declined over the second half of the 20th century, down from extreme levels: the top 10% share was above 55% between 1900 and 1960, and is close to 40% in 2021. Over the past four decades, two movements are observed: a reduction in top 10% income share in the 2000s, followed by an increase since the early 2010s in the context of a generalized drop in incomes.

Table 1: *Inequality outlook*

	Income		Wealth	
	Avg. Income (PPP €)	Share of total (%)	Avg. Wealth (PPP €)	Share of total (%)
Full population	17,200	100%	31,000	100%
Bottom 50%	5,600	16.2%	3,500	5.7%
Middle 40%	17,600	41.0%	27,900	36.1%
Top 10%	73,500	42.8%	180,300	58.2%
Top 1%	300,800	17.5%	795,200	25.7%
Top 10% to Bot. 50% Income gap		1 to 13		
Female labor share		37%		
GHG footprint		6,5 tCO2 / pers.		
Transparency index		6,5 / 20		

Interpretation: See glossary for definitions of concepts and indicators.
Sources and series: wir2022.wid.world/methodology.

Figure 1: *Top 10% and bottom 50% income shares in Argentina, 1900-2021*

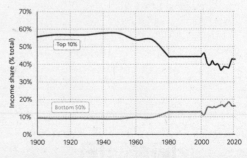

Interpretation: The Top 10% income share is equal to 43% in 2021. Income is measured after the operation of pensions and unemployment insurance systems and before income tax.
Sources and series: see wir2022.wid.world/methodology and Chancel and Piketty (2021).

2: €1 PPP = $PPP 1.4 = ARS 66.0

Wealth inequality maintained at an extreme level

Average household wealth has more than doubled in Argentina since 1995 but wealth inequality has remained at very high levels, with a top 10% wealth share oscillating between 60 and 70%. In 2021, the top 10% owns €PPP180,300 (ARS 11,903,540) on average, while the bottom 50% own €PPP3,500 or ARS234,090 (less than 6% of the total) in 2021. Argentinian wealth inequality is slightly lower than in the rest of Latin America but remains very high from an international standpoint.

Gender inequality

In Argentina, the female labor income share is equal to 37%. This value places Argentina slightly above the Latin American average (35%). Female labor income share is close to levels in Western Europe (38%), lower than Eastern Europe (41%) but higher than in Asia (21% excluding China) or sub-Saharan Africa (28%). Since 1990, the female labor share has been increasing slowly (+4 p.p).

Carbon inequality

The average per capita greenhouse gas footprint in Argentina is equal to 6.5 tCO2e. The bottom 50%, middle 40% and top 10% were on average responsible for respectively 3.5, 7 and 19tCO2e/capita in 2019. Average emissions are high compared with other Latin American countries (average per capita GHG consumption in Brazil is equal to 5 tCO2e) but lower than in high-income countries such as Germany Canada and Japan (around 11-19 tonnes).

Figure 2: *Wealth distribution in Argentina, 1995-2021*

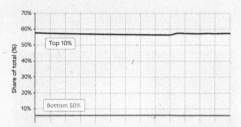

Interpretation: In 2021, the wealthiest 10% of the population own 58% of total household wealth. Household wealth is the sum of all financial assets (e.g. stock, bonds) and non-financial assets (e.g. housing), net of debts.
Sources and series: *wir2022.wid.world/methodology.*

Figure 3: *Female labor income share in Argentina, 1990-2020*

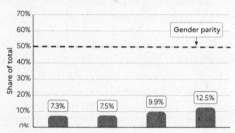

Interpretation: The share of total labor income accruing to women in 2020 is close to 37%.

Source and series: *wir2022.wid.world/methodology.*

Table 2: *Carbon table*

	Avg. GHG footprint (tCO2e/capita)
Full population	6.5
Top 1%	58.0
Top 10%	19.0
Middle 40%	7.0
Bottom 50%	3.5

Interpretation: The table presents average CO2 emissions of different groups of the population in 2019. Emissions take into account carbon embedded in consumption and investment portfolios.
Sources and series: *wir2022.wid.world/methodology.*

AUSTRALIA

(POP. 25,656,000 (2021))

Income inequality in Australia

Australia is a high-income country. The average per adult national income is equal to €PPP40,000 (AUD83,850).[3] This is comparable with other developed countries such as France (€PPP36,300) and Canada (€PPP38,000). While the bottom 50% earns €PPP13,000 (AUD27,110), the top 10% earns on average 10 times more (€PPP134,000 or AUD281,720).

Income inequality in the long run

Income inequality in Australia has been rising steadily since the early 1980s. Forty years ago, the top 10% income share was below 25%, it reached 30% at the turn of the century, and nears 34% in 2021. This trend stands in contrast with the 1900-1970 period, when top incomes experienced a severe drop, making 1970s Australia one of the most equal countries on the planet. The 2010s has been a lost decade, in particular for the bottom 50%, whose incomes are slightly under their level 10 years ago.

3: €1 PPP = $PPP 1.4 = AUD 2.1

Table 1: *Inequality outlook*

	Income		Wealth	
	Avg. Income (PPP €)	Share of total (%)	Avg. Wealth (PPP €)	Share of total (%)
Full population	40,000	100%	228,700	100%
Bottom 50%	12,900	16.2%	27,800	6.1%
Middle 40%	50,200	50.2%	215,700	37.7%
Top 10%	134,200	33.6%	1,285,400	56.2%
Top 1%	513,300	12.9%	5,419,300	23.7%
Top 10% to Bot. 50% Income gap	1 to 10			
Female labor share	37%			
GHG footprint	19,6 tCO2 / pers.			
Transparency index	9 / 20			

Interpretation: See glossary for definitions of concepts and indicators.
Sources and series: wir2022.wid.world/methodology.

Figure 1: *Top 10% and bottom 50% income shares in Australia, 1900-2021*

Interpretation: The Top 10% income share is equal to 34% in 2021. Income is measured after the operation of pensions and unemployement insurance systems and before income tax.
Sources and series: see wir2022.wid.world/methodology and Chancel and Piketty (2021).

Wealth inequality

Wealth inequalities in Australia have remained stable at a medium level since the mid-1990s. The share of the bottom 50% of total national wealth is around 6%, while the middle 40% and top 10% own around 38% and 56% respectively of all personal wealth.

Gender inequality

In Australia, the female labor income share is equal to 37%. This level is comparable with those in Western Europe (38%) and North America (38%), lower than in Eastern Europe (41%) and higher than in Asia (21%, excluding China) and sub-Saharan Africa (28%). Women's labor share is increasing slowly and has grown by four percentage points since 1990.

Carbon inequality

Average carbon emissions in Australia are close to 20 tCO2e/capita, one of the highest levels in the world and comparable with those in the US (21 tCO2e/capita). The bottom 50%, middle 40% and top 10% of the population respectively emit 10, 22 and 60 tonnes of carbon every year. Since 1990, carbon emissions have been slowly decreasing in the country: average emissions have gone down by two tonnes. This decrease took place in the poorest categories of population: while the bottom 50% and middle 40% decreased emissions by two and five tonnes, the top 10 % increased their emissions by 13 tonnes.

Figure 2: **Wealth distribution in Australia, 1995-2021**

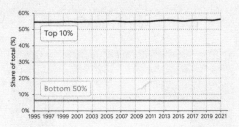

Interpretation: In 2021, the wealthiest 10% of the population own 56% of total household wealth. Household wealth is the sum of all financial assets (e.g. stock, bonds) and non-financial assets (e.g. housing), net of debts.
Sources and series: wir2022.wid.world/methodology.

Figure 3: *Female labor income share in Australia, 1990-2020*

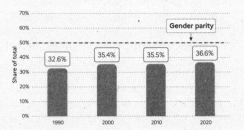

Interpretation: *The share of total labor income accruing to women in 2020 is close to 37%.*
Source and series: *wir2022.wid.world/methodology.*

Table 2: **Carbon table**

	Avg. GHG footprint (tCO2e/capita)
Full population	19.6
Top 1%	196.0
Top 10%	60.2
Middle 40%	21.8
Bottom 50%	9.7

Interpretation: *The table presents average CO2 emissions of different groups of the population in 2019. Emissions take into account carbon embedded in consumption and investment portfolios.*
Sources and series: *wir2022.wid.world/methodology.*

BRAZIL

(POP. 213,993,000 (2021))

The top 10% earn more than half of total income

In Brazil, the average national income of the adult population is €PPP14,000 (BRL,43,680).[4] While the bottom 50% earns €PPP2,800 (BRL8,800), the top 10% earns almost 30 times more (€PPP82,000 or BRL255,760). Brazil is one of the most unequal countries in the world: the top 10% captures 59% of total national income while the bottom half of the population takes only around 10%. Inequalities in Brazil are higher than in the US, where the top 10% captures 45% of total national income, and China, where it is 42%.

Income inequality since the 2000s

Income inequality in Brazil has long been marked by extreme levels. Available estimates suggest that the top 10% income share has always been higher than 50%. Since the 2000s, wage inequality has been reduced in Brazil and millions of individuals lifted out of poverty, largely thanks to government programs such as the increase in the minimum wage or Bolsa Família. At the same time, in the absence of major tax and land reform, overall income inequality has remained virtually unchanged, with the bottom 50% capturing around 10% of national income and the top 10% about half of it.

4: €1 PPP = $PPP 1.4 = BRL 3.1

Table 1: *Inequality outlook*

	Income		Wealth	
	Avg. Income (PPP €)	Share of total (%)	Avg. Wealth (PPP €)	Share of total (%)
Full population	14,000	100%	36,700	100%
Bottom 50%	2,800	10.1%	-300	-0.4%
Middle 40%	11,000	31.4%	18,800	20.6%
Top 10%	81,900	58.6%	292,700	79.8%
Top 1%	372,000	26.6%	1,793,900	48.9%
Top 10% to Bot. 50% Income gap	1 to 29			
Female labor share	39%			
GHG footprint	4,6 tCO2 / pers.			
Transparency index	5,5 / 20			

Interpretation: See glossary for definitions of concepts and indicators.
Sources and series: wir2022.wid.world/methodology.

Figure 1: *Top 10% and bottom 50% income shares in Brazil, 2000-2021*

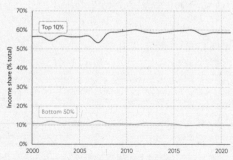

Interpretation: The Top 10% income share is equal to 59% in 2021. Income is measured after the operation of pensions and unemployment insurance systems and before income tax.
Sources and series: see wir2022.wid.world/methodology, Chancel and Piketty (2021) and Morgan (2017).

■ Extreme levels of wealth inequality, still on the rise

Wealth inequality in Brazil is also among the highest in the world. In 2021, the poorest half of the population does not own wealth (compared with 6% in Argentina, for example), whereas the top 1% of the population owns about half of total wealth. Available data suggests that wealth inequality has increased since the mid-1990s in a context of financial deregulation and no major tax reform.

■ Gender inequality

In Brazil, the female labor income share is equal to 38.5% of all labor income. This is slightly higher than in other Latin American countries, including Argentina (37%) and Colombia (36%). Compared with other countries, the growth in labor income share is particularly significant in Brazil: between 1990 and 2019, it grew by 10 points. Gender inequality levels are now equal to the average in Western Europe (38%).

■ Carbon inequality

The average per capita greenhouse gas footprint in Brazil is equal to 4.6 tCO2e. The bottom 50%, middle 40% and top 10% are on average responsible for respectively around 2, 4.5 and 18 tCO2e/capita. Average emissions are lower than in Argentina (6.5 tCO2e) and Europe. Brazil has a very specific place in climate mitigation policies because of the importance of the Amazon forest on its territory. Representing half of remaining rain forest in the world, the deforestation of the Amazon puts Brazil at the center of global environmental debates. Recent studies suggest that the forest is on the brink of becoming a source of carbon emissions, rather than a carbon sink.

Figure 2: **Wealth distribution in Brazil, 1995-2021**

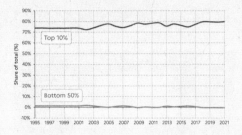

Interpretation: *In 2021, the wealthiest 10% of the population own 80% of total household wealth. Household wealth is the sum of all financial assets (e.g. stock, bonds) and non-financial assets (e.g. housing), net of debts.*
Sources and series: *wir2022.wid.world/methodology.*

Figure 3: *Female labor income share in Brazil, 1990-2020*

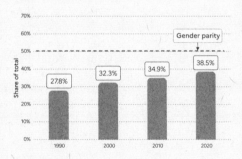

Interpretation: *The share of total labor income accruing to women in 2020 is close to 39%.*
Source and series: *wir2022.wid.world/methodology.*

Table 2: **Carbon table**

	Avg. GHG footprint (tCO2e/capita)
Full population	4.6
Top 1%	72.1
Top 10%	17.7
Middle 40%	4.3
Bottom 50%	2.2

Interpretation: *The table presents average CO2 emissions of different groups of the population in 2019. Emissions take into account carbon embedded in consumption and investment portfolios.*
Sources and series: *wir2022.wid.world/methodology.*

CANADA

(POP. 38,006,000 (2021))

Inequality in Canada

In Canada, the average national income of the adult population is €PPP38,000 (CAD65,590.)[5] While the bottom 50% earns €PPP12,000 (CAD20,440), the top 10% earns on average 13 times more (€PPP156,000 or CAD266,950).Canada is a country with high levels of inequality, midway between the US and Europe. The ratio between the incomes of the top 10% and the bottom 50% is equal to 13, compared with nine for the European Union and 17 for the US. While the average Canadian earns 30% more than the average citizen of the European Union (in purchasing parity terms), the poorest half of Canadians earn 85% less than the poorest half of Western Europeans.

Income inequality in the long run

Income inequality in Canada has been rising significantly over the past 40 years. In 1980, the top 10% income share was close to 35% and the bottom 50% captured almost 20% of national income. Inequality in Canada dropped after the Second World War and was maintained at low levels from the 1950 to the 1980s thanks to a mix of capital control and social policies, in a context of high economic growth. Since the 1980s, financialization, deregulation and lower taxes contributed to rising inequalities, though the rise was not as fast as in the US.

5: €1 PPP = $PPP 1.4 = CAD 1.7

Table 1: *Inequality outlook*

	Income		Wealth	
	Avg. Income (PPP €)	Share of total (%)	Avg. Wealth (PPP €)	Share of total (%)
Full population	38,300	100%	220,700	100%
Bottom 50%	11,900	15.6%	25,700	5.8%
Middle 40%	41,900	43.7%	201,500	36.5%
Top 10%	156,000	40.7%	1,272,800	57.7%
Top 1%	566,900	14.8%	5,512,400	25.0%
Top 10% to Bot. 50% Income gap			1 to 13	
Female labor share			38%	
GHG footprint			19,4 tCO2 / pers.	
Transparency index			9 / 20	

Interpretation: See glossary for definitions of concepts and indicators.
Sources and series: wir2022.wid.world/methodology.

Figure 1: *Top 10% and bottom 50% income shares in Canada, 1900-2021*

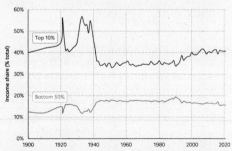

Interpretation: The Top 10% income share is equal to 41% in 2021. Income is measured after the operation of pensions and unemployment insurance systems and before income tax.
Sources and series: see wir2022.wid.world/methodology, and Chancel and Piketty (2021).

A wealthy country, with high levels of wealth inequality

Canada is a wealthy country, with an average wealth of €PPP220,700 (CAD377,680). The bottom 50% holds on average €PPP25,700 (CAD43,950), and these figures rise to €PPP202,000 (CAD914,110) and €PPP 1,273,000 (CAD5,602,434) for the middle 40% and top 10%, respectively. This is comparable with Western European countries such as France (respectively bottom 50%, middle 40% and top 10% average wealth of 22,300, 203,000 and 1,356,000 €PPP). Since the mid-1990s, wealth inequality levels have remained relatively stable in the country with the shares of the bottom 50%, middle 40% and top 10% equal to around 6%, 37% and 58% respectively.

Gender inequality

In Canada, the female labor income share is 38%. This share is slightly lower than in the US (39%). It is higher than the average in sub-Saharan Africa (28%), Asia (21%, excluding China) and Western Europe (38%), but lower than in Eastern Europe (41%). The growth of the female labor income share has been moderate since 1991 (+ 4 p.p.).

Carbon inequality

Canada is one of the highest emitters in the world in per capita terms. Average per capita emissions are equal to 19.4 tCO2e. This is lower than in the US (21 tCO2e) but much higher than in Germany (11) and China (8). Since 1990, emissions have decreased by 3.1 tonnes of carbon per person. While the bottom 50% and middle 40% have reduced their emissions by 3.5 and 4.5 tonnes respectively per person, emissions of the top 10% have increased by around 4 tonnes per person. Canada's official objective is to reach 12.3 tCO2e/capita by 2030. To reduce their carbon footprint to this level, the top 10% and the middle 40% will have to reduce emissions by around 48 and eight tonnes per person, respectively.

Figure 2: **Wealth distribution in Canada, 1995-2021**

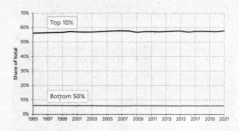

Interpretation: *In 2021, the wealthiest 10% of the population own 58% of total household wealth. Household wealth is the sum of all financial assets (e.g. stock, bonds) and non-financial assets (e.g. housing), net of debts.*
Sources and series: *wir2022.wid.world/methodology.*

Figure 3: *Female labor income share in Canada, 1990-2020*

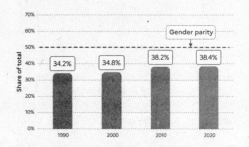

Interpretation: *The share of total labor income accruing to women in 2020 is close to 38%.*
Source and series: *wir2022.wid.world/methodology.*

Table 2: **Carbon table**

	Avg. GHG footprint (tCO2e/capita)
Full population	19.4
Top 1%	190.2
Top 10%	60.3
Middle 40%	20.9
Bottom 50%	10.0

Interpretation: *The table presents average CO2 emissions of different groups of the population in 2019. Emissions take into account carbon embedded in consumption and investment portfolios.*
Sources and series: *wir2022.wid.world/methodology.*

CHILE

(POP. 19,212,000 (2021))

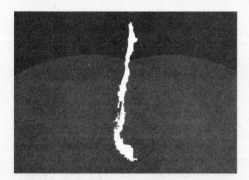

Extreme income inequality in Chile

In Chile, the average national income of the adult population is €PPP22,100 (or CLP14,083,780).[6] While the bottom 50% earns €PPP4,500 (CLP2,866,570), the top 10% earns almost 30 times more (€PPP130,200 or CLP82,966,190). The bottom 50% in Chile earn only 10% of total income, while the top 10% share is equal to almost 60%. The country is one of the most unequal in Latin America. These levels are comparable with inequalities in Brazil, where the bottom 50% share is also close to 10%.

Income inequality in the long run

Available estimates suggest that inequality in Chile has been extreme over the past 120 years, with a top 10% income share constantly around 55%-60% and a bottom 50% income share around 9-10%. The persistence of extreme inequality in Chile, even after the end of the military dictatorship (1973-1990), has recently triggered a wave of social protests. In 2019-2020, Chileans went to the streets to protest against a dual economy system characterized by an economic elite living according to wealthy North American standards on the one hand, and a very poor working class and increasingly pauperized middle class on the other.

6: €1 PPP = $PPP 1.4 = 637.2

Table 1: *Inequality outlook*

	Income		Wealth	
	Avg. Income (PPP €)	Share of total (%)	Avg. Wealth (PPP €)	Share of total (%)
Full population	22,100	100%	53,900	100%
Bottom 50%	4,500	10.2%	-600	-0.6%
Middle 40%	17,100	30.9%	27,100	20.1%
Top 10%	130,200	58.9%	433,400	80.4%
Top 1%	585,100	26.5%	2,670,300	49.6%
Top 10% to Bot. 50% Income gap		1 to 29		
Female labor share		38%		
GHG footprint		6,3 tCO2 / pers.		
Transparency index		8 / 20		

Interpretation: See glossary for definitions of concepts and indicators.
Sources and series: wir2022.wid.world/methodology.

Figure 1: *Top 10% and bottom 50% income shares in Chile, 1980-2021*

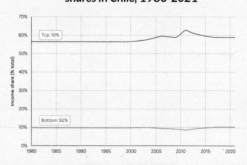

Interpretation: The Top 10% income share is equal to 59% in 2021. Income is measured after the operation of pensions and unemployment insurance systems and before income tax.
Sources and series: see wir2022.wid.world/methodology, and Chancel and Piketty (2021).

The poorest half owns no wealth, the richest 1% owns half of it

In 2021, the average wealth for the bottom 50% in Chile is negative, with a high number of Chilean in debt. On the other hand, the top 10% and top 1% of the population respectively hold 80% of the total (€PPP433,000 on average, CLP276,160,350) and 50% of the total (€PPP2,670,000 on average, CLP1,701,429,350). In the last 25 years, these extreme levels of inequalities have continuously increased. Between 1995 and 2021, the average wealth of the poorest half has remained around zero. Simultaneously, the averages of the top 10% and top 1% have more than doubled.

Gender inequality

In Chile, the female labor income share is equal to 38%. This is very close to other Latin American countries, including Argentina (37%) and Brazil (38%). Similar to Brazil, the decrease in gender inequality in Chile has been significant in the last 30 years. Between 1991 and 2021, female labor income share has increased by 14 points.

Carbon inequality

Unsurprisingly, carbon inequalities in the country are also very high. The average carbon consumption is around 6 tCO2e/capita. While the top 10% emit on average 26 tonnes every year, the bottom 50% and middle 40% emit respectively three and six tonnes. Between 1990 and 2011, the average carbon footprint in Chile went from 3.7 tonnes to 6.3 tonnes. Since then, it has stabilized.

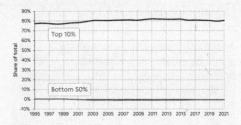

Figure 2: *Wealth distribution in Chile, 1995-2021*

Interpretation: *In 2021, the wealthiest 10% of the population own 80% of total household wealth. Household wealth is the sum of all financial assets (e.g. stock, bonds) and non-financial assets (e.g. housing), net of debts.*
Sources and series: *wir2022.wid.world/methodology.*

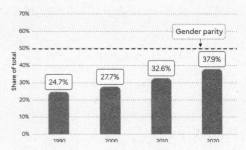

Figure 3: *Female labor income share in Chile, 1990-2020*

Interpretation: *The share of total labor income accruing to women in 2020 is close to 33%.*
Source and series: *wir2022.wid.world/methodology.*

Table 2: *Carbon table*

	Avg. GHG footprint (tCO2e/capita)
Full population	6.3
Top 1%	108.2
Top 10%	26.1
Middle 40%	5.8
Bottom 50%	2.7

Interpretation: *The table presents average CO2 emissions of different groups of the population in 2019. Emissions take into account carbon embedded in consumption and investment portfolios.*
Sources and series: *wir2022.wid.world/methodology.*

CHINA

(POP. 1,411,132,000 (2021))

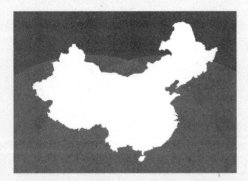

▇ Income inequality in China

In China, the average national income of the adult population is €PPP17,600 (or CNY88,870).[7] While the bottom 50% earns €PPP5,100 (CNY25,520), the top 10% earns on average 14 times more (€PPP73,400 or CNY370,210). This gap between incomes of the bottom 50% and the top 10% is higher than the inequalities observed in Europe, but below that of the US (17) and India (21).

▇ Income inequality in the long run

Economic inequality in China followed a U-shape trajectory over the course of the 20th century. The establishment of the People's Republic of China in 1949 was associated with a fall in inequality levels in the context of a general decline in incomes. The post-1978 economic reforms led to fast-rising average incomes as well as growing inequality until the middle of the first decade of the 2000s. Post-2005, investments in health, education and infrastructure in rural areas, helped to keep inequality in check, but wealth inequality continued to increase at the very top of the social pyramid (see below).

Table 1: **Inequality outlook**

	Income		Wealth	
	Avg. Income (PPP €)	Share of total (%)	Avg. Wealth (PPP €)	Share of total (%)
Full population	17,600	100%	86,100	100%
Bottom 50%	5,100	14.4%	11,000	6.4%
Middle 40%	19,400	44.0%	55,600	25.8%
Top 10%	73,400	41.7%	583,400	67.8%
Top 1%	246,600	14.0%	2,621,300	30.5%
Top 10% to Bot. 50% Income gap	1 to 14			
Female labor share	33%			
GHG footprint	8 tCO2 / pers.			
Transparency index	6,5 / 20			

Interpretation: See glossary for definitions of concepts and indicators.
Sources and series: wir2022.wid.world/methodology.

Figure 1: **Top 10% and bottom 50% income shares in China, 1900-2021**

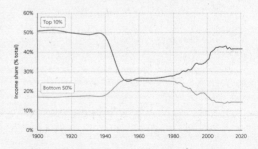

Interpretation: The Top 10% income share is equal to 42% in 2021. Income is measured after the operation of pensions and unemployment insurance systems and before income tax.
Sources and series: see wir2022.wid.world/methodology, and Chancel and Piketty (2021).

7: €1 PPP = $PPP 1.4 = CNY 5.0

A constant rise in wealth inequality

The average wealth of the bottom 50%, middle 40% and top 10% is equal to €PPP11,000, €PPP56,000 and €PPP583,000 respectively (CNY55,270, CNY280,500 and CNY2,943,907). Overall, the top 10% in China own almost 70% of total national wealth. Wealth inequality in China is higher than the levels found in India (where the share of the top 10% is equal to 64%) and comparable with inequality levels in the US (71%). Since the 1990s, wealth inequality has been on the rise.

Gender inequality

Here, China is an exception within Asia. The female labor income share is higher than the average in the region (33% vs. 21%) and in Japan (28%). Contrary to the general trend, however, female labor income share in the country is currently declining. Between 1991 and 2019, it decreased by six percentage points.

On average, the top 10% in China emit 10 times more emissions than the bottom 50%

Although China is by far the world's largest emitter in aggregate due to the size of its population, its per capita footprint consumption is lower than European levels and equal to 8 tCO2e/capita. This value is comparable with France's carbon footprint (8.7 tCO2e/hab), but inequality levels are much higher. The bottom 50%, middle 40% and top 10% are on average responsible for respectively three, seven and 36 tonnes of CO2e/capita. Since 1990, average per capita emissions have notably increased, rising from 2.7 tCO2e/capita to 8 tCO2e/capita. The emissions of the top 10% increased faster than the average, from around 7 tCO2e/capita to over 30 tCO2e/capita. In comparison, the bottom 50% only increased their emissions from 1.5 to 3.0 tCO2e/capita over the period.

Figure 2: **Wealth distribution in China, 1995-2021**

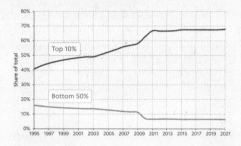

Interpretation: In 2021, the wealthiest 10% of the population own 68% of total household wealth. Household wealth is the sum of all financial assets (e.g. stock, bonds) and non-financial assets (e.g. housing), net of debts.
Sources and series: *wir2022.wid.world/methodology.*

Figure 3: *Female labor income share in China, 1990-2020*

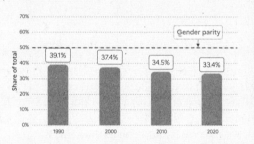

Interpretation: The share of total labor income accruing to women in 2020 is close to 38%.
Source and series: *wir2022.wid.world/methodology.*

Table 2: **Carbon table**

	Avg. GHG footprint (tCO2e/capita)
Full population	8.0
Top 1%	138.9
Top 10%	36.4
Middle 40%	7.2
Bottom 50%	3.0

Interpretation: The table presents average CO2 emissions of different groups of the population in 2019. Emissions take into account carbon embedded in consumption and investment portfolios.
Sources and series: *wir2022.wid.world/methodology.*

FRANCE

(POP. 67,035,000 (2021))

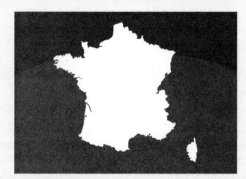

Income inequality in France

In France, the average national income is €PPP36,300 (or €38,360).[8] While the bottom 50% earns €PPP16,500 (€17,430), the top 10% earns on average seven times more (€PPP117,000 or €123,610). This gap between incomes of the bottom 50% and the top 10% is smaller than some other European countries, including Germany (10), and comparable with others, including the UK (8.8). This ratio is much smaller than in the US (17) and China (14).

Income inequality in the long run

Income inequality in France declined significantly over the course of 20th century, a decline partly due to the impacts of the First and Second World Wars, the 1929 crisis and the fall of foreign assets, as well as to the post-WWII development of the social state, and pro-labor policies implemented after the 1968 social protests. After 1983, a wave of deregulation and liberalization policies partly reversed the downwards trend. More recently, top-end inequality has increased as a result of tax cuts concentrated on wealthiest income groups.

Table 1: *Inequality outlook*

	Income		Wealth	
	Avg. Income (PPP €)	Share of total (%)	Avg. Wealth (PPP €)	Share of total (%)
Full population	36,300	100%	228,000	100%
Bottom 50%	16,500	22.7%	22,300	4.9%
Middle 40%	40,900	45.1%	203,100	35.6%
Top 10%	116,900	32.2%	1,355,800	59.5%
Top 1%	357,000	9.8%	6,162,900	27.0%
Top 10% to Bot. 50% Income gap	1 to 7			
Female labor share	41%			
GHG footprint	8,7 tCO2 / pers.			
Transparency index	15 / 20			

Interpretation: See glossary for definitions of concepts and indicators.
Sources and series: wir2022.wid.world/methodology.

Figure 1: *Top 10% and bottom 50% income shares in France, 1900-2021*

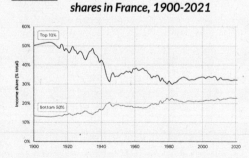

Interpretation: The Top 10% income share is equal to 32% in 2021. Income is measured after the operation of pensions and unemployment insurance systems and before income tax.
Sources and series: see wir2022.wid.world/methodology, and Chancel and Piketty (2021).

8: €1 PPP = $PPP 1.4 = € 1.1

A continued rise in wealth inequality

The average wealth for the top 10%, middle 40% and bottom 50% groups in France is respectively equal to €PPP1,356,000, €PPP203,000 and €PPP22,300 (€1,432,950, €214,640 and €23,560). Wealth inequalities in France are much higher than income inequalities and continue to rise. Wealth inequality levels are, however, lower than in China (where the top 10% own 67% of the wealth) and the US (where 66% of the wealth is concentrated in the top 10). In Europe, French inequality levels are comparable with those in the UK (where the top 10% holds 57% of national wealth).

Gender inequality

In France, the female labor income share is equal to 41%. This share is higher than the UK (38%) and the Western European average (38%). It is higher than the average in sub-Saharan Africa (28%), Asia (21%, excluding China) and North America (38%), but slightly lower than in Eastern Europe (41%). Since 1990, changes in the female labor income share in France have followed the general Western European trend, with a moderate increase over 30 years (+ 5 p.p.).

Carbon inequality

The average yearly GHG consumption in France is equal to 8.7 tonnes of CO_2e per capita. While the bottom 50% emits on average 5 tCO_2e, the top 10% is responsible for nearly 25 tCO_2e in emissions per capita. While emissions among the bottom 50% have declined by 29% since 1990, top 10% emissions decreased by 18%. Official carbon mitigation objectives for France amount to reaching an average of around 5 tCO_2e/capita by 2030. Bottom 50% emissions are close to this level already, while the top 10% would need to cut their individual emissions by almost 20 tCO_2e to get there.

Figure 2: **Wealth distribution in France, 1900-2021**

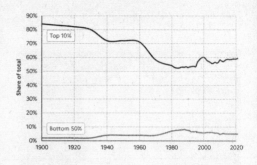

Interpretation: *In 2000, the wealthiest 10% of the population owned 60% of total household wealth. Household wealth is the sum of all financial assets (e.g. stock, bonds) and non-financial assets (e.g. housing), net of debts.*
Sources and series: *wir2022.wid.world/methodology.*

Figure 3: *Female labor income share in France, 1990-2020*

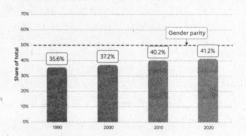

Interpretation: *The share of total labor income accruing to women in 2020 is close to 41%.*
Source and series: *wir2022.wid.world/methodology.*

Table 2: **Carbon table**

	Avg. GHG footprint (tCO2e/capita)
Full population	8.7
Top 1%	77.5
Top 10%	24.7
Middle 40%	9.3
Bottom 50%	5.0

Interpretation: *The table presents average CO2 emissions of different groups of the population in 2019. Emissions take into account carbon embedded in consumption and investment portfolios.*
Sources and series: *wir2022.wid.world/methodology.*

GERMANY

(POP. 84,588,000 (2021))

Income inequality in Germany

In Germany, the average national income of the adult population is €PPP39,900.[9] While the bottom 50% earns €PPP15,200, the top 10% earns on average 10 times more (€PPP148,000). This ratio is higher than in France (7), but smaller than in the US (17) and China (14).

Income inequality in the long run

Income inequality in Germany decreased substantially between 1917 and 1970. At the beginning of the 20th century, estimates suggest that more than half of national income accrued to the top 10% of the population, while around 15% went to the bottom 50%. Top incomes were barely affected by the hyperinflation that was followed by the 1929 crisis and the Second World War. Inequality was further reduced between the 1960 and the 1980s, thanks to a combination of progressive income and wealth taxes in a context of high growth rates for all, and in particular for low and middle income earners. The top 10% income share rose significantly after 1980, partly driven by liberalization policies.

Table 1: **Inequality outlook**

	Income		Wealth	
	Avg. Income (PPP €)	Share of total (%)	Avg. Wealth (PPP €)	Share of total (%)
Full population	39,900	100%	163,500	100%
Bottom 50%	15,200	19.0%	10,900	3.4%
Middle 40%	43,900	43.9%	151,700	37.1%
Top 10%	148,000	37.1%	973,600	59.6%
Top 1%	509,800	12.8%	4,853,200	29.7%
Top 10% to Bot. 50% Income gap	1 to 10			
Female labor share	36%			
GHG footprint	11,3 tCO2 / pers.			
Transparency index	10 / 20			

Interpretation: See glossary for definitions of concepts and indicators.
Sources and series: wir2022.wid.world/methodology.

Figure 1: **Top 10% and bottom 50% income shares in Germany, 1900-2021**

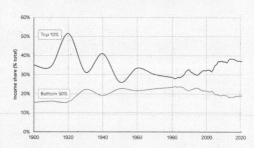

Interpretation: The Top 10% income share is equal to 37% in 2021. Income is measured after the operation of pensions and unemployment insurance systems and before income tax.
Sources and series: see wir2022.wid.world/methodology, and Chancel and Piketty (2021).

9: €1 PPP = $PPP 1.4 = € 1.1

Wealth inequality in Germany

Wealth inequality in Germany has followed a similar pattern to income inequality. The top 1% wealth share was slightly above 45% in the early 20th century and dropped to 20-25% in the 1990s, before slightly increasing over the past 30 years. From an international perspective, wealth inequality in Germany is similar to that of other European countries, for example France and the UK, and below the US (where the top 1% wealth share is close to 40%).

Gender inequality

In Germany, the female labor income share is equal to 36%. This is comparable with levels observed across Western Europe, although slightly lower than in France (41%) and the UK (38%). It is higher than the average in sub-Saharan Africa (28%), and Asia (21%, excluding China). The female labor income share has grown by about 6 p.p. since 1990.

Germany is one of the highest emitters in the European Union

Within the European Union, Germany is one of the highest CO2 emitters. While average footprint emissions in the EU are 9.5 tCO2e/capita, in Germany, they are above 11 tCO2e/capita. The top 10% emit on average 34 tons, i.e. six times more than the bottom 50%. Germany has pledged to cut its territorial emissions by 55% before 2030, compared with 1990 levels. This would mean reaching a per capita emissions average close to 6.5 tCO2e/capita - approximately the current level of the poorest half of the population.

Figure 2: **Wealth distribution in Germany, 1995-2021**

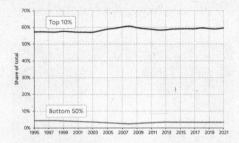

Interpretation: *In 2021, the wealthiest 10% of the population own 60% of total household wealth. Household wealth is the sum of all financial assets (e.g. stock, bonds) and non-financial assets (e.g. housing), net of debts.*
Sources and series: *wir2022.wid.world/methodology.*

Figure 3: *Female labor income share in Germany, 1990-2020*

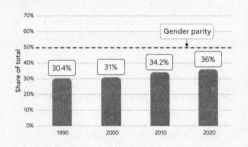

Interpretation: *The share of total labor income accruing to women in 2020 is close to 36%.*
Source and series: *wir2022.wid.world/methodology.*

Table 2: **Carbon table**

	Avg. GHG footprint (tCO2e/capita)
Full population	11.3
Top 1%	117.8
Top 10%	34.1
Middle 40%	12.2
Bottom 50%	5.9

Interpretation: *The table presents average CO2 emissions of different groups of the population in 2019. Emissions take into account carbon embedded in consumption and investment portfolios.*
Sources and series: *wir2022.wid.world/methodology.*

INDIA

(POP. 1,393,409,000 (2021))

Extreme income inequalities in India

The average national income of the Indian adult population is €PPP7,400 (or INR204,200).[10] While the bottom 50% earns €PPP2 000 (INR53,610), the top 10% earns more than 20 times more (€PPP42 500 or INR1,166,520). While the top 10% and top 1% hold respectively 57% and 22% of total national income, the bottom 50% share has gone down to 13%. India stands out as a poor and very unequal country, with an affluent elite.

Income inequality in the long run : a historical high

Indian income inequality was very high under British colonial rule (1858-1947), with a top 10% income share around 50%. After independence, socialist-inspired five-year plans contributed to reducing this share to 35-40%. Since the mid-1980s, deregulation and liberalization policies have led to one of the most extreme increases in income and wealth inequality observed in the world. While the top 1% has largely benefited from economic reforms, growth among low and middle income groups has been relatively slow and poverty persists . Over the past three years, the quality of inequality data released by the government has seriously deteriorated, making it particularly difficult to assess recent inequality changes.

10: €1 PPP = $PPP 1.4 = INR 27.5

Table 1: *Inequality outlook*

	Income		Wealth	
	Avg. Income (PPP €)	Share of total (%)	Avg. Wealth (PPP €)	Share of total (%)
Full population	7,400	100%	35,800	100%
Bottom 50%	2,000	13.1%	4,200	5.9%
Middle 40%	5,500	29.7%	26,400	29.5%
Top 10%	42,500	57.1%	231,300	64.6%
Top 1%	161,600	21.7%	1,181,400	33.0%
Top 10% to Bot. 50% Income gap	1 to 22			
Female labor share	18%			
GHG footprint	2,2 tCO2 / pers.			
Transparency index	5,5 / 20			

Interpretation: See glossary for definitions of concepts and indicators.
Sources and series: wir2022.wid.world/methodology.

Figure 1: *Top 10% and bottom 50% income shares in India, 1900-2021*

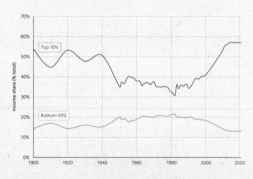

Interpretation: The Top 10% income share is equal to 57% in 2021. Income is measured after the operation of pensions and unemployment insurance systems and before income tax.
Sources and series: see wir2022.wid.world/methodology.

Wealth inequality

Average household wealth in India is equal to €PPP35,800 or INR983,010 (compared with €PPP86,100 in China). The bottom 50% own almost nothing, with an average wealth of €PPP4,200 (6% of the total, INR115,000). The middle class is also relatively poor (with an average wealth of only €PPP26,400 or INR723,930, 29.5% of the total) as compared with the top 10% and 1% who own respectively €PPP231,300 (65% of the total) and over €PPP1.2 million (33%), INR6,354,070, and INR32,449,360.

Gender inequality

Gender inequalities in India are very high. The female labor income share is equal to 18%. This is significantly lower than the average in Asia (21%, excluding China). This value is one of the lowest in the world, slightly higher than the average share in Middle East (15%). The significant increase observed since 1990 (+8 p.p.) has been insufficient to lift women's labor income share to the regional average.

Carbon inequality

India is a low carbon emitter: the average per capita consumption of greenhouse gas is equal to just over 2 tCO2e. These levels are typically comparable with carbon footprints in sub-Saharan African countries. The bottom 50%, middle 40% and top 10% respectively consume 1, 2, and 9 tCO2e/capita. A person in the bottom 50% of the population in India is responsible for, on average, five times fewer emissions than the average person in the bottom 50% in the European Union and 10 times fewer than the average person in the bottom 50% in the US.

Figure 2: **Wealth distribution in India, 1995-2021**

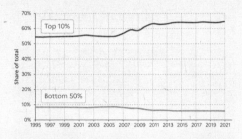

Interpretation: *In 2021, the wealthiest 10% of the population own 65% of total household wealth. Household wealth is the sum of all financial assets (e.g. stock, bonds) and non-financial assets (e.g. housing), net of debts.*
Sources and series: *wir2022.wid.world/methodology.*

Figure 3: *Female labor income share in India, 1990-2020*

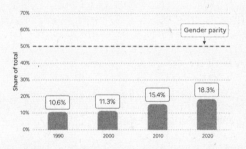

Interpretation: *The share of total labor income accruing to women in 2020 is close to 18%.*
Source and series: *wir2022.wid.world/methodology.*

Table 2: **Carbon table**

	Avg. GHG footprint (tCO2e/capita)
Full population	2.2
Top 1%	32.4
Top 10%	8.8
Middle 40%	2.0
Bottom 50%	1.0

Interpretation: *The table presents average CO2 emissions of different groups of the population in 2019. Emissions take into account carbon embedded in consumption and investment portfolios.*
Sources and series: *wir2022.wid.world/methodology.*

INDONESIA

(POP. 44,617,000 (2021))

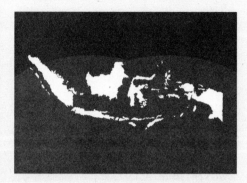

Income inequality in Indonesia

In Indonesia, the average national income of the adult population is €PPP11,700 (or IDR69,030,990).[11] While the bottom 50% earns €PPP2,900 (IDR22,612,000), the top 10% earns on average 19 times more (€PPP56,100 or IDR285,073,820).

Income inequality in the long run

Historical estimates for inequality in Indonesia reveal that the top 10% income share has oscillated around 40-50% since 1900. Inequality has slightly increased since the 1980s, after significant but short-spanned ups and downs in the late 1990s and early 2000s.

Table 1: *Inequality outlook*

	Income		Wealth	
	Avg. Income (PPP €)	Share of total (%)	Avg. Wealth (PPP €)	Share of total (%)
Full population	11,700	100%	17,550	100%
Bottom 50%	2,900	12.4%	1,916	5.5%
Middle 40%	11,600	39.6%	15,067	34.3%
Top 10%	56,100	48.0%	105,651	60.2%
Top 1%	213,400	18.3%	515,268	29.4%
Top 10% to Bot. 50% Income gap		1 to 19		
Female labor share		25%		
GHG footprint		3,3 tCO2 / pers.		
Transparency index		6 / 20		

Interpretation: See glossary for definitions of concepts and indicators.
Sources and series: wir2022.wid.world/methodology.

Figure 1: *Top 10% and bottom 50% income shares in Indonesia, 1900-2021*

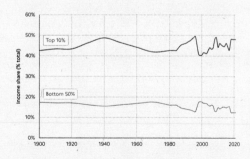

Interpretation: The Top 10% income share is equal to 48% in 2021. Income is measured after the operation of pensions and unemployment insurance systems and before income tax.
Sources and series: see wir2022.wid.world/methodology, and Chancel and Piketty (2021).

11: €1 PPP = $PPP 1.4 = IDR 5911.7

Wealth inequality

Indonesia has millions of poor people. The bottom 50% of the population, representing more than 135 million people, has an average wealth of €PPP1,916 (IDR8,159,830) and holds just over 5% of total national revenue. Since 1999, Indonesia has seen a significant growth in wealth levels. While the 1995 average was €PPP14,600 (IDR86,310,820) this has multiplied by four to reach €PPP52,530 in 2021 (IDR310,540,544). However, this growth has left the huge wealth inequality almost unchanged.

Gender inequality

Indonesian gender inequalities are significant, the female labor income share in the country is equal to 25%. This level of inequality is slightly higher than the average in Asia (21%, excluding China). The female labor income share is lower than in Japan (28%) and Korea (32%) but significantly higher than in India (18%). As in many countries around the world, we observe a small upwards trend for female labor income share since 1991: it has gone up by four percentage points.

Carbon inequality

Carbon emissions in Indonesia are relatively low: on average, an individual emits three tonnes of greenhouse gas per year. This is more than in India (2 tCO2e/capita) but less than in other Asian countries, including China (8 tCO2e/capita) and Japan (12 tCO2e/capita). The bottom 50% emits 1.4 tonnes in contrast to 11.8 tonnes for the top 10%.

Figure 2: **Wealth distribution in Indonesia, 1995-2021**

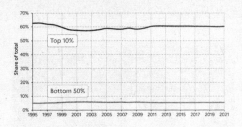

Interpretation: *In 2021, the wealthiest 10% of the population own 60% of total household wealth. Household wealth is the sum of all financial assets (e.g. stock, bonds) and non-financial assets (e.g. housing), net of debts.*
Sources and series: *wir2022.wid.world/methodology.*

Figure 3: *Female labor income share in Indonesia, 1990-2020*

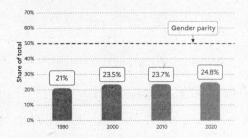

Interpretation: *The share of total labor income accruing to women in 2020 is close to 25%.*
Source and series: *wir2022.wid.world/methodology.*

Table 2: **Carbon table**

	Avg. GHG footprint (tCO2e/capita)
Full population	3.3
Top 1%	42.2
Top 10%	11.8
Middle 40%	3.5
Bottom 50%	1.4

Interpretation: *The table presents average CO2 emissions of different groups of the population in 2019. Emissions take into account carbon embedded in consumption and investment portfolios.*
Sources and series: *wir2022.wid.world/methodology.*

ISRAEL

(POP. 8,790,000 (2021))

High income inequalities in a high-income country

Israel is an affluent country. The average national income for the adult population is equal to €PPP43,100 (or ILS223,040).[12] This is higher than affluent Western European countries such as France (€PPP36,300) and the UK (€PPP32,700) but lower than the US (€PPP54,300). However, Israel is one of the most unequal high-income countries. The bottom 50% of the population earn on average €PPP11,200 or ILS57,900, while the top 10% earn 19 times more (€PPP211,900, ILS1,096,300). Thus, inequality levels are similar to those in the US, with the bottom 50% of the population earning 13% of total national income, while the top 10% share is 49%.

Evolution of income inequality

Overall, income inequality has remained at a very high level in Israel over the past 30 years. Liberalization reforms of the of mid-1980s and 1990s led to a marked increase. While inequalities have slightly decreased since 2012, they remain at a very high level, in the context of a highly segregated society.

Table 1: **Inequality outlook**

	Income		Wealth	
	Avg. Income (PPP €)	Share of total (%)	Avg. Wealth (PPP €)	Share of total (%)
Full population	43,100	100%	129,100	100%
Bottom 50%	11,200	13.0%	12,800	5.0%
Middle 40%	40,800	37.9%	105,600	32.7%
Top 10%	211,900	49.2%	804,700	62.3%
Top 1%	713,500	16.6%	4,017,600	31.1%
Top 10% to Bot. 50% Income gap	1 to 19			
Female labor share	38%			
GHG footprint	12,5 tCO2 / pers.			
Transparency index	3 / 20			

Interpretation: See glossary for definitions of concepts and indicators.
Sources and series: wir2022.wid.world/methodology.

Figure 1: **Top 10% and bottom 50% income shares in Israel, 1980-2021**

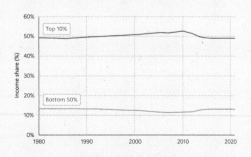

Interpretation: The Top 10% income share is equal to 49% in 2021. Income is measured after the operation of pensions and unemployment insurance systems and before income tax.
Sources and series: see wir2022.wid.world/methodology.

12: €1 PPP = $PPP 1.4 = ILS 5.2

Wealth inequality

Average household wealth is equal to €PPP129,100 (ILS668,050), the average for the bottom 50% and top 10% are respectively equal to €PPP12,800 and €PPP804,700 (ILS 66,280 and 4,163,120). This means that the bottom 50% of the population holds only 5% of total national wealth, while the top 10% holds 62%.

Gender inequality

The female labor income share in Israel is equal to 38%. This level of inequality is comparable with levels in North America (38%). Gender inequality is slightly higher than in Western Europe but significantly lower than in the neighboring Middle East countries (15%). In the first part of the 21st century, inequalities decreased quickly, with female labor income share gaining 10 points between 1991 and 2019.

Carbon inequality

Carbon consumption in Israel is significantly above world average. With 12.5 tonnes of CO2 equivalent per capita, yearly greenhouse gas emissions are higher than the average in the EU. They are, however, lower than in the US (21 tCO2e/capita) and Canada (20 tCO2e/capita). While the bottom 50% and middle 40% of the population respectively emit 6.7 and 13 tonnes of CO2 equivalent every year, the top 10% emits 40 tonnes.

Figure 2: **Wealth distribution in Israel, 1995-2021**

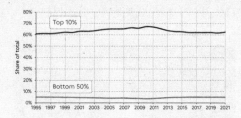

Interpretation: In 2021, the wealthiest 10% of the population own 62% of total household wealth. Household wealth is the sum of all financial assets (e.g. stock, bonds) and non-financial assets (e.g. housing), net of debts.
Sources and series: wir2022.wid.world/methodology.

Figure 3: *Female labor income share in Israel, 1990-2020*

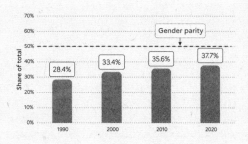

Interpretation: The share of total labor income accruing to women in 2020 is close to 38%.
Source and series: wir2022.wid.world/methodology.

Table 2: **Carbon table**

	Avg. GHG footprint (tCO2e/capita)
Full population	12.5
Top 1%	130.3
Top 10%	40.3
Middle 40%	13.0
Bottom 50%	6.7

Interpretation: *The table presents average CO2 emissions of different groups of the population in 2019. Emissions take into account carbon embedded in consumption and investment portfolios.*
Sources and series: *wir2022.wid.world/methodology.*

ITALY

(POP. 60,753,000 (2021))

Income inequality in Italy

In Italy, the average national income of the adult population is €PPP29,100 (or €27,340),[13] which is below some Western European countries including France and Germany (€PPP36,300 and 39,900, respectively) but similar to the average income in Spain (30,600). While the bottom 50% earns €PPP12 100 (21% of the total) or €11,320, the top 10% earns on average eight times more (€PPP93,900 or €1,166,520, 32% of the total).

Income inequality in the long run

Income inequality in Italy declined considerably over the course of the 20th century, following the military, political and economic shocks of the period 1910-1940s as well as the effects of post-WWII policies. But since the early 1980s, the top 10% income share rose considerably, by 8-10 p.p., while the bottom 50% share dropped from 27% to 21%. Between 2007 and 2019, the bottom 50% average incomes dropped by 15%, while national income per adult dropped by 12% as a result of the austerity policies that followed the financial crisis and the European debt crisis of 2012-2014.

Table 1: **Inequality outlook**

	Income		Wealth	
	Avg. Income (PPP €)	Share of total (%)	Avg. Wealth (PPP €)	Share of total (%)
Full population	29,100	100%	185,000	100%
Bottom 50%	12,100	20.7%	36,800	10.0%
Middle 40%	34,300	47.1%	196,000	42.4%
Top 10%	93,900	32.2%	882,200	47.7%
Top 1%	253,700	8.7%	3,336,500	18.0%
Top 10% to Bot. 50% Income gap	1 to 8			
Female labor share	36%			
GHG footprint	9,1 tCO2 / pers.			
Transparency index	13 / 20			

Interpretation: See glossary for definitions of concepts and indicators.
Sources and series: wir2022.wid.world/methodology.

Figure 1: **Top 10% and bottom 50% income shares Italy, 1900-2021**

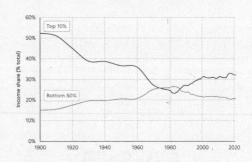

Interpretation: *The Top 10% income share is equal to 32% in 2021. Income is measured after the operation of pensions and unemployment insurance systems and before income tax.*
Sources and series: *see wir2022.wid.world/methodology.*

13: €1 PPP = $PPP 1.4 = € 0.9

Wealth inequality

Italy is one of the countries with the highest wealth to income ratio. This implies that knowing the structure of wealth distribution in the country is crucial to a proper evaluation of the trends in inequalities. Wealth concentration in Italy in 2021 is high, but lower than most European Union countries. In 2021, the top 10% hold 48%, while the middle 40% and the bottom 50% respectively hold 42% and 10%.

Gender inequality

Gender inequalities in Italy are slightly higher than in other Western European countries. The female labor income share in the country is equal to 36%, which is close to values in North America (38%). This value is higher than in sub-Saharan Africa (28%) and Asia (21%, excluding China) but significantly lower than in the Eastern European region (41%). We observe a recent significant decrease of gender inequalities in the country, with female labor income share gaining six points in the last 30 years.

Carbon inequality

In Italy, the average greenhouse gas production is around 9 tCO2e/capita. This is similar to European countries such as France (9 tonnes) and the UK (10 tonnes). The top 10% emit 24 tonnes in 2021 compared with five tonnes for the bottom 50%. Between 1990 and 2021, emissions in Italy decreased by around three tonnes of CO2e/capita on average. While emissions among the top 10% have dropped by 8% since 1990, the bottom 50% recorded a 32% drop in its emissions. These dynamics are partly due to a stronger drop in incomes among the poor than among the rich after the lost decade of 2007-2017.

Figure 2: **Wealth distribution in Italy, 1995-2021**

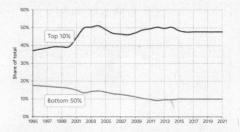

Interpretation: *In 2021, the wealthiest 10% of the population own 48% of total household wealth. Household wealth is the sum of all financial assets (e.g. stock, bonds) and non-financial assets (e.g. housing), net of debts.*
Sources and series: *wir2022.wid.world/methodology.*

Figure 3: *Female labor income share in Italy, 1990-2020*

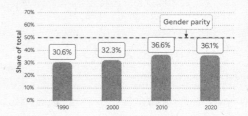

Interpretation: *The share of total labor income accruing to women in 2020 is close to 36%.*
Source and series: *wir2022.wid.world/methodology.*

Table 2: **Carbon table**

	Avg. GHG footprint (tCO2e/capita)
Full population	9.1
Top 1%	63.0
Top 10%	23.8
Middle 40%	10.3
Bottom 50%	5.2

Interpretation: *The table presents average CO2 emissions of different groups of the population in 2019. Emissions take into account carbon embedded in consumption and investment portfolios.*
Sources and series: *wir2022.wid.world/methodology.*

JAPAN

(POP. 124,851,000 (2021))

Rising inequalities since the 1980s

In Japan, the average national income of the adult population is €PPP30,500 (or JPY4,313,160).[14] While the bottom 50% earns €PPP10,200 (JPY1,447,440), the top 10% earns on average 13 times more (€PPP137 000 or JPY19,363,880).

Income inequality in the long run

Income inequality in Japan dropped considerably after the Second World War and was maintained at low levels through the 1950-1980s thanks to the consolidation of a generous welfare system and a series of capital control policies. During that period, the top 10% income share oscillated around 30-35%. Financial deregulation and liberalization in the 1980s created a rise in inequalities. The asset price bubble burst in 1991 and the subsequent secular stagnation of average incomes was accompanied by a further increase in the top 10% income share, from 40% in the early 1990s to close to 45% in 2021.

Table 1: **Inequality outlook**

	Income		Wealth	
	Avg. Income (PPP €)	Share of total (%)	Avg. Wealth (PPP €)	Share of total (%)
Full population	30,500	100%	181,500	100%
Bottom 50%	10,200	16.8%	20,900	5.8%
Middle 40%	29,200	38.3%	165,600	36.5%
Top 10%	137,000	44.9%	1,048,200	57.8%
Top 1%	400,000	13.1%	4,439,200	24.5%
Top 10% to Bot. 50% Income gap	1 to 13			
Female labor share	28%			
GHG footprint	11.9 tCO2 / pers.			
Transparency index	6 / 20			

Interpretation: *See glossary for definitions of concepts and indicators.*
Sources and series: *wir2022.wid.world/methodology.*

Figure 1: **Top 10% and bottom 50% income shares in Japan, 1900-2021**

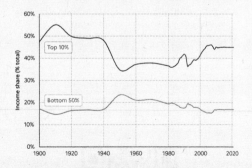

Interpretation: *The Top 10% income share is equal to 45% in 2021. Income is measured after the operation of pensions and unemployment insurance systems and before income tax.*
Sources and series: *see wir2022.wid.world/methodology.*

14: €1 PPP = $PPP 1.4 = JPY 141.4

Wealth inequalities

Japan is a relatively wealthy country: the average household wealth is equal to €PPP181,500 (JPY25,660,220). This is significantly above the Asian average and comparable with Western Europe levels. Wealth distribution in Japan is very unequal, but not more than in Western Europe countries. Since 1995, wealth shares have remained broadly stable, with the bottom 50%, middle 40% and top 10% holding on average respectively 6%, 36% and 58% of total wealth.

Gender inequality

The female labor income share in Japan is equal to 28%. This is comparable with levels in Korea (32%) but higher than in India (18%). Overall, these shares are higher than in sub-Saharan Africa (28%) and MENA countries (15%) but lower than in Western and Eastern Europe (respectively 38% and 41%). Following the general world trend, we observe a continuous increase in women's income share since 1990. During this period, it went up by six percentage points.

Carbon inequality

Japanese carbon emissions (12 tCO2e/capita) are significantly above the Asian average and slightly over Western European averages (9.5 tons). Contrary to the increasing trend in Asian countries, per capita emissions in Japan have remained stable since 1990. The bottom 50% emits slightly over six tons while the top 10% emits close to 38 tons per capita.

Figure 2: *Wealth distribution in Japan, 1995-2021*

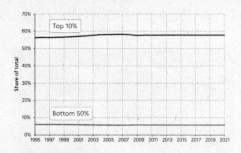

Interpretation: *In 2021, the wealthiest 10% of the population own 58% of total household wealth. Household wealth is the sum of all financial assets (e.g. stock, bonds) and non-financial assets (e.g. housing), net of debts.*
Sources and series: *wir2022.wid.world/methodology.*

Figure 3: *Female labor income share in Japan, 1990-2020*

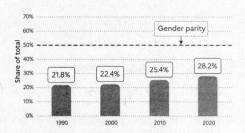

Interpretation: *The share of total labor income accruing to women in 2020 is close to 28%.*
Source and series: *wir2022.wid.world/methodology.*

Table 2: *Carbon table*

	Avg. GHG footprint (tCO2e/capita)
Full population	11.9
Top 1%	109.2
Top 10%	37.9
Middle 40%	12.4
Bottom 50%	6.3

Interpretation: *The table presents average CO2 emissions of different groups of the population in 2019. Emissions take into account carbon embedded in consumption and investment portfolios.*
Sources and series: *wir2022.wid.world/methodology.*

MEXICO

(POP. 129,789,000 (2021))

◾ One of the most unequal countries in the world

In Mexico, the average national income of the adult population is €PPP17,300 (or MXN232,790).[16] While the bottom 50% earns €PPP3,200 (MXN42,700, 9% of the total), the top 10% earns more than 30 times more (€PPP99,400 or MXN1,335,030, 57% of the total).

◾ Income inequality in the long run

Unlike large European, Asian and North American economies, available data suggest that Mexico did not experience a strong reduction in inequality over the 20th century. In fact, income inequality in Mexico has been extreme throughout the past and present centuries. The top 10% income share has oscillated around 55%-60% over that period, while the bottom 50% has been constant at around 8-10%, making of Mexico one of the most unequal countries on earth.

Table 1: **Inequality outlook**

	Income		Wealth	
	Avg. Income (PPP €)	Share of total (%)	Avg. Wealth (PPP €)	Share of total (%)
Full population	17,300	100%	62,100	100%
Bottom 50%	3,200	9.2%	-200	-0.2%
Middle 40%	14,500	33.5%	33,300	21.5%
Top 10%	99,400	57.4%	488,400	78.7%
Top 1%	452,900	26.1%	2,910,300	46.9%
Top 10% to Bot. 50% Income gap	1 to 31			
Female labor share	33%			
GHG footprint	4.8 tCO2 / pers.			
Transparency index	8.5 / 20			

Interpretation: *See glossary for definitions of concepts and indicators.*
Sources and series: *wir2022.wid.world/methodology.*

Figure 1: **Top 10% and bottom 50% income shares in Mexico, 2000-2021**

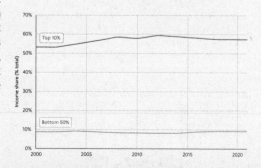

Interpretation: *The Top 10% income share is equal to 57% in 2021. Income is measured after the operation of pensions and unemployment insurance systems and before income tax.*
Sources and series: *see wir2022.wid.world/methodology, and Chancel and Piketty (2021).*

16: €1 PPP = $PPP 1.4 = MXN 13.4

Wealth inequality

Average household wealth in Mexico amounts to €PPP62,000 (MXN833,660). The poorest half of the population is deprived of wealth: its net wealth is negative, meaning that this group has on average more debts than assets. This is in stark contrast to the top 10% of the population, which owns on average €PPP488,000 (or MXN6,561,490, 62% of the total).

Gender inequality

The female labor income share in Mexico stands at 33%. This is below the average in Latin America (35%) and countries such as Brazil (38%) and Argentina (37%). This share is just slightly above the average in sub-Saharan Africa (28%) and significantly below levels in Western and Eastern Europe (respectively 38% and 41%). However, since 1990, the female labor income share has increased quite significantly, by nine percentage points.

Carbon inequality

Carbon inequalities are also very high in Mexico. Average carbon emissions are equal to around five tonnes per capita. While the bottom 50% of the population emits fewer than 2 tCO2e/capita, emissions for the top 10% of the population are more than 10 times higher (20t). These levels of inequalities are significantly higher than in Brazil (where the top 10% of the population emit eight times more than the bottom 50%) and comparable with China (12).

Figure 2: **Wealth distribution in Mexico, 1995-2021**

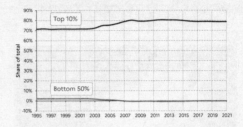

Interpretation: *In 2021, the wealthiest 10% of the population own 79% of total household wealth. Household wealth is the sum of all financial assets (e.g. stock, bonds) and non-financial assets (e.g. housing), net of debts.*
Sources and series: *wir2022.wid.world/methodology.*

Figure 3: *Female labor income share in Mexico, 1990-2020*

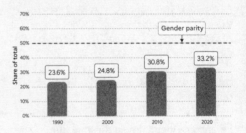

Interpretation: *The share of total labor income accruing to women in 2020 is close to 33%.*
Source and series: *wir2022.wid.world/methodology.*

Table 2: **Carbon table**

	Avg. GHG footprint (tCO2e/capita)
Full population	4.8
Top 1%	83.7
Top 10%	20.0
Middle 40%	4.5
Bottom 50%	1.9

Interpretation: *The table presents average CO2 emissions of different groups of the population in 2019. Emissions take into account carbon embedded in consumption and investment portfolios.*
Sources and series: *wir2022.wid.world/methodology.*

MOROCCO

(POP. 44,617,000 (2021))

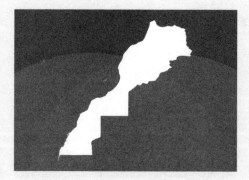

Income inequality in Morocco

In Morocco, the average national income of the adult population is €PPP7,800 (or MAD43,130).[17] Income inequality in Morocco is high and characterized by a relatively poor middle class: the bottom 50% earns €PPP2,100 (MAD11,700, close to 13.5% of the total), the middle earns on average €PPP7,200 (MAD39,910, 37% of the total) and the top 10% earns €PPP38,700 (MAD213,210, 49.5% of the total).

Income inequality in Morocco since the 1980s

Inequality has remained high over the past 40 years in Morocco. Despite slight shifts, the top 10% share has never been under 48% and the bottom 50% never over 14%.

Table 1: **Inequality outlook**

	Income		Wealth	
	Avg. Income (PPP €)	Share of total (%)	Avg. Wealth (PPP €)	Share of total (%)
Full population	7,800	100%	19,300	100%
Bottom 50%	2,100	13.6%	1,700	4.5%
Middle 40%	7,200	37.0%	15,600	32.3%
Top 10%	38,700	49.4%	121,900	63.2%
Top 1%	118,500	15.1%	585,500	30.4%
Top 10% to Bot. 50% Income gap	1 to 18			
Female labor share	14%			
GHG footprint	3.3 tCO2 / pers.			
Transparency index	1.5 / 20			

Interpretation: See glossary for definitions of concepts and indicators.
Sources and series: wir2022.wid.world/methodology.

Figure 1: **Top 10% and bottom 50% income shares in Morocco, 1980-2021**

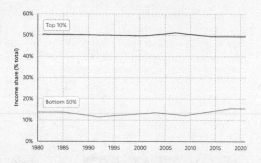

Interpretation: The Top 10% income share is equal to 49% in 2021. Income is measured after the operation of pensions and unemployment insurance systems and before income tax.
Sources and series: see wir2022.wid.world/methodology.

17: €1 PPP = $PPP 1.4 = MAD 5.5

Wealth inequality

Wealth inequality in Morocco is extreme: the top 10% of the population own more than 63% of the total, whereas the bottom 50% own less than 5% of it. While the average household wealth in the country is equal to €PPP19,300 (MAD106,300), the bottom 50% possesses an average of €PPP1,700 (or MAD9,510). In comparison, the average for the top 10% and top 1% are equal to €PPP121,900 and €PPP585,500 (MAD671,870 and 3,227,020).

Gender inequality

Women's income share in Morocco is extremely low (14%), and below even the MENA region average of 15%. The female labor income share is slightly above that of Algeria (13%) but lower than in Tunisia (19%). Between 1990 and 2005, the female labor income share rose up by four points but since then, it has fallen by more than 1 p.p.

Carbon inequality

Carbon consumption in Morocco is also very low. Average emissions are just over 3 tCO2e/capita. While the bottom 50% and middle 40% respectively emit 1.7 and 3.5, the top 10% emit 11tCO2e/capita.

Figure 2: *Wealth distribution in Morocco, 1995-2021*

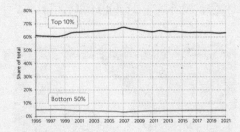

Interpretation: *In 2021, the wealthiest 10% of the population own 63% of total household wealth. Household wealth is the sum of all financial assets (e.g. stock, bonds) and non-financial assets (e.g. housing), net of debts.*
Sources and series: *wir2022.wid.world/methodology.*

Figure 3: *Female labor income share in Morocco, 1990-2020*

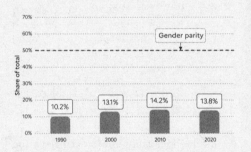

Interpretation: *The share of total labor income accruing to women in 2020 is close to 14%.*
Source and series: wir2022.wid.world/methodology.

Table 2: **Carbon table**

	Avg. GHG footprint (tCO2e/capita)
Full population	3.3
Top 1%	33.2
Top 10%	11.2
Middle 40%	3.5
Bottom 50%	1.7

Interpretation: *The table presents average CO2 emissions of different groups of the population in 2019. Emissions take into account carbon embedded in consumption and investment portfolios.*
Sources and series: *wir2022.wid.world/methodology.*

NIGERIA

(POP. 211,401,000 (2021))

Income inequality in Nigeria

In Nigeria, the average national income is equal to €PPP7,600 (or NGN1,895,630).[18] The top 10% earn on average €PPP32,700 or NGN8,098,350 (this group makes 43% of national income). In comparison, the bottom 50% earn a yearly average of €PPP2,400 (NGN587,583, or 16% of total national income). This level of inequality is similar to that in China, higher than in Europe and lower than in North America.

Inequality in Nigeria over the past decades

Available estimates are scarce for Nigeria but sources suggest that inequality has remained at relatively high levels since the 1990s. Still, after 2010, a decrease in inequality was observed. This decrease was first marked by relatively fast-rising bottom and middle incomes in 2010-2015, but following the 2016 growth slowdown, average incomes have been trending downwards.

Table 1: **Inequality outlook**

	Income		Wealth	
	Avg. Income (PPP €)	Share of total (%)	Avg. Wealth (PPP €)	Share of total (%)
Full population	7,600	100%	26,600	100%
Bottom 50%	2,400	15.5%	3,000	5.7%
Middle 40%	8,000	41.8%	24,100	36.2%
Top 10%	32,700	42.7%	154,300	58.1%
Top 1%	88,600	11.6%	669,500	25.2%
Top 10% to Bot. 50% Income gap	1 to 14			
Female labor share	28%			
GHG footprint	1.6 tCO2 / pers.			
Transparency index	0.5 / 20			

Interpretation: See glossary for definitions of concepts and indicators.
Sources and series: wir2022.wid.world/methodology.

Figure 1: **Top 10% and bottom 50% income shares in Nigeria, 1990-2021**

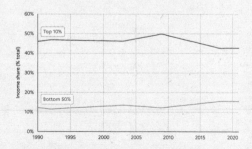

Interpretation: The Top 10% income share is equal to 43% in 2021. Income is measured after the operation of pensions and unemployment insurance systems and before income tax.
Sources and series: see wir2022.wid.world/methodology.

18: €1 PPP = $PPP 1.4 = NGN 248.0

Wealth inequality

Wealth inequalities in Nigeria are very high. While the average household wealth in the country is €PPP26,600 (NGN6,592,200), the bottom 50% wealth is just over €PPP3,000 (NGN754,770, less than 6% of the total). In contrast, top 10% wealth is equal to €PPP154,300 or NGN38,277,170 (58% of the total).

Gender inequality

In Nigeria, the female income labor share is equal to 28%. This is within the sub-Saharan African average but lower than in South Africa, where women's labor incomes is 36% of the total. These gender inequality levels are lower than in MENA countries (where women earn on average 15% of labor income) and Asia (21%, excluding China) but higher than in Latin America (where the female share is 35%).

Carbon inequality

Carbon consumption in Nigeria is extremely low. Average emissions are equal to 1.6 tCO2e/capita. This is lower than North African countries, for example Morocco (3t). While the bottom 50% and middle 40% respectively emit one and two tonnes, the top 10% emits slightly over four tonnes. This means that a Nigerian from the richest 10% of the population emits over 2 times less carbon than a poor American from the bottom 50%.

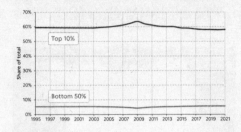

Figure 2: **Wealth distribution in Nigeria, 1995-2021**

Interpretation: *In 2021, the wealthiest 10% of the population own 58% of total household wealth. Household wealth is the sum of all financial assets (e.g. stock, bonds) and non-financial assets (e.g. housing), net of debts.*
Sources and series: *wir2022.wid.world/methodology.*

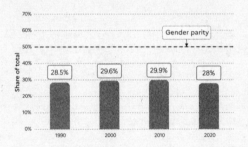

Figure 3: *Female labor income share in Nigeria, 1990-2020*

Interpretation: *The share of total labor income accruing to women in 2020 is close to 28%.*
Source and series: *wir2022.wid.world/methodology.*

Table 2: **Carbon table**

	Avg. GHG footprint (tCO2e/capita)
Full population	1.6
Top 1%	9.2
Top 10%	4.4
Middle 40%	1.8
Bottom 50%	0.9

Interpretation: *The table presents average CO2 emissions of different groups of the population in 2019. Emissions take into account carbon embedded in consumption and investment portfolios.*
Sources and series: *wir2022.wid.world/methodology.*

POLAND

(POP. 37,797,000 (2021))

Income inequality in Poland

In Poland, the average national income of the adult population is €PPP26,600 (or PLN68,950).[19] While the bottom 50% earns €PPP10 400 (PLN26,850, 19.5% of the total), the top 10% earns on average 10 times more (€PPP100,400 or PLN260,260, almost 38% of the total). Income inequality in Poland is relatively high for a European country: the share earned by the top 10% is similar to that in Germany but significantly higher than other neighboring countries.

Income inequality in Poland since the 1990s

Since 1990 there has been a spectacular increase of inequality in Poland. In 1990, the bottom 50% captured 28% of national income whereas in 2021 they gain only 20%. The share of the top 10% increased from 20% to 38%. This increase is similar to that of other former Eastern Bloc countries, including Russia, which experienced an extreme rise of inequality in the context of a series of liberalization and privatizations policies which primarily favored wealthy groups.

Table 1: *Inequality outlook*

	Income		Wealth	
	Avg. Income (PPP €)	Share of total (%)	Avg. Wealth (PPP €)	Share of total (%)
Full population	26,600	100%	49,400	100%
Bottom 50%	10,400	19.5%	-700	-0.7%
Middle 40%	28,500	42.8%	48,000	38.9%
Top 10%	100,400	37.8%	305,300	61.8%
Top 1%	395,800	14.9%	1,497,300	30.3%
Top 10% to Bot. 50% Income gap	1 to 10			
Female labor share	40%			
GHG footprint	9.4 tCO2 / pers.			
Transparency index	8.5 / 20			

Interpretation: See glossary for definitions of concepts and indicators.
Sources and series: wir2022.wid.world/methodology.

Figure 1: *Top 10% and bottom 50% income shares in Poland, 1980-2021*

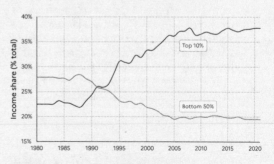

Interpretation: The Top 10% income share is equal to 38% in 2021. Income is measured after the operation of pensions and unemployment insurance systems and before income tax.
Sources and series: see wir2022.wid.world/methodology.

19: €1 PPP = $PPP 1.4 = PLN 2.6

Wealth inequality

Average household wealth in Poland is low compared with Western European countries and medium within Eastern Europe. It is equal to €PPP49,400 (PLN127,950), which is comparable with Russia (€PPP52,000) and slightly higher than Turkey (€PPP39,000). The average wealth of the top 10% is about €PPP305,000 or PLN791,130 (62% of the total), while the middle 40% owns about €PPP48,000 or PLN124,430 (39% of the total). In comparison, the bottom 50% average wealth is negative (-1% of the total): this group has more debts than assets.

Gender inequality

In Poland, the female labor income share is equal to 40%. This value is significantly above the world average (35%). Poland was part of the ex-Soviet bloc, which encouraged women's participation in the labor market. In general, women in Eastern European countries earn a larger share of total income than in the rest of the world (41% on average for countries in the former Eastern bloc). In Poland, women's income share is equal to that in Spain (40%). In recent years, the share of total income earned by women in Poland has remained stable at around 40%.

Carbon inequality

Average carbon emissions in Poland are equal to 9.4 tCO2e/capita. While Poland is much poorer than Western European countries, its emissions levels are comparable because a large share of its electricity is generated from coal. Average emissions are similar to those in the UK (10) and France (9). The bottom 50% emit on average 5.3 tonnes of CO2 equivalent every year, the top 10% emit around five times more (27t).

Figure 2: **Wealth distribution in Poland, 1995-2021**

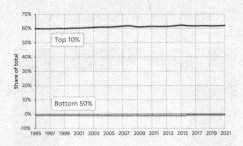

Interpretation: *In 2021, the wealthiest 10% of the population own 62% of total household wealth. Household wealth is the sum of all financial assets (e.g. stock, bonds) and non-financial assets (e.g. housing), net of debts.*
Sources and series: *wir2022.wid.world/methodology.*

Figure 3: *Female labor income share in Poland, 1990-2020*

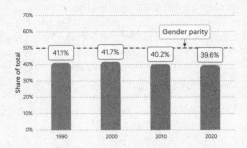

Interpretation: *The share of total labor income accruing to women in 2020 is close to 40%.*
Source and series: *wir2022.wid.world/methodology.*

Table 2: **Carbon table**

	Avg. GHG footprint (tCO2e/capita)
Full population	9.4
Top 1%	91.8
Top 10%	27.2
Middle 40%	10.2
Bottom 50%	5.3

Interpretation: *The table presents average CO2 emissions of different groups of the population in 2019. Emissions take into account carbon embedded in consumption and investment portfolios.*
Sources and series: *wir2022.wid.world/methodology.*

RUSSIA

(POP. 147,185,000 (2021))

Income inequality in Russia

In Russia, the average national income is equal to €PPP22,500 (or RUB896,150).[20] While the bottom 50% earns €PPP7 700 or RUB304,350 (17% of total income), the top 10% earns on average 14 times more (€PPP104,600 or RUB4,160,690, 46% of the total).

Income inequality in the long run

In the early 20th century, income inequality in Russia was especially high (the top 10% income share was close to 50%), but it dropped significantly after the 1917 revolution. After the implosion of the Soviet Union in 1991 and the subsequent "shock therapy" (a mixture of abrupt privatizations and deregulation), incomes at the bottom and the middle of the distribution declined. Conversely, the very rich gained substantially from the new economic regime, large-scale privatizations and very little control over financial flows. Tax evasion among wealthy Russians is particularly high.

Table 1: **Inequality outlook**

	Income		Wealth	
	Avg. Income (PPP €)	Share of total (%)	Avg. Wealth (PPP €)	Share of total (%)
Full population	22,500	100%	52,700	100%
Bottom 50%	7,700	17.0%	3,300	3.1%
Middle 40%	20,600	36.6%	30,000	22.8%
Top 10%	104,600	46.4%	390,400	74.1%
Top 1%	483,200	21.5%	2,512,000	47.7%
Top 10% to Bot. 50% Income gap	1 to 14			
Female labor share	40%			
GHG footprint	12.3 tCO2 / pers.			
Transparency index	4.5 / 20			

Interpretation: See glossary for definitions of concepts and indicators.
Sources and series: wir2022.wid.world/methodology.

Figure 1: **Top 10% and bottom 50% income shares in Russia, 1900-2021**

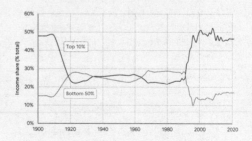

Interpretation: The Top 10% income share is equal to 46% in 2021. Income is measured after the operation of pensions and unemployment insurance systems and before income tax.
Sources and series: see wir2022.wid.world/methodology, and Chancel and Piketty (2021).

20: €1 PPP = $PPP 1.4 = RUB 39.8

Wealth inequalities also on the rise

The transition to capitalism in Russia has also led to increased wealth accumulation in the country. Since the early 1990s, the share of the top 10% in net national wealth has risen to more than 70%, making the distribution of wealth in Russia one of the most polarized in the world.

Gender inequality

In Russia, the female labor income share is equal to 40%. This value is significantly above the world average (35%). Historically, the USSR encouraged women's participation in the labor market and so in general, women in Eastern European countries hold a larger share of total income than in the rest of the world (41% in average in countries of the Eastern bloc). In Russia, women's income share is higher than Western European countries such as the UK (38%). The share of total income that women earn in Russia has gone up moderately in the last 30 years, gaining three percentage points.

Carbon inequality

The average carbon footprint in Russia is equal to 12.3 tCO2e/capita. This is higher than the average country in the European Union (9.5t), but smaller than high-emitting countries such as the United States (21t) and Canada (19t). Since the early 1990s and the fall of the Soviet Union, per capita emissions have dropped significantly (by around 30%). The emissions of the bottom 50% stand at seven tons in 2021 (five tons below their 1990 value), while emissions of the top 10% reach 42 tons in 2021, up by around five tons since 1990.

Figure 2: **Wealth distribution in Russia, 1995-2021**

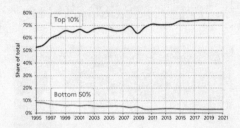

Interpretation: *In 2021, the wealthiest 10% of the population own 74% of total household wealth. Household wealth is the sum of all financial assets (e.g. stock, bonds) and non-financial assets (e.g. housing), net of debts.*
Sources and series: *wir2022.wid.world/methodology.*

Figure 3: *Female labor income share in Russia, 1990-2020*

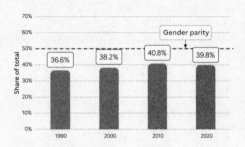

Interpretation: *The share of total labor income accruing to women in 2020 is close to 40%.*
Source and series: *wir2022.wid.world/methodology.*

Table 2: **Carbon table**

	Avg. GHG footprint (tCO2e/capita)
Full population	12.3
Top 1%	186.1
Top 10%	41.7
Middle 40%	11.7
Bottom 50%	6.8

Interpretation: *The table presents average CO2 emissions of different groups of the population in 2019. Emissions take into account carbon embedded in consumption and investment portfolios.*
Sources and series: *wir2022.wid.world/methodology.*

SOUTH AFRICA

(POP. 59,012,000 (2021))

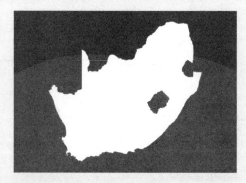

▨ One of the world's most unequal countries

In South Africa, the average national income of the adult population is €PPP12,400 (or ZAR117,260).[26] While the bottom 50% earns €PPP1,300 (ZAR12,340), the top 10% earns more than 60 times more (€PPP82,500 or ZAR780,300). In 2021, the top 10% in South Africa earn more than 65% of total national income and the bottom 50% just 5.3% of the total.

▨ South African income inequality

Available estimates suggest that income inequality in South Africa has been extreme throughout the 20th and 21st centuries. The top 10% income share oscillated between 50 and 65% in this period, whereas the bottom 50% of the population has never captured more than 5-10% of national income. While democratic rights were extended to the totality of the population after the end of apartheid in 1991, extreme economic inequalities have persisted and been exacerbated. Post-apartheid governments have not implemented structural economic reforms (including land, tax and social security reforms) sufficient to challenge the dual economy system.

Table 1: *Inequality outlook*

	Income		Wealth	
	Avg. Income (PPP €)	Share of total (%)	Avg. Wealth (PPP €)	Share of total (%)
Full population	12,400	100%	32,300	100%
Bottom 50%	1,300	5.3%	-1,600	-2.4%
Middle 40%	8,700	28.2%	13,500	16.8%
Top 10%	82,500	66.5%	276,700	85.7%
Top 1%	272,000	21.9%	1,777,300	55.0%
Top 10% to Bot. 50% Income gap		1 to 63		
Female labor share		36%		
GHG footprint		7.2 tCO2 / pers.		
Transparency index		8.5 / 20		

Interpretation: *See glossary for definitions of concepts and indicators.*
Sources and series: *wir2022.wid.world/methodology.*

Figure 1: *Top 10% and bottom 50% income shares in South Africa, 1900-2021*

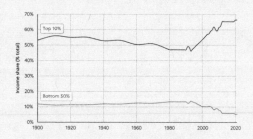

Interpretation: *The Top 10% income share is equal to 67% in 2021. Income is measured after the operation of pensions and unemployment insurance systems and before income tax.*
Sources and series: *see wir2022.wid.world/methodology, and Chancel and Piketty (2021).*

26: €1 PPP = $PPP 1.4 = ZAR 9.5

Wealth inequality

While the richest South Africans have wealth levels broadly comparable with those of affluent Western Europeans, the bottom 50% in South Africa own no wealth at all. The top 10% own close to 86% of total wealth and the share of the bottom 50% is negative, meaning that the group has more debts than assets. Since 1990, the average household wealth for the bottom 50% has remained under zero.

Gender inequality

South Africa stands out as an exception in the sub-Saharan African region. The country's female labor income share is equal to 36%, which is significantly higher than the regional average (28%). Gender inequalities in South Africa are comparable with levels observed in Western Europe (where the average earnings of women are equal to 38% of total national income on average).

Carbon inequality

South Africa is one of the highest emitters in Africa. On average, GHG emissions per capita are equal to 7.2 tCO2e/capita. This is slightly fewer than in China (8.0) and France (8.7) but considerably more than in other African countries, including Kenya (1.4), and is well over the sub-Saharan African average. On average, the top 10% emit 10 times more emissions than the bottom 50%. Since the early 1990s, these high levels of carbon inequality have remained constant.

Figure 2: **Wealth distribution in South Africa, 1995-2021**

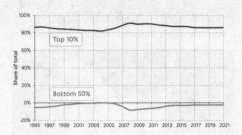

Interpretation: In 2021, the wealthiest 10% of the population own 86% of total household wealth. Household wealth is the sum of all financial assets (e.g. stock, bonds) and non-financial assets (e.g. housing), net of debts.
Sources and series: wir2022.wid.world/methodology.

Figure 3: Female labor income share in South Africa, 1990-2020

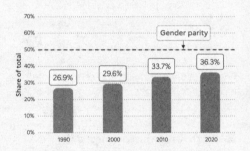

Interpretation: The share of total labor income accruing to women in 2020 is close to 36%.
Source and series: wir2022.wid.world/methodology.

Table 2: **Carbon table**

	Avg. GHG footprint (tCO2e/capita)
Full population	7.2
Top 1%	116.4
Top 10%	31.3
Middle 40%	6.5
Bottom 50%	3.0

Interpretation: The table presents average CO2 emissions of different groups of the population in 2019. Emissions take into account carbon embedded in consumption and investment portfolios.
Sources and series: wir2022.wid.world/methodology.

SOUTH KOREA

(POP. 51,656,000 (2021))

▪ Income inequality in Korea

In Korea, the average national income of the adult population is €PPP33,000 (or KRW38,426,130),[15] a level close to that of affluent Western European countries. Inequality is higher than in Western Europe and closer to that observed in the United States. The bottom 50% earns €PPP10,600 or KRW12,326,845 (16% of the total), the top 10% earns on average 14 times more (€PPP153,200 or KRW178,508,110), 46% of the total).

▪ A spectacular rise of income inequality in Korea

South Korea is one of the four "Asian Tigers" which underwent rapid industrialization and economic development between the 1960s and the 1990s. This development came with liberalization and deregulation economic policies in a context of weak social protection. As a result, inequality grew substantially over the period, the top 10% share rising from 35% to 45% since 1990, at the expense of the bottom 50% which dropped from 21% to below 16%.

Table 1: *Inequality outlook*

	Income		Wealth	
	Avg. Income (PPP €)	Share of total (%)	Avg. Wealth (PPP €)	Share of total (%)
Full population	33,000	100%	179,700	100%
Bottom 50%	10,600	16.0%	20,200	5.6%
Middle 40%	30,900	37.5%	161,100	35.9%
Top 10%	153,200	46.5%	1,051,300	58.5%
Top 1%	485,200	14.7%	4,571,400	25.4%

Top 10% to Bot. 50% Income gap	1 to 14
Female labor share	32%
GHG footprint	14.7 tCO2 / pers.
Transparency index	10.5 / 20

Interpretation: See glossary for definitions of concepts and indicators.
***Sources and series**: wir2022.wid.world/methodology.*

Figure 1: *Top 10% and bottom 50% income shares in South Korea, 1980-2021*

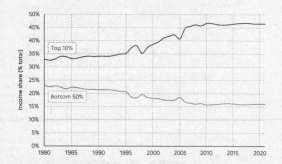

Interpretation: *The Top 10% income share is equal to 46% in 2021. Income is measured after the operation of pensions and unemployment insurance systems and before income tax.*
***Sources and series:** see wir2022.wid.world/methodology.*

15: €1 PPP = $PPP 1.4 = KRW 1165.3

A wealthy country with medium levels of wealth inequality

South Korea is one of the wealthiest Asian countries. The average household wealth is equal to €PPP179,700 (KRW209,317,180). This is more than twice the average in China and eight times more than in India. Wealth inequality is very high, though. The share of total wealth held by the bottom 50%, middle 40% and top 10% is equal to 6%, 36% and 59% respectively. Inequality levels have increased in the last 30 years, with the middle class and working classes recording a slight decline in their share of total wealth, to the benefit of the top 10%.

Gender inequality

The female labor income share in Korea is equal to 32%. This is higher than levels in Japan (28%) and India (18%). Overall, these shares are higher than in sub-Saharan Africa (28%) or MENA countries (15%) but remain lower than in Western and Eastern Europe (respectively 38% and 41%). Following the general world trend, we observe a small but continuous increase in women's income share since 1990. During this period, it went up by five percentage points.

Carbon inequality

Korea is a high carbon emitter. Per capita greenhouse gas emissions are equal to 14.7 tCO2e on average. This is more than in China (8t) but less than in the US (21t) and Canada (19t). During the 1990s, carbon emissions in South Korea went up significantly. Average emissions increased by 66% over their 1990 level. While emissions in the bottom 50% increased by 43%, they increased by almost 200% for the top 10%.

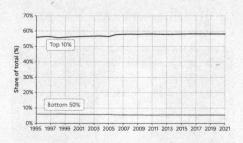

Figure 2: **Wealth distribution in South Korea, 1995-2021**

Interpretation: *In 2021, the wealthiest 10% of the population own 59% of total household wealth. Household wealth is the sum of all financial assets (e.g. stock, bonds) and non-financial assets (e.g. housing), net of debts.*
Sources and series: *wir2022.wid.world/methodology.*

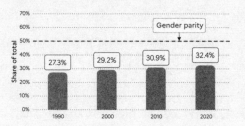

Figure 3: *Female labor income share in South Korea, 1990-2020*

Interpretation: *The share of total labor income accruing to women in 2020 is close to 32%.*
Source and series: *wir2022.wid.world/methodology.*

Table 2: **Carbon table**

	Avg. GHG footprint (tCO2e/capita)
Full population	14.7
Top 1%	180.0
Top 10%	54.5
Middle 40%	14.9
Bottom 50%	6.6

Interpretation: *The table presents average CO2 emissions of different groups of the population in 2019. Emissions take into account carbon embedded in consumption and investment portfolios.*
Sources and series: *wir2022.wid.world/methodology.*

SPAIN

(POP. 46,329,000 (2021))

Income inequality in Spain

In Spain, the average national income of the adult population is €PPP30,600 (or €26,560).[21] While the bottom 50% earns €PPP12,900 (€11,220), the top 10% earns on average eight times more (€PPP 105,500 or €91,560, 34.5% of the total). Spain is a relatively equal country compared with its European neighbors: the top 10% captures 34.5% of national income, while the bottom 50% has 21%. Inequality levels are similar to those in France and lower than in Germany.

Income inequality in the long run

Income inequality in Spain declined significantly over the course of 20th century, following the trend in other European countries (the top 10% share was above 50% in 1900 and dropped to 35% in the 1960s). Over the next 40 years, income inequality was maintained at relatively low levels, but then the country went through important economic turnarounds. After the fast growth of 1995-2005, the 2008-2014 financial crisis depressed average incomes, including those of the bottom 50%. It is only since 2015 that the poorest half of the population has recovered its pre-2007 average income level.

Table 1: *Inequality outlook*

	Income		Wealth	
	Avg. Income (PPP €)	Share of total (%)	Avg. Wealth (PPP €)	Share of total (%)
Full population	30,600	100%	164,106	100%
Bottom 50%	12,900	21.1%	27,095	6.7%
Middle 40%	34,000	44.4%	186,158	35.8%
Top 10%	105,500	34.5%	1,168,685	57.6%
Top 1%	378,800	12.4%	4,919,665	24.2%
Top 10% to Bot. 50% Income gap	1 to 8			
Female labor share	40%			
GHG footprint	7,7 tCO2 / pers.			
Transparency index	10 / 20			

Interpretation: *See glossary for definitions of concepts and indicators.*
Sources and series: *wir2022.wid.world/methodology.*

Figure 1: *Top 10% and bottom 50% income shares in Spain, 1900-2021*

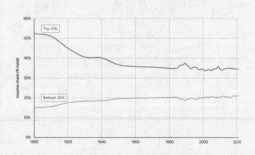

Interpretation: *The Top 10% income share is equal to 35% in 2021. Income is measured after the operation of pensions and unemployment insurance systems and before income tax.*
Sources and series: *see wir2022.wid.world/methodology, and Chancel and Piketty (2021).*

21: €1 PPP = $PPP 1.4 = € 0.9

Wealth inequality

The richest 10% of the population in Spain owns 58% of total wealth, while the bottom 50% owns 7% of wealth. Over the past 30 years, despite financial booms and busts, the wealth share of the top 10% has remained largely stable. This relative stability can be explained by the fact that the richest Spaniards sold part of their housing assets during the bust of the real estate bubble in 2008.

Gender inequality

Female labor income share in Spain in 2021 is equal to 40%. This is comparable with levels in France (41%), and higher than in the UK (38%). This level of inequality is close to the average in Western Europe (38%), but lower than in Eastern Europe (41%). Women's share of total labor income in the country has increased significantly since the beginning of the century. Between 1990 and 2019, it grew by 15 percentage points, which is more than the general Western European trend (six percentage points during the period).

Carbon inequality

In Spain, average carbon emissions are equal to 8 tCO2e/capita. This is in between the rates of neighboring countries Portugal (6t) and France (9t). While the bottom 50% emits 4.6 tCO2e/capita, the top 10% emits five times more (21t). Between 1990 and 2006, with a stable growth, benefiting also the poorest population groups, carbon emissions in Spain grew from 8.9 to 12.3 tCO2e/capita. Emissions for the bottom 50% increased by over two tonnes, up to 7.5. After the financial crisis, in a context of economic depression, carbon emissions decreased steadily.

Figure 2: **Wealth distribution in Spain, 1995-2021**

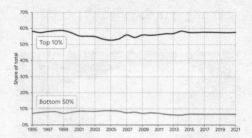

Interpretation: *In 2021, the wealthiest 10% of the population own 58% of total household wealth. Household wealth is the sum of all financial assets (e.g. stock, bonds) and non-financial assets (e.g. housing), net of debts.*
Sources and series: *wir2022.wid.world/methodology.*

Figure 3: *Female labor income share in Spain, 1990-2020*

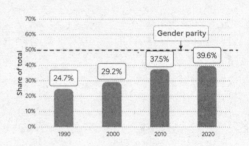

Interpretation: *The share of total labor income accruing to women in 2020 is close to 40%.*
Source and series: *wir2022.wid.world/methodology.*

Table 2: **Carbon table**

	Avg. GHG footprint (tCO2e/capita)
Full population	7.7
Top 1%	64.7
Top 10%	20.8
Middle 40%	8.3
Bottom 50%	4.6

Interpretation: *The table presents average CO2 emissions of different groups of the population in 2019. Emissions take into account carbon embedded in consumption and investment portfolios.*
Sources and series: *wir2022.wid.world/methodology.*

SWEDEN

(POP. 9,870,000 (2021))

Income inequality in Sweden

In Sweden, the average national income of the adult population is €PPP45,200 (or SEK557,960).[22] While the bottom 50% earns €PPP21,500 (SEK265,380), the top 10% earns on average 6 times more (€PPP139,000 or SEK1,717,450). Sweden is one of the least unequal countries in terms of income in Europe and the world, with the top 10% of the population earning just over 30% of total national income and the bottom 50% earning almost 24% of national income.

Long run inequality

Sweden was one of the most unequal countries in Europe in the late 19th and early 20th centuries and democratic rights were tied to wealth ownership. The expansion of democracy and growing support for the Swedish socialist party paved the way for the development of the Swedish welfare state, which led to a large-scale drop in inequalities, accompanied by fast-rising average incomes for the vast majority of the population. While inequalities have risen in Sweden since the 1980s (the top 10% share rose by about 5 p.p. since then), the country remains one of the most equal nations on earth in 2021.

Table 1: Inequality outlook

	Income		Wealth	
	Avg. Income (PPP €)	Share of total (%)	Avg. Wealth (PPP €)	Share of total (%)
Full population	45,200	100%	197,100	100%
Bottom 50%	21,500	23.8%	23,000	5.8%
Middle 40%	51,400	45.4%	178,400	36.2%
Top 10%	139,200	30.8%	1,142,800	58.0%
Top 1%	476,900	10.5%	5,389,400	27.3%
Top 10% to Bot. 50% Income gap	1 to 6			
Female labor share	42%			
GHG footprint	9.5 tCO2 / pers.			
Transparency index	14.5 / 20			

Interpretation: See glossary for definitions of concepts and indicators.
Sources and series: wir2022.wid.world/methodology.

Figure 1: Top 10% and bottom 50% income shares in Sweden, 1900-2021

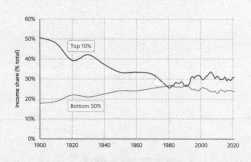

Interpretation: The Top 10% income share is equal to 31% in 2021. Income is measured after the operation of pensions and unemployment insurance systems and before income tax.
Sources and series: see wir2022.wid.world/methodology, and Chancel and Piketty (2021).

22: €1 PPP = $PPP 1.4 = SEK 12.3

Wealth inequality

While income inequalities are relatively low in Sweden, wealth inequality remains high, comparable with countries such as France and Germany. In 2021, the bottom 50%, middle 40% and top 10% respectively hold 6%, 36% and 58% of total national wealth.

Gender inequality

The female income labor share in Sweden is equal to 42% of the total. This value is significantly above the Western Europe average of 38% and slightly higher than in the former Eastern bloc countries (41%). This share has increased from around 39% in 1991.

Carbon inequality

The average carbon footprint in Sweden is equal to 9.5 tCO2e/capita. This is similar to the European Union average. The top 10% emit on average 28 tonnes of CO2e every year. In comparison, the bottom 50% emit five times less (5.4 tonnes).

Figure 2: **Wealth distribution in Sweden, 1995-2021**

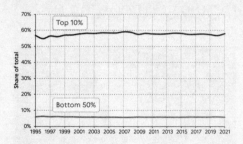

Interpretation: *In 2021, the wealthiest 10% of the population own 58% of total household wealth. Household wealth is the sum of all financial assets (e.g. stock, bonds) and non-financial assets (e.g. housing), net of debts.*
Sources and series: *wir2022.wid.world/methodology.*

Figure 3: *Female labor income share in Sweden, 1990-2020*

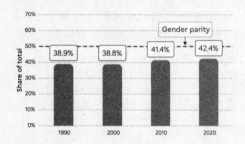

Interpretation: *The share of total labor income accruing to women in 2020 is close to 42%.*
Source and series: *wir2022.wid.world/methodology.*

Table 2: **Carbon table**

	Avg. GHG footprint (tCO2e/capita)
Full population	9.5
Top 1%	97.3
Top 10%	27.9
Middle 40%	10.1
Bottom 50%	5.4

Interpretation: *The table presents average CO2 emissions of different groups of the population in 2019. Emissions take into account carbon embedded in consumption and investment portfolios.*
Sources and series: *wir2022.wid.world/methodology.*

TURKEY

(POP. 85,043,000 (2021))

Income inequality in Turkey

In Turkey, the average national income of the adult population is €PPP27,400 (or TRY85,010).[23] While the bottom 50% earns €PPP6,500 (TRY20,260), the top 10% earns on average 23 times more (€PPP149,400 or TRY463,020). The top 10% captures 54.5% of total income while the bottom 50% takes 12%.

Income inequality over the past three decades

Estimates of inequalities in Turkey are very limited: the country's transparency index is 3/20. Sources suggest that after a decline in inequality during the 1980-1990s, inequality has risen over the past 15 years. The recent economic slowdown (2018-2021) has depressed the average incomes of all population groups.

Table 1: **Inequality outlook**

	Income		Wealth	
	Avg. Income (PPP €)	Share of total (%)	Avg. Wealth (PPP €)	Share of total (%)
Full population	27,400	100%	39,100	100%
Bottom 50%	6,500	11.9%	2,900	3.7%
Middle 40%	23,100	33.6%	28,200	28.9%
Top 10%	149,400	54.5%	263,800	67.5%
Top 1%	516,700	18.8%	1,442,500	36.9%
Top 10% to Bot. 50% Income gap	1 to 23			
Female labor share	23%			
GHG footprint	6.3 tCO2 / pers.			
Transparency index	3 / 20			

Interpretation: See glossary for definitions of concepts and indicators.
Sources and series: wir2022.wid.world/methodology.

Figure 1: **Top 10% and bottom 50% income shares in Turkey, 1990-2021**

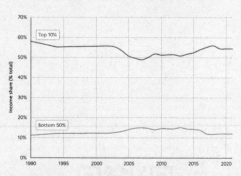

Interpretation: The Top 10% income share is equal to 54% in 2021. Income is measured after the operation of pensions and unemployment insurance systems and before income tax.
Sources and series: see wir2022.wid.world/methodology, and Chancel and Piketty (2021).

23: €1 PPP = $PPP 1.4 = TRY 3.1

Wealth inequality

In the last 25 years, average wealth in Turkey has more than doubled, to €PPP39,100 in 2021 (TRY121,160). In terms of wealth, Turkey appears to be more unequal than other countries with comparable wealth levels. In 2021, the bottom 50%, middle 40% and top 10% respectively hold 4%, 29% and 68% of total national wealth. This means that there is still a high number of very poor people, with the bottom 50% holding on average less than €PPP 2,900 (or TRY 8,910).

Gender inequality

The female labor income share in Turkey is equal to 23%. This is higher than in MENA countries (where women earn on average 15% of the total) but lower than neighboring European countries including Greece (37%) and Bulgaria (43%). After stagnating between 1990 and 2005, women's earnings in the country have since gone up by six percentage points.

Carbon inequality

Average carbon emissions in Turkey are around 6 tCO2e/capita. While the bottom 50% of the population emit just under 3.1 tons, the top 10% emit seven times more (22.6 tCO2e/capita). With the general increase in living standards in the early 21st century, carbon emissions have slightly increased in Turkey (by around one tonne since 1990).

Figure 2: **Wealth distribution in Turkey, 1995-2021**

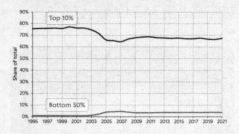

Interpretation: *In 2021, the wealthiest 10% of the population own 68% of total household wealth. Household wealth is the sum of all financial assets (e.g. stock, bonds) and non-financial assets (e.g. housing), net of debts.*
Sources and series: *wir2022.wid.world/methodology.*

Figure 3: *Female labor income share in Turkey, 1990-2020*

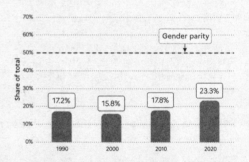

Interpretation: *The share of total labor income accruing to women in 2020 is close to 23%.*
Source and series: *wir2022.wid.world/methodology.*

Table 2: **Carbon table**

	Avg. GHG footprint (tCO2e/capita)
Full population	6.3
Top 1%	75.0
Top 10%	22.6
Middle 40%	6.3
Bottom 50%	3.1

Interpretation: *The table presents average CO2 emissions of different groups of the population in 2019. Emissions take into account carbon embedded in consumption and investment portfolios.*
Sources and series: *wir2022.wid.world/methodology.*

UNITED KINGDOM

(POP. 67, 286, 000 (2021))

▇ Income inequality in the United Kingdom

In the United Kingdom, the average national income is €PPP32,700 (or GBP32,720).[24] While the bottom 50% earns €PPP13,300, the top 10% earns on average nine times more (€PPP116,700). The top 10% captures over 36% of total income and the bottom 50% less than 20% of it. The gap between top 10% and bottom 50% incomes is smaller than in some European countries, including Germany and Poland (10) but higher than others, for example France (6) and Sweden (7). This gap is much smaller than in the US (21) and China (14).

▇ Income inequality in the long run

The United Kingdom was one the most unequal countries on earth in the early 20th century, with a top 10% income share over 55%, close to levels recorded in Latin America in 2021. The military and economic shocks of the 1910-1940s and decolonization processes hit top incomes hard. In the 1950s, the development of the social state in the UK further reduced inequality in a context of high average income growth rates. The neoliberal turnaround of the early 1980s led to a significant increase in the top 10% share, by around 10 p.p. The financial crisis of 2008 slowed this increase but also depressed average incomes: these were lower in late 2019 than 10 years before.

24: €1 PPP = $PPP 1.4 = GBP 1.0

Table 1: Inequality outlook

	Income		Wealth	
	Avg. Income (PPP €)	Share of total (%)	Avg. Wealth (PPP €)	Share of total (%)
Full population	32,700	100%	214,100	100%
Bottom 50%	13,300	20.4%	19,900	4.6%
Middle 40%	36,000	44.0%	204,700	38.2%
Top 10%	116,700	35.7%	1,223,200	57.1%
Top 1%	413,900	12.7%	4,559,200	21.3%
Top 10% to Bot. 50% Income gap	1 to 9			
Female labor share	38%			
GHG footprint	9.9 tCO2 / pers.			
Transparency index	15.5 / 20			

Interpretation: See glossary for definitions of concepts and indicators.
Sources and series: wir2022.wid.world/methodology.

Figure 1: Top 10% and bottom 50% income shares in the United Kingdom, 1900-2021

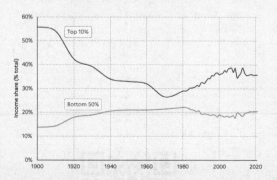

Interpretation: The Top 10% income share is equal to 36% in 2021. Income is measured after the operation of pensions and unemployment insurance systems and before income tax.
Sources and series: see wir2022.wid.world/methodology, and Chancel and Piketty (2021).

■ A strong decline in wealth inequality in the 20th century followed by a slow rise

In 2021, average household wealth stands at €PPP214,000. The bottom 50% owns 5% of household wealth and the top 10% owns 57% of it. In the early 1900s, the top 10% UK wealth share was extreme, i.e. above 90% of the total. Wealth inequalities strongly declined over the 20th century (1910-1980) and mostly during the 1950s-1970s. Since the mid-1980s, the declining trend has been reversed but so far, the rise in wealth has been slower than for income.

■ Gender inequality

In the UK, the female labor income share is equal to 38%. This is lower than France (41%) and equal to the Western European average (38%). It is higher than the average in sub-Saharan Africa (28%), Asia (21%, excluding China) and comparable with North America (38%), but lower than in Eastern Europe (41%). Since 1990, we observe a significant increase in female labor income share, with a gain of eight points over 30 years.

■ Carbon inequality

Starting from a very high level, the UK has had one of the most important decreases in GHG emissions since 1990 and has now reached average EU levels. In 1990, average emissions in the UK were around 15 tCO2e/capita. In 2020, they are fewer than 10 tons. The UK has set an ambitious carbon target to limit its emissions up to around 5.2 tonnes per capita by 2035.

Figure 2: *Wealth distribution in the United Kingdom, 1900-2021*

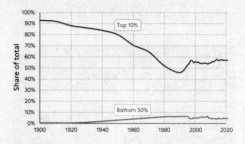

Interpretation: *In 2021, the wealthiest 10% of the population own 57% of total household wealth. Household wealth is the sum of all financial assets (e.g. stock, bonds) and non-financial assets (e.g. housing), net of debts.*
Sources and series: *wir2022.wid.world/methodology.*

Figure 3: *Female labor income share in the United Kingdom, 1990-2020*

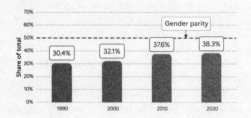

Interpretation: *The share of total labor income accruing to women in 2020 is close to 38%.*
Source and series: *wir2022.wid.world/methodology.*

Table 2: *Carbon table*

	Avg. GHG footprint (tCO2e/capita)
Full population	9.9
Top 1%	76.6
Top 10%	27.7
Middle 40%	10.9
Bottom 50%	5.6

Interpretation: *The table presents average CO2 emissions of different groups of the population in 2019. Emissions take into account carbon embedded in consumption and investment portfolios.*
Sources and series: *wir2022.wid.world/methodology.*

UNITED STATES

(POP. 333,148,000 (2021))

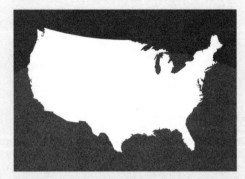

■ Income inequality in the US is among the highest among rich countries

In the US, the average national income of the adult population is €PPP54,300 (or USD77,090).[25] While the bottom 50% earns €PPP14,500 (USD20,520) per person, the top 10% earns on average 17 times more (€PPP246,800 or USD350,440). The ratio of 17 between incomes of the top 10% and the bottom 50% is significantly higher than in European countries (ranging from 6 to 10) and in China (14). The top 10% captures 45.5% of total income while just 13.3% goes to the bottom 50%.

■ Income inequality is back to historical highs

The top 10% income share in the US dropped significantly after the Second World War (from slightly below 50% in the 1930s to 35-40% in the 1950-1960s), under the effect of strong capital control policies and a rise in federal spending, accompanied by strongly progressive taxation. The 1950-1980s were also marked by rapidly rising average incomes. From the early 1980s onward, deregulation, privatizations, decreases in tax progressivity and a decline in union coverage all contributed to a formidable rise in the top 10% income share (from around 34% in 1980 to 45% in 2021) and a drop in the bottom 50% (from 19% to 13%).

25: €1 PPP = $PPP 1.4 = USD 1.4

Table 1: *Inequality outlook*

	Income		Wealth	
	Avg. Income (PPP €)	Share of total (%)	Avg. Wealth (PPP €)	Share of total (%)
Full population	54,300	100%	283,600	100%
Bottom 50%	14,500	13.3%	8,500	1.5%
Middle 40%	56,000	41.2%	197,300	27.8%
Top 10%	246,800	45.5%	2,004,400	70.7%
Top 1%	1,018,700	18.8%	9,890,300	34.9%
Top 10% to Bot. 50% Income gap		1 to 17		
Female labor share		39%		
GHG footprint		21.1 tCO2 / pers.		
Transparency index		15.5 / 20		

Interpretation: See glossary for definitions of concepts and indicators.
Sources and series: wir2022.wid.world/methodology.

Figure 1: *Top 10% and bottom 50% income shares in the United States, 1900-2021*

Interpretation: The Top 10% income share is equal to 46% in 2021. Income is measured after the operation of pensions and unemployment insurance systems and before income tax.
Sources and series: see wir2022.wid.world/methodology, and Chancel and Piketty (2021).

Wealth inequality

Wealth inequality levels in the contemporary US are close to those observed at the beginning of the 20th century, with a top 10% wealth share above 70%. Wealth inequality has followed similar dynamics as income over the past century. In 2021, average wealth for the top 10%, middle 40% and bottom 50% are respectively equal to €PPP2,004,400, €PPP197,300 and €PPP8,500 (USD2,846,360, USD280,150 and USD12,130). The share of total wealth owned by the poorest half of the US population is extremely small (1.5% of the total). While average household wealth in the US is 3.5 times higher than in China, the bottom 50% of the US population owns less wealth than the Chinese bottom 50%, in purchasing power parity terms.

Gender inequality

In the US, the female labor income share is equal to 39%. This stands in between Canada (38%) and Russia (40%), and significantly above China (33%). While the share has risen in the US since 1990 (up from 34%), progress remains slow. Women's representation among richest income groups is particularly low in 2021: among the top 1% of earners, women make up only 12% of earnings.

Carbon inequality

The US is one of the highest GHG emitters in the world. The average American is responsible for more than 21 tonnes of CO2e every year (twice as much as the average person in the EU). The bottom 50%, middle 40% and top 10% emit respectively 10, 22 and 75 tCO2e/capita. Since 1990, average per capita emissions have remained broadly stable among the top 10% and have decreased from 28 to 22 tCO2e/capita among the middle 40%. The US has pledged to cut, by 2030, half its emissions compared with 1990 levels, corresponding to emissions of around 10 tCO2e/capita.

Figure 2: **Wealth distribution in the United States, 1913-2021**

Interpretation: *In 2020, the wealthiest 10% of the population own 71% of total household wealth. Household wealth is the sum of all financial assets (e.g. stock, bonds) and non-financial assets (e.g. housing), net of debts.*
Sources and series: *wir2022.wid.world/methodology.*

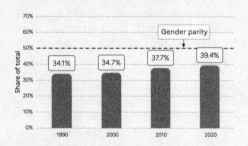

Figure 3: *Female labor income share in the United States, 1990-2020*

Interpretation: *The share of total labor income accruing to women in 2020 is close to 39%.*
Source and series: *wir2022.wid.world/methodology.*

Table 2: **Carbon table**

	Avg. GHG footprint (tCO2e/capita)
Full population	21.1
Top 1%	269.3
Top 10%	74.7
Middle 40%	22.0
Bottom 50%	9.7

Interpretation: *The table presents average CO2 emissions of different groups of the population in 2019. Emissions take into account carbon embedded in consumption and investment portfolios.*
Sources and series: *wir2022.wid.world/methodology.*

NOTES

WIR2022.WID.WORLD

WORLD
INEQUALITY LAB